WHEN WOMEN BECOME PRIESTS

WHEN WOMEN BECOME PRIESTS

The Catholic Women's Ordination Debate

KELLEY A. RAAB

COLUMBIA UNIVERSITY PRESS
NEW YORK

A portion of chapter 4 was first published as "Nancy Jay and a Feminist
Psychology of Sacrifice," *Journal of Feminist Studies in Religion* 13, no. 1 (Spring
1997): 75–89. Reprinted by permission of the *Journal of Feminist Studies in
Religion*.

A portion of chapter 5 was first published as "Christology Crossing Boundaries:
The Threat of Imaging Christ as Other Than a White Male," *Pastoral Psychology*
45, no. 5 (1997): 389–399. Reprinted by permission of the Human Sciences
Press.

Schaeffer, Pamela, "Woman Cuts Into Liturgy, Asks to Be Priest," *National
Catholic Reporter* 34, no. 14 (February 1998): 5. Reprinted by permission of the
publisher.

Library of Congress Cataloging-in-Publication Data
Raab, Kelley A.
    When women become priests: the Catholic women's ordination debate /
Kelley A. Raab.
        p. cm.
    Includes bibliographical references and index.
    ISBN 0–231–11334–X (alk. paper)—ISBN 0–231–11335–8 (pbk. : alk.
paper)
    1. Psychoanalysis and religion 2. Psychoanalysis and feminism 3. Women
priests. 4. Catholic Church—Clergy. I. Title.

BF175.4.R44 R23 2000
262'.142'082—dc21   99–049657

To Nancy U. Raab

and in memory of

Spencer O. Raab

CONTENTS

ACKNOWLEDGMENTS

This project began in the mid-1980s as my doctoral dissertation at the University of Ottawa. While it has changed substantially since then, many of the ideas for the book were first conceptualized when I was a Ph.D. student in the Religious Studies Program. First and foremost, I am indebted to my doctoral adviser, Naomi Goldenberg. She has been an excellent mentor. More than anyone else, Naomi has supported this project over the years. Two other women scholars in Ottawa who helped me flesh out some of the preliminary ideas for the book are Elisabeth Lacelle and Caryll Steffens. To them I also owe thanks.

Since this book has gone through many stages, there are many other people to acknowledge along the way. I especially thank colleagues within the American Academy of Religion for their support. Among them are Catherine Roach, Diane Jonte-Pace, and William Beers. The chapter on sacrifice was honed through presentation of several papers that received helpful feedback. Tom Huffman encouraged me to present those papers, and he read innumerable drafts of them. He also edited the introduction and assisted me with numerous computer problems. James Jones read an earlier draft of the manuscript and made suggestions concerning structure. Young Mi Angela Pak read a later draft and helped me fine-tune my arguments.

I thank my editor at Columbia University Press, John Michel, and his assistant editor, Alexander Thorp, for their commitment to the book. Thanks also go to the anonymous reviewer for the press. Her detailed comments on each chapter contributed significantly to the book's final shape. Jan McInroy was an excellent copy editor. I am also grateful to the Episcopal priests and laypersons whom I interviewed for this project. Their responses provided direction for the book and made me feel that my efforts were worthwhile.

Thanks as well go to the National Endowment for the Humanities, which provided me with a summer stipend in 1994 to study with Peter Gay at Yale University. The Women's Studies Program at Northeastern University in Boston provided a congenial research environment when I took a leave of absence from my teaching position at Westmar University during 1994–1995 to write a major draft of the book. In addition, Nebraska Wesleyan University allowed me a leave of absence from my teaching responsibilities during 1998–1999 to complete the final draft. The librarians at Nebraska Wesleyan, especially Irma Sarata and Janet Lu, were extremely helpful in tracking down bibliographic sources. I was also able to use the Bridwell Library at Southern Methodist University for bibliographic information. My student research assistant at Nebraska Wesleyan during the spring of 1998, Pauletta Lehn, assisted me enormously in updating my bibliography on the Catholic women's ordination debate.

I thank my mother, Nancy U. Raab, and my brother, Stephen Raab, for their faith in me over the years. I also wish to acknowledge Coleman Brown of Colgate University, who first encouraged my intellectual pursuits in religious studies. Finally, immeasurable thanks go to Dan Scott, who provided support during the last year of research and writing.

WHEN WOMEN BECOME PRIESTS

1

INTRODUCTION

This book is about what will happen when women become Catholic priests. Specifically, it concerns how women clergy will affect the celebration of the sacraments, in particular the Eucharist. While many books focus on why women should be Catholic priests, none have entertained this question: what difference will it make when the priest is a woman? Beginning with this question will lead to answers to other questions, such as why the Vatican is so resistant to the idea of ordaining women. These questions move us beyond the current point of stagnation concerning the Vatican's refusal to admit women to the priesthood. Entertaining just what women priests might mean will result, I submit, in enormous progress in the Catholic women's ordination debate.

To make my position clear at the outset, I should say that I wholeheartedly support the ordination of women to the priesthood. Since there are as yet no Catholic women priests, the topic "when the priest is a woman" is by necessity somewhat hypothetical. I say "somewhat" because the example of women Episcopal clergy offers clues concerning what Catholic women priests would be like. So we do have women priests, but not Catholic women priests. This book uses a psychological approach to address the question of what difference women priests would make.

I believe that the crux of the controversy about women priests in the Catholic Church revolves not only around issues of religious leadership but also around concerns about the nature of God and Christ. The heart of my argument is that women priests celebrating mass challenge traditional understandings of priesthood and

Eucharist, which in turn leads to reenvisioning other core dimensions of theology. These changes have yet to be fully recognized in the Episcopal Church, but at some level they continue to fuel resistance to female Episcopal clergy.

The small amount of literature available on Episcopal women's eucharistic ministries suggests that when women preside at the altar, latent maternal themes in the Eucharist become apparent. Motifs of feeding and nurturing are more prominent, the sacrament is perceived as more "embodied," women experience greater connectedness and self-affirmation, Christ and God are imaged as female, and women's blood and suffering are correlated with Christ's. Episcopal women clergy at the altar reveal that the impact of women priests goes deeper than attaining equality between the sexes; it extends to the *theology* of the Eucharist itself.[1]

Because gender issues are central to the debate, feminist theology and its focus on women's experiences will be important to my analysis. I am not wedded to papal doctrine, nor to the work of Catholic theologians teaching in Catholic schools. Many books on women's ordination from a strictly Catholic perspective have already been written. The issue has become so encrusted that it sorely needs a fresh perspective. A broader focus on women's experiences is required. The experiences of women of color—brought to light through womanist, *mujerista*, and Asian American women's theology—help to bring a desperately needed new vision. I hope that this book will open the door to further exploration into the subject of Catholic women priests from many different vantage points.

The psychological theories that I utilize are drawn largely from a school of thought known as object relations theory, but I also make use of Freud and French feminist psychoanalytic thinkers, particularly Luce Irigaray and Julia Kristeva. Each of these theories makes a unique contribution to the women's ordination debate: Freud in his notions of the unconscious, and French feminists and object relations theorists in their emphasis on the pre-Oedipal period of development, when the relationship with the mother is central. All offer insight into issues of gender, symbolism, and power.

My interest in using a psychological methodology stems from a desire to deepen understanding of religious beliefs and practices—

not to debunk them. It should be noted, however, that psychoanalytic theories of religion frequently conform to one of two models. The first, perhaps best known as a "reductive" model, tends to explain all religious phenomena in terms of purely psychological categories. In this model, a psychological origin is found in early childhood for religious experiences and concepts of God without the necessity of acknowledging a transcendent origin. Freud's famous theories of "religion as an illusion" and of God as a "projection of an omnipotent father" are examples of this type of approach. Its proponents most frequently profess an atheistic or agnostic leaning, and, to theologians, they may seem to present an acontextual, ahistorical model that ignores the complexities of such phenomena as religious symbols and creedal beliefs.

A second model for a psychological understanding of religion offers an interpretive framework without negating the possible existence of a transcendent reality. This is the model to which I subscribe. This type of approach views psychoanalysis as a means of broadening and deepening the study of religion. For example, Erik Erikson's eight stages of psychosocial development have been fruitfully applied to stages of faith development by James Fowler.[2] During the first stage, trust versus mistrust, the child gains the capacity for faith if the world seems secure and the child is allowed to develop a healthy sense of trust in her or his surroundings. Religion can affect the second stage, autonomy versus shame and doubt, depending on whether religious teaching encourages shame-based feelings or a sense of self-reliance and independence. Ana-Maria Rizzuto's *The Birth of the Living God: A Psychoanalytic Study* offers another example of this second type of approach. Rizzuto is interested not in whether there is a God but in how one's psychological constitution informs and is illuminated by his or her religious orientation. Rizzuto offers, by means of case studies, a psychological analysis of the formation of "God representations" and correlates them with Freud's stages of psychosexual development.[3]

My interest in the Catholic women's ordination debate stems from a desire to expand public understanding of underlying concerns of gender, symbolism, and power. In so doing, I wish to educate the reader concerning questions regarding Catholic women's

ordination that are deeper and more enduring than those encountered in the popular media. While my research focuses in part on
the significance of early infant-mother interactions for religious ritual, my intention is neither to reduce eucharistic experience to longing for the womb nor to ahistoricize it. The theology of the
Eucharist has a long history apart from my attempt to provide psychological analysis. Yet people "experience" the Eucharist in ways
that can be explored psychologically, and their experiences set the
stage for theology. In using psychoanalytic theory to clarify and aug-
ment issues of religion and gender in the context of the Catholic
Eucharist, I hope to provide a common meeting ground between
the fields of theology and psychology. By means of a psychological
approach, I wish to show that theology is not static but constantly
evolving and that a useful way to approach topics of religion is
through understanding how people perceive themselves and the
world around them.

What does a psychological methodology offer to the women's
ordination debate that other perspectives have not provided
already? It allows a more profound analysis of the issues of gender,
symbolism, and power that are involved in this controversy. Two
recent books, for example, address the effects that the advent of
Episcopal women priests has had on the church. *Women Priests: The
First Years*, a collection of essays by Anglican women clergy,
explores changes observed by Anglican women priests since the
ordination of women was approved in England in 1992 and makes
several important points. First, women feel affirmed in the church.[4]
A majority of women experience the "rightness" and "naturalness"
of seeing a woman at the altar or in pastoral situations.[5] Many
parishioners mention the special gifts that women have for ministry,
including their sensitivity, their willingness to talk about problems,
and their gentleness in bereavement work.[6] Second, many believe
that the ordination of women may help to correct the mistaken theology that God is male.[7] Women priests evoke neglected images of
God, such as mother and midwife, and those strands of Christian
spirituality that have emphasized the nurturing, tender, and intimate
aspects of God.[8] It follows that there will likely be greater demand
for more inclusive language during services.[9] Third, new styles of

leadership will emerge, including a more collaborative style achieved by negotiation.[10] The second book, *Crossing the Boundary: What Will Women Priests Mean?*, also speaks to the significance of women priests for the Anglican Church, suggesting, for example, that sexuality and spirituality will be co-present at the altar[11] and that women priests will symbolize general acceptance of women's sexuality.[12] In addition, women may bring special gifts in the areas of spiritual direction and retreat-leading, as well as the desire to make connections and to work holistically.[13] Finally, women priests raise questions and offer insights into the nature of God.[14] The first generation of women priests will bring their symbolic value as outsiders: when they break the bread, they will be particularly powerful signs of God's seeking love.[15]

These two books make important contributions to the significance of women clergy for the Episcopal Church. While they offer a number of insights, they also prompt more questions. I believe that a psychological methodology provides the best way to respond to these questions. For example, *why* do women parishioners feel affirmed in the church when women are at the altar? Do women bring a different physical presence to the celebration? If so, are there other gender differences that would affect priesthood? *How* do women clergy evoke maternal images of God? What is the connection between priesthood and images of God and between inclusive language and women priests? *Why* and *how* will sexuality be co-present with spirituality at the altar when women are celebrating? What effect will this have on the experience of parishioners? What effect will it have on the church at large?

A psychological approach enables us to explore in greater depth and breadth some of the issues that have already emerged concerning the effects of women priests. The questions above can be organized into four broad queries: (1) What difference would women priests make for the priesthood? (2) What difference would women priests make for the parishioner? (3) What difference would women priests make for theology? (4) What difference would women priests make for the church? I also discuss additional avenues of inquiry that are opened up by these questions, largely through interviews with Episcopal women clergy on their experiences of sacrament.

During 1988–1989 and 1998, I conducted interviews with fifteen Episcopal priests and three Episcopal laypersons (see the appendix). In addition to the literature on women priests, the ethnographic data provided by these interviews shed a great deal of light on the contemporary Catholic women's ordination debate. The reader must first understand, however, how study of the Episcopal Church speaks to the debate about women priests in the Catholic Church.

In the United States, women have been officially ordained in the Episcopal Church since 1977. Statistics indicate that the number of women priests has increased steadily over the past twenty years. From 1982 to 1987, for example, the number of Episcopal women clergy in the United States doubled, from 603 to 1,167.[16] According to official diocesan reports as of January 1, 1987, 6 percent of all Episcopal priests were women and 31 percent of all U.S. Episcopal deacons were women.[17] According to the 1998 *Episcopal Clerical Directory*, the number of women priests had increased to 1,955. Women clergy constitute 13.8 percent of all those listed in the *Directory*, and 45.8 percent of all Episcopal deacons are women. In contrast, in 1998 only 2.5 percent of all U.S. bishops were women.[18] These figures indicate that though women priests still constitute a minority of all Episcopal clergy in the United States, they do exist in significant numbers to enable study.

The Episcopal Church is one of the most recent Christian sacramental traditions to allow women to serve as eucharistic celebrants. Unfortunately, there is a dearth of material on the impact of women priests on the Episcopal Church as a whole, and in particular on sacramental ministries. Writing and research abound on issues concerning the ordination of women to the Episcopal priesthood. Notwithstanding the two books mentioned, however, very little has been published about what difference it makes that the priest is a woman.[19] The Episcopal Church, like the Catholic Church, for the most part still seems stuck on the "fact" of women clergy.

In order to explore the effects of Catholic women priests on sacramental ministries, one needs to understand the correlation between Episcopalian and Roman Catholic eucharistic theologies. Among Western Christian traditions, the Episcopal Church is generally considered to be closest to Roman Catholicism in its theology, liturgy, and church structure. Theologically, there is a wide divergence among Episcopalians with regard to both the nature of the Eucharist and the role of the celebrant. High Anglicans—or "Anglo-Catholics"—generally adhere to transubstantiation (i.e., the bread and wine are changed into the body and blood of Christ), to the recurrent sacrifice of Christ in the mass, and to the notion that the eucharistic celebrant directly represents Christ at Calvary. Low Anglicans, in contrast, tend to believe in consubstantiation (i.e., there is no change in the substance of bread and wine to body and blood of Christ) and in the priest as a representative of the community rather than of Christ per se. They also deemphasize the Eucharist as a sacrifice. The low Anglican perspective, of course, is a more Protestant understanding of the Eucharist and the celebrant. It is significant, however, that both high and low Anglicans are part of the same Episcopal hierarchical structure—consisting of a lineage of archbishop, bishops, priests, deacons, and laypersons.

Ethnographic material on Episcopal women priests advances additional questions concerning the impact of women priests on priesthood, parishioner, theology, and church. Because these subject areas are fundamentally intertwined, one cannot talk about changes that women priests would bring to the church without addressing their effects in the other three areas. Here I briefly address each of these four topics and identify specific themes and queries to be discussed in subsequent chapters.

PRIESTHOOD

According to one clergywoman I interviewed, the ordination of women has broadened the understanding of ministry. Women celebrating the Eucharist give the priesthood a completeness it did not have before. Lay ministry, according to this priest, is perhaps an outgrowth of ordaining women. People can see that anybody—not just males—can be called simply as a Christian believer. Women priests themselves, however, have expressed ambivalence over their own priestly authority. This ambivalence may have much to do with a traditional, hierarchical notion of priesthood, in which the priest is set apart from the people. Kathleen Greider notes, for example, that many women testify to being on the receiving end of oppressive priestly authority. She asks: "Will women shape a priestly ministry that shares power, or will we fall prey to the same temptations of power-over that have corrupted the ministries of some priests before us?"[20] Greider proposes that ambivalence is inherent in the priestly function of ministry. It seems likely as well that women, because they have been in positions to suffer from misuse of authority, are more aware of this ambivalence than men are.

Lesley Stevens, who conducted a study of 108 Anglican clergy-women in 1989, also has observed that women priests demonstrate ambivalence about their authority, as well as the desire to rework it into nonhierarchical forms. More than one half (53 percent) of those she surveyed acknowledged that "leadership style" was the locus of the greatest change that has resulted in the Episcopal Church from the advent of women priests. In particular, respondents describe female leadership as "more personal," "less authoritarian," "inclusive of others," "collegial," "facilitative," "non-hierarchical," and "the exercise of authority without power-seeking." Not surprisingly, Stevens found that for some women priests, this style emerged as a consequence of their own negative experiences of subordination: "Women have a particular sensitivity to the experience of being oppressed and are exploring new patterns of using and sharing power."[21] Authority, according to Stevens, manifests itself in the preference for an egalitarian style of authority in ritual. Stevens notes that "horizontal" is the term most often used to describe this approach, in which the focus is "communal." Some women priests responded that the celebrant's role is shared with the whole community.[22]

Interestingly, a laywoman informed me that women celebrants are perceived differently because there is still a sense that a woman presiding is forbidden, wrong, problematic. Women priests bring a whole different sense of history to the celebration than do men. Women presiders in her view, like women preachers, have to struggle with their gender identity: many feel that either they have to be nonthreatening, gentle, and motherly or they need to behave as much like the men as possible. Women presiding at the Eucharist, she explained, have no models for what a woman eucharistic presider is like. The only models are male.

A male priest suggested to me that the kinds of differences women make are only beginning to be manifested. For the first ten years, women followed male role models. Except for the pitch of their voices, he stated, they were indistinguishable from men. Now some women are beginning to rethink what they are doing, in his view, and to find more "congenial" ways to do things. These women are trying to be less hierarchical and more intimate. He explained that women are endeavoring to find their own style.

The above material on leadership style and priestly authority raises additional questions, to which I will respond through a psychological approach. How, for example, do different leadership styles affect the way priesthood is understood? What is problematic for women priests and others about their expressions of authority? What difference does it make for priesthood that women presiders have historically been forbidden?

PARISHIONER

Ethnographic material indicates that from the point of view of the parishioner, women priests have a different physical presence. Responses to Stevens's survey on the theme of physical presence draw attention to such effects as voice, gesture, and "attention to detail." Several women priests explained in the survey that they recite the liturgy more slowly than their male colleagues in order to ensure that all are following the words. In addition, some hypothesized that a female body at the altar has significant impact, giving a whole new meaning to Christ's words "This is my body." Greider recalls a story that, for the priest concerned, highlighted the connection between her own blood and the consecrated cup of wine:

> One Communion Sunday morning, the woman priest got
> her menstrual period just before worship began. She says, "I
> felt ill all during the worship. When I was saying the words

of institution, I felt like I was going through the motions, but as I lifted the chalice I was startled by my own thought: Am I unclean? I could hardly believe the thought had crossed my mind. Then I spoke the words: 'This is my blood, . . . poured out for you and for many, for the forgiveness of sins.' *No,* I thought, *I am not unclean. I, too, know that blood is the essence of life.*"[23]

A woman priest I interviewed related that it is difficult to get people to talk about the images they experience when she celebrates the Eucharist. They say that what she does with her hands is "so wonderful" and that her voice is "so wonderful," but they do not go any further. She told me:

Women priests hold themselves differently, they say the words differently, they move their hands differently. The gestures women started have been picked up by a lot of the men. Women are not different from men in the sense of "true-womanhood." However, they are different in an historical sense, that what it means to be a woman in this culture is very different from what it means to be male. In this sense, gender does matter, and shapes the way we do the celebration.

One male priest I interviewed related that most men react to having a woman celebrant with "I don't know what this is going to be like." There is some fear. Among the reactions he heard afterward was: "Well, that didn't hurt. It wasn't any different." Another male reaction he heard was: "This is better in many respects, because it is fairer." For men, he explained, having women clergy is a "justice and fairness" issue. On the other hand, for women, in his view, having a woman celebrant is more of an experiential issue. Women's reactions to a female celebrant include a moving experience of self-affirmation within the life of the church, in which they feel greater comfort, welcome, and support for their own "being."

Several Episcopal laywomen I spoke with acknowledged differences in their experience of the Eucharist when women are celebrants. One woman told me, for example, that women celebrants make her feel included in the church on a gut level. She feels an identification that she does not feel when a man presides. The difference, she stated, perhaps lies in the symbols: when she looks at the altar when a woman is celebrating, she realizes that there is really no part of the church where *she* could not play a role. She feels affirmed in who she is as a woman. Another laywoman indicated that she cannot look at a woman presiding at the Eucharist without being aware of "all the women who struggled and fought and prayed and worked to make it possible for her to stand there." One clergywoman I spoke with, however, explained that she is always conscious of the fact that there may be someone in the congregation who will not take communion because she is celebrating. She struggles with the notion that her ministry may be keeping an individual away from the sacrament.

The above material whets the appetite for further exploration of the effects of women priests on parishioners' experience. What new meaning, for example, is given to Christ's words, "This is my body"? What "images" do parishioners experience when women celebrate the Eucharist? How does menstruation attest to women's presence as a contested presence? Why are there ambivalence and resistance to women as celebrants?

THEOLOGY

In addition to the impact of women presiders on parishioners' experience, women presiders also affect theology, as indicated by two quotations from John Morgan's book *Women Priests*:

> Symbolically, I believe the woman at the altar enlarges people's understandings and imaginings about God. In prayers and in celebration, the ordained person is representative of the people to God and God to the people. If the image is always male, God is represented only as male. As women are included symbolically as representative people, the image of God is larger. The feminine becomes more than the Spirit dimension. Sonship begins to include daughters and the understanding of us all as children becomes stronger.[24]

Something subtly different is happening when a woman
stands at the altar—our experience of the sacrament is
changed. Women, being more embodied [i.e.,historically
associated more with body], say more about the incarnation-
al dimension of God, about the nurturing, physical, enduring aspects, being as opposed to doing. Women, being more
related than men on the whole, have an edge in the pastoral
dimension of ministry.[25]

One woman priest told me that a lot of women say that to see
"their own" being mirrored at the altar has been a very powerful
experience for them. Another clergywoman indicated that the first
comments she heard regarding her celebration were these: "When I
hear you celebrating the Eucharist, I hear Christ. When I see you,
Christ is there."

Two male priests I spoke with expressed resistance to women's
ordination, largely on theological grounds. Women presiders, for
one, foul up the symbolism of the uniqueness of the incarnation, as
well as confuse people about the nature of the Christian community gathered around the table with Jesus as the host. The Scriptures,
according to this priest, are very clear about the uniqueness of the
incarnation of Jesus Christ as a male; he stated that Jesus was the
Son of God and not the Child of God. The Bible, in his view, gives
meaning to the male symbol without "adding value" to maleness. He
explained:

If then a priest is the host of the memorial feast at which
Christ is really present, then if this is the Last Supper, we
don't use . . . champagne and croissants because he didn't
use that. It seems to me the issue of the modern church is
the uniqueness of the incarnation and that we make a terri-
ble mistake when in our own sacramental symbolism we
make the host a question mark.

Another male priest expressed extreme ambivalence regarding
women presiding at the altar, and women priests in general, stating:

The priest in the Eucharist is traditionally seen as standing in the place of Christ—as *alter Christus*. If you change the symbol, you're going to change the theological reflections on that symbol. One of the things that bothered me in seminary was the dichotomy many feminists created between the Jesus of history and the Christ of faith. It was an attempt to downplay the maleness of Jesus. This struck me as questionable Christology.

Ordaining women, in this priest's view, has initiated a number of theological questions that people are just beginning to think about. For example, having a woman stand in the place of Christ raises the question of whether a woman can represent Christ. Further questions arise: What is it about Christ that a woman represents? That a man represents? That a man cannot? He argued that the Jesus of history/Christ of faith begins to break down with a woman celebrant. Other questions are also raised by the above ethnographic material: What is the relationship between symbol and metaphor? Do women priests evoke female images of God that are nonmaternal as well? How do women clergy influence Christology?

CHURCH

Some of the most profound changes caused by the advent of women clergy pertain to the church as a whole. One woman priest, for example, told me that she sees women in a prophetic role, questioning the patriarchal foundation of institutional Christianity. She worries, however, about perpetuating patriarchal values in a female style. How can she be in the institution but not of it? Another believes that clergywomen are helping to peel away the false dichotomy of women as either figures on a pedestal or little children. She states that women really have to "work on themselves" when they see a woman at the altar. Women have grown up, in her view, forcing themselves into a role, "sort of like shaping yourself into some strangely shaped shoes, [and] gradually you come to think that's the way your foot is really shaped." Women priests help women get rid of "barnacles," those self-images that weigh them down. She also thinks that women clergy have helped to soften some of the gender lines in families.

In the view of a third woman priest interviewed, clergywomen have brought a nurturing dimension to the church. As well, women clergy are more willing to be vulnerable and to use their own experiences to build bridges with the laity. Because of this they bring a human dimension to the priesthood, conveying a message of equality. This priest also believes that more women clergy than men clergy are sympathetic to issues regarding homosexuality. She explained: "Women know what it feels like to be excluded. Women know what it feels like to be invisible . . . to be marginalized, to not count, to be stereotyped." Women clergy are also, in her view, much more empowering of laypeople and more interested in coming to a consensus than in ruling by majority. The advent of women priests, she stated, is changing the way the church communicates.

Another woman priest I spoke with believes that women clergy can help mediate inevitable tensions in the Episcopal Church. She also suggested that women clergy are helping the Episcopal Church to develop a more global ministry. Parishioners are saying, "How do I take what I'm getting from the church into my world? How do I change my world with my relationship with God?" She believes that this in part may be a result of women's not having to focus as much energy on achieving goals within church walls. The advent of women priests, she observed, has also brought greater awareness within the church to women's issues, such as domestic violence and sexual abuse. In addition, women clergy serve as role models for female parishioners on how to be both a spiritual person and a professional and family person.

In the view of one male priest, one of the fruits of women priests is that they have provided a greater sense of tactile ministry. Women's role at the altar has expressed the fullness of humanity in a different way. As a result of socialization, women have brought a more nurturing, relational presence to the Eucharist. Women priests he knows have been more willing to show emotion within the role of priest, which has given permission to men to admit their own feelings.

Similarly, a laywoman explained that women priests bring different life experiences to the Episcopal Church. Growing up female, bearing children, and childrearing affect women's preaching, their relationships with parishioners, and the way they preside at liturgy. Women clergy also bring a perspective that is rooted in the struggles they have had to endure to become priests. Women's ordination creates a space in the church that was not there before: "It expands the horizons. It makes new possibilities. I think any time the church does something like that—opens a door that's been closed before—you don't altogether know what the outcome . . . will be."

An important question that arises from the above ethnographic material is this: Are women really more nurturing and relational than men? If so, will they always be that way? I believe that a psychological methodology can be used to answer many of the questions I have asked concerning the effects of women priests on priesthood, parishioner, theology, and church. Without the benefit of a psychological approach, readers would likely misunderstand *how* and *why* women priests would make a difference. They also might not fully understand the roots and extent of the widespread ambivalence and resistance to women priests. In addition, without such a perspective, it is likely that readers would not fully appreciate the *depth* and *breadth* of difference that women priests would bring, or the ways in which women priests would enhance the future of the Catholic faith.

OUTLINE OF THE BOOK

What difference will women priests make? Subsequent chapters present five main ideas pertinent to the women's ordination debate in the Catholic Church. These five arguments are expressed in the chapter titles: (1) Gender Reversal, (2) Maternal Envy, (3) Sacrifice, (4) Christ as a Woman, and (5) Gender, Sex, and God. Each idea in some way addresses the primary question of what difference it will make when the priest is a woman. The arguments offer a framework for interpreting the ethnographic data on

Episcopal women priests, which is drawn upon throughout the book.

Chapter 2 examines the Vatican's reasoning behind the prohibition of women priests. This reasoning is found in the 1976 Vatican "Declaration on the Question of the Admission of Women to the Ministerial Priesthood," four drafts of a pastoral letter in response, and a 1994 apostolic letter also issued by the Vatican. The evidence presented in these documents can be summarized in three points: tradition, natural resemblance, and bridegroom or nuptial imagery. I will not entertain these arguments in detail here, but I do wish to point out that all three have been challenged by Catholic scholars and theologians. Something else, something deeper, must be going on. A close examination of the arguments from natural resemblance and bridegroom imagery discloses important information about the nature of priesthood and church. For example, my findings indicate that the contemporary Catholic understandings of priesthood and church are at variance with early conceptions of them. While the arguments against women clergy are based on the premise that gender difference *prohibits* women from becoming priests, I show that both the Catholic priesthood and the notion of church have "feminine," particularly maternal, origins.

The first argument leads to the second. Since the arguments leveled against women clergy from tradition, natural resemblance, and bridegroom imagery have been declared unsound by certain Catholic scholars and theologians, why not at least permit dialogue on the women's ordination issue? In chapter 2 I propose that maternal themes run even deeper, to the theology of the Eucharist itself. A key premise is that the Catholic Eucharist at heart expresses pre-Oedipal themes, that is, dynamics emerging from the early relationship between mother and infant. The issue of a "feminine" priesthood populated by a solely male clergy is also addressed. I submit that, psychologically, opposition to women priests is fueled by unconscious dynamics concerning male gender identity issues, proclivities that are not easily overcome by education or a will toward fairness. Using object relations theory, I explore ways in which these dynamics express themselves culturally.

While chapters 2 and 3 explain the perpetuation of a solely male clergy, chapters 4, 5, and 6 examine the significance of women priests for eucharistic theology and experience. Sacrifice, a central component of Catholic eucharistic theology, is the focus of chapter 4. The third main idea is that ritual sacrifice can be redeemed from its patriarchal underpinnings as a violent, misogynistic act and read to express something fundamental about the human condition—in particular, needs for separation and communion and the dialectic that these requirements generate. A central question is the meaning of Jesus' words "This is my body" when that body is a woman's. The impact of women's physical presence at the altar on parishioners' experience is examined, including women's blood as sacrificial blood. I advance the notion that acknowledging women's traditional roles as feeders and nurturers would transform current understandings of ritual sacrifice. Psychologically, priesthood as a site of transference also becomes a subject of investigation. I suggest that women celebrants, much like the female analyst in a psychotherapeutic situation, would serve as a template for maternal transferences. These transferences would be both positive and negative, and in particular would concern issues of separation-connection germane to the infant-mother relationship.

The fourth argument is based on the notion that the priest acts *in persona Christi*, in the person of Christ, when celebrating the Eucharist. Feminist theory, as well as the work of feminist, womanist, *mujerista*, and Asian American women theologians in the area of Christology, allows us to posit that women celebrants would bring unique resources to eucharistic theology and experience. I argue that, psychologically, while male priests reinforce paternal transferences and a "Father-God" image, women clergy evoke a pre-Oedipal God representation, and hence a female Christ. This discussion speaks to many of the questions concerning Christology, especially how women would represent Christ to parishioners. Using theories of symbol and metaphor, it also responds to the query of what images parishioners experience when women celebrate the Eucharist. In addition, using psychological theory, I analyze how and why some women feel affirmed while others do not, as well as continued resistance and ambivalence to women as priests by men.

In chapter 6, I draw upon French feminist psychoanalytic theory to further explore the significance of women priests acting in the person of Christ. At this point questions concerning priesthood, parishioners' experience, theology, and church truly converge. My final argument is that the gender of the celebrant influences theology about God and sexuality. The work of Luce Irigaray and Julia Kristeva further advances my claim that the Eucharist is a site for emergence of pre-Oedipal issues. I suggest that in a Kristevan paradigm, the woman at the altar becomes a locus for suffering, birth, and death in the context of maternal—instead of paternal—generativity. Kristeva's work makes possible additional exploration of the influence of gender difference on priesthood. The importance of the female voice, of gesture, and of body is taken into account. On the other hand, by drawing upon Irigaray, we can speculate on ways in which women clergy would bring nonmaternal dimensions, such as the erotic and mother-daughter issues, to eucharistic theology and experience. An Irigarayan model also suggests that body and spirit are intertwined, allowing discussion of the relationship between sexuality and the sacred. How sexuality would be co-present with spirituality becomes a major focus, as well as the issues raised by sexuality for Christology.

Chapter 7 entertains the question "What needs to happen for women to become priests?" The historic struggle of Episcopal women to become priests is examined, as well as current movements toward women's ordination within Catholicism. In conclusion, I discuss how I have answered the questions asked in the introduction, subjects that remain to be explored, and a tentative direction for future work.

I will end this chapter by saying a few words about my own experience with ritual, for to a large extent, this book concerns the power of ritual to transform a social institution and the individuals within it. The ability of ritual to renew and reform is what first drew me to study it. I have always been interested in ritual to some degree. As a child I frequently attended church with my mother while other kids were in Sunday school. While I do not have strong memories of what I heard, I do remember the rituals: hymns, sermons, confession, communion. In college I had my first experience of a woman celebrant, the assistant chaplain. A United Church of Christ minister, Pat Dutcher planted seeds suggesting that women too could stand at the altar and consecrate the elements.

When in seminary in the early 1980s, I was first exposed to alternative liturgies. One of my professors, Phil Anderson, was trained as a Gestalt therapist, and he began to open my eyes to the transformative power of ritual. Specifically, he used creative visualization to help students address blocks in their spiritual development. He emphasized ways in which language can restrict or empower one's progress. I began to see ritualizing as a way of creating an alternative reality, as opening an avenue for individual and social change.

My interviews with Episcopal women priests have convinced me that this is possible within the context of an institutional structure. During the course of my research, I myself saw an Episcopal woman celebrate the Eucharist for the first time. The event was more powerful for me than my earlier college experience with a woman celebrant. I think that was because I knew that the understanding of sacrament was different and because the church setting was Anglo-Catholic. It was clear to me that this woman was representing Christ. When she said the words of institution, I felt as though *her* body was being broken for me. I had never encountered a female Christ image like this before. As a result, I experienced myself intuitively affirmed and much more included in the service. The event helped me understand the power of ritual in a fresh way.

2

GENDER REVERSAL

Any woman who has organized and presided over a meal, be it banquet or family, could preside over the Eucharist (with training). Maybe that is why I feel so at home at the altar. At the altar I publicly give thanks, rejoice, praise and celebrate my being at one with God, in Christ in the power of the spirit.
—*From John Morgan,* Women Priests

Women of all time have made babies within their bodies. In this sense they are the vessels of life. They transform food—bread and wine—into the body and blood of their children. They are the first priests in a very physical sense.
—*Rosemary Luckett, "Women Make Eucharist Too"*

On what grounds does the Vatican claim women cannot become priests? Through examining the 1976 Vatican declaration on women clergy, the ensuing four drafts of a pastoral letter on women, and the 1994 papal apostolic letter *Ordinatio Sacerdotalis*, we discover that the Vatican's ban on women priests is based largely on arguments made from tradition, natural resemblance, and "bridegroom" imagery.[1] These documents are explored in detail, for I believe they serve as a screen for what is really going on in the Eucharist, i.e., a gender reversal of male and female reproductive and nurturing roles. Gender reversal in the Eucharist is but one aspect of the broader phenomenon of male identification with women, a development that has taken place on many societal levels.

I am convinced that a gender reversal of women's functions and roles in the context of a male priesthood is found in the two primary arguments against women priests. Gender reversal in the

Eucharist becomes especially apparent when Jesus' feminine identification in the early church and in medieval Christianity becomes a focus of attention, and when the biblical roots of the ritual in the Last Supper are examined. An analysis of the tradition and natural resemblance arguments, as well as the corollary argument to natural resemblance, bridegroom imagery, exposes this thinking as a screen for gender reversal in the Eucharist.

Specifically, a close study of natural resemblance and bridegroom imagery reveals the following: (1) the hiding of Jesus' feminine qualities, (2) the appropriation of these qualities by the priestly role, (3) the cloaking of feminine symbolism in the bridegroom symbol, (4) a false emphasis on Jesus' genitals, and (5) the restriction of representations of birth and feeding to celibate male priests. In order to illustrate these points, I first discuss gender reversal as a general phenomenon, then give some background on the women's ordination debate in the Catholic Church, focusing in particular on the 1976 Vatican declaration and the 1994 apostolic letter. This discussion provides a context for exploring the Vatican's arguments more thoroughly.

Since the primary goal of this chapter is to illuminate a pervasive type of male dominance of women—which I term *gender reversal*—in the context of the Catholic Eucharist, it makes sense to clarify my terminology. *Gender*, using R. W. Connell's understanding of the term, refers to "practice organized in terms of, or in relation to, the reproductive division of people into male and female."[2] While a number of other definitions have been offered, most scholars agree that gender determines what is considered male and what is considered female in our society. Gender, unlike anatomical sex, however, is the *cultural* construction of maleness and femaleness. In this context, *reversal* refers to an inversion of roles or values such that a traditionally female role, often associated with a low societal value, takes on a high value when enacted by males. In this sense, gender reversal involves male appropriation of female roles and the simultaneous prohibition of women from performing those same roles.

In the Sambia of New Guinea, for example, men carry out a monthly nosebleeding ritual simulating menstruation, while popular belief is that women's blood flow is polluting and dangerous. Ritual nosebleeding is thought to be a necessary step in the development of virulent masculinity in this highly patriarchal culture; that is, it is necessary in order to become part of the male "club."[3] As well, in the Genesis creation story a male God creates a man, who in turn gives birth to a woman from his rib. This story inverts the actual process of men's birth from women, denying women a reproductive role in the Jewish and Christian mythology of creation. Gender reversal in the Eucharist includes both men's appropriation of female reproductive and nurturing functions and the barring of women's expression of those same functions.

Gender reversal occurs cross-culturally. As a phenomenon of male-dominated society (which can also be termed an "androcentric-patriarchal worldview"),[4] it rests upon several assumptions. One is co-optation and cover-up of female power. Historically, politically, religiously, biologically, and psychologically, men have appropriated and denied female capacities. Marija Gimbutas's work on the Neolithic civilization of the goddess suggests that the earliest known cultures were matrifocal, probably with shared power between men and women. Religiously, priestesses presided over all temple functions. Goddess worship paid homage to the female ability to bear life, to nurture it, and to regenerate monthly.[5] In turn, the line between biological dependence on the mother and psychological attachment to her cannot be sharply drawn. As will be shown in subsequent chapters, psychologically, even as the infant is drawing nurture from the breast, he/she perceives himself/herself to be merged with the mother. Cultural male suppression of women is bent on keeping hidden this primal and primary power.

Another assumption upon which gender reversal rests is a stark differentiation between what is considered masculine and what is considered feminine. It has been suggested that societies in which the line between male and female is more sharply drawn tend to be more male-dominated, while societies in which it is less so lean more toward shared power.[6] Yet even in the latter, gender identity issues remain influential at a deep psychological level, particularly for men. While I will argue that gender identity is predominantly a male issue, women's identity is in turn prescribed by the male gaze. Witness the persistent obsession with body image, manifested in diet books, eating disorders, and cosmetic surgery. Women's gains in political representation in the U.S. House and Senate have been coupled with a "backlash" against feminism, described by Susan Faludi.[7] Too much blurring of gender roles sets off a vigilant attempt to reestablish the boundaries between who men are and who women are and what they can do and become.

Instances of gender reversal are found in at least four of the major world religions—Christianity, Judaism, Islam, and Hinduism. It is not coincidental that each has been heavily influenced by an androcentric-patriarchal worldview. The male creation story is a cornerstone event in the three Western traditions mentioned. In Hinduism, the belief that an individual must be transformed into a male in order to be spiritually liberated reinforces male privilege and control.[8] Ironically, this final state, described by mystics as one of loss of distinctions between self and other, is analogous to the period of primal infant-mother harmony in the womb. While Hindu philosophical texts recognize the female as the ultimate source of existence, Asian cultures influenced by this religion remain sexist in the social and political spheres.

The Vatican refuses to consider the ordination of women as Catholic priests. Significantly, four drafts of a response to women's concerns—all of which upheld the Vatican view on women's ordination—have been voted down by American bishops. Meanwhile, Vatican officials cling tightly to the worn notion of "complementarity" of roles between men and women and to the idea that there must exist an anatomical "natural resemblance" between the priest and Christ.

THE CATHOLIC WOMEN'S ORDINATION DEBATE

Once a rarity, women clergy are today much more common in many Christian denominations. A majority of the mainline Protestant denominations, for example, have been ordaining women since at least the 1950s. The Congregationalist tradition dates the ordination of women to the late 1800s. Moreover, the Quaker and Unitarian traditions have long histories of women in leadership roles. The most recent tradition to ordain women in the United States is the Episcopal Church, which began to do so in 1977. These are landmark events within the history of the Christian tradition, illustrating that women have made giant steps toward overcoming sexism in many denominations. It is no longer uncommon to see women in the pulpit of many a liberal Protestant church, and numerous women are sole pastors of such churches. This was not the case during my youth in the 1960s and 1970s: the first woman I ever heard preach was the assistant chaplain of my college, in the late 1970s.

For other Christian traditions, the ordained ministry remains closed to women. Among these are the Roman Catholic Church, the Eastern Orthodox Church, the Lutheran Church–Missouri Synod, the Southern Baptist Church, and the Church of Jesus Christ of the Latter-day Saints. When I moved to Nebraska in 1995, I discovered several other denominations that do not ordain women, such as the Berean Church and the Lutheran Church–Wisconsin Synod. In the United States and Canada, Roman Catholicism is by far the largest tradition still to deny ordination to women. In the United States, 20 to 25 percent of the population is Roman Catholic.

Ordination remains out of bounds for Catholic women despite their lengthy history of involvement in church ministries,[9] a shortage of priests, and a recent Gallup poll showing that in 1992 Catholics favored women priests by a margin of 67 percent. Interestingly, even pressure from such national groups as Call to Action and the Women's Ordination Conference have not swayed the pope from his stand against women priests. However, as a result of the influence of Pope John XXIII and the reforms of Vatican II—a series of councils held from 1962 to 1965—women can now serve as lay readers and distributors of the Eucharist. Yet because they remain barred from the priesthood, women are restricted from leading sacramental functions and from participating in church leadership in any way, shape, or form. This means that women cannot officially—i.e., in the capacity of a priest—baptize,[10] confirm, offer penance, marry, give last rites, say mass, or receive holy orders. Many Catholic women, tired of waiting for official recognition, are "unofficially officiating" at some of the sacraments, in particular the Eucharist. In one parish that I know of, this was done publicly, and when the bishop found out about it the presiding priest was transferred and replaced by a more conservative one. The new priest immediately fired the woman from her position as assistant.

It should be mentioned that not all Catholic feminists, and certainly not all Catholic women, are in favor of women clergy. This at first sounds like an oxymoron, but one rationale is that admitting women to the priesthood would essentially be a form of co-optation by the existing androcentric-patriarchal worldview. In other words, ordaining women would require asking them to be like men and to fit into a masculinist system. Women who advocate this position argue that instead of pushing for ordination, a more suitable feminist strategy would be to break down the present clerical caste system, so that administering the sacraments is not prohibited to all nonordained persons.[11]

This view is not without merit. There are several ways to dismantle clerical caste, however, only one of which is to allow nonpriests to perform the sacraments. Another method of attacking clerical hierarchy would be to allow more types of people, including women and married men, to celebrate the sacraments. Currently, in my opinion, this seems the more realistic choice. The Catholic Church has been hierarchical for so long that it seems easier to try to bring more types of people into it than to out-and-out disassemble the hierarchy, although I believe the latter will be a necessary byproduct of the former. Catholic feminist theologian Anne Carr believes, for example, that women priests would further the transformation of the priesthood from a bureaucratic, hierarchical, "male-dominated club" to an open, collegial, "spiritual service of unity."[12] Granted, this will take time, and at present I know of no women Episcopal priests who feel that the Episcopal Church has become egalitarian. Yet, as shown, the advent of women Episcopal priests has brought significant changes to the Episcopal tradition.

It is important to note that despite the hope for a more egalitarian priesthood, Catholic feminists remain divided on the issue of women's ordination. The risks and benefits to Catholic women are perhaps weighed differently by an insider than by a non-Catholic like myself. Among the risks, as described by Catholic Mary Hunt, are ordaining women into an irrelevant, anachronistic church, giving them a low-paying "women's job in patriarchy," and attracting women who are more conservative than their constituents. Hunt observes, for example, that many women who are Catholic by tradition no longer attend church and do not find Christianity uniquely valid. Among the benefits of women's ordination are breaking down one of the last bastions of patriarchy (that alone is a worthy cause, in my estimation), placing women in decision-making roles, and stimulating them globally to be religious agents.[13] The pro-ordination movement continues to grow despite mixed views, and several Catholic bishops have spoken out in favor of women priests.[14]

Historically, the struggle for ordination had its inception at the beginning of the century. Antoinette Iadorola suggests that the movement for women clergy may have originated from the Saint Joan's Alliance, a group formed in 1911 to work for women's suffrage.[15] This organization actively petitioned for women's ordination since the early 1960s.[16] The rising feminist consciousness of the sixties led another group of women to form the Leadership Conference of Women Religious, whose specific purpose was to examine women's status within the Catholic Church. Ordination has been one of the issues under examination.[17] In addition, a third group of women, the Women's Ordination Conference (WOC), has aggressively pursued the question of women priests. Ruth Fitzpatrick, former president of the WOC, periodically requested conferences with the pope—requests that were systematically ignored.

1976 Vatican Declaration

These different groups in various ways put pressure on the Vatican to discuss the issue of women clergy. That pressure eventually led to the 1976 "Declaration on the Question of the Admission of Women to the Ministerial Priesthood," also known as *Inter Insigniores*.[18] This document gives the following six reasons for the continued prohibition of women priests:

1. Tradition: The Catholic Church has never felt that priestly ordination can validly be conferred on women.

2. Attitude of Christ: While Christ was sympathetic toward women, he did not call any women to become part of the twelve disciples.

3. Practice of the Apostles: The apostolic community remained faithful to the attitude of Jesus toward women and did not confer ordination upon any prominent woman of the Gospels.

4. Normativity: This involves preserving an unbroken tradition throughout the history of the Church.

5. Mystery of Christ: When Christ's role in the Eucharist is to be expressed sacramentally, there would not be a "natural resemblance" between Christ and the minister if the role of Christ were not taken by a man.

6. Ministerial Calling: Here is found the vocational argument—the priesthood is a calling, and women are not called to it.

The declaration provoked a flurry of responses from Catholic theologians and laypersons alike. Since the declaration, four drafts of a pastoral letter have attempted to wrestle with such issues as the "meaning and dignity" of being a woman and of women's status in church and society.[19] Ironically, the drafts only barely touch upon women's ordination, primarily to dismiss it. Two reasons, summarizing the six in the declaration, prevail for pushing aside discussion on women clergy. One is that the present teaching is said to rest on unbroken tradition and is considered to be of divine revelation.[20] The other, dubbed the "natural resemblance" argument, is that only men can adequately symbolize Christ in the sacrament of the Eucharist. Corollary to the natural resemblance argument is the notion that the priest must be male to symbolize a "bridegroom" adequately, the church being the "bride."

As will be shown, the three chief arguments given by the Vatican against women priests (tradition, natural resemblance, and bridegroom imagery) are clearly refutable. Many scholars contend that the Vatican in actuality has no theological basis on which to continue to prohibit the ordination of women. Equally glaring is the ethical injustice being perpetuated. While the Vatican maintains that women are in no way inferior to men, exclusion of women from the priesthood implies their subjection, domination, and lack of power. Throughout the pastoral drafts, the notion of "complementarity" shackles women to stereotypes of "womanly" virtues, roles, and functions. These include being chaste, finding fulfillment in motherhood, being submissive, and doing service for the good of others. While not always negative, these roles become restrictive when they are the only options available.[21]

1994 Apostolic Letter

On May 22, 1994, Pope John Paul II issued an apostolic letter, known as *Ordinatio Sacerdotalis*, to the world's Catholic bishops. The following November the Vatican Congregation for the Doctrine of the Faith (CDF), a church body whose intent is to safeguard and promote authentic Catholic teaching, publicly responded to the letter. Father James Roberts notes that the letter, "given its authoritative content and severely demanding tone, will create a crisis of major proportions in the church. The consequences will affect numerous areas of church doctrine, discipline and sacramental life, let alone the Church's ecumenical relationships with other Christian churches."[22] Two points in the letter received media attention: the pope's declaration that women will not be ordained as priests and that this doctrine is to be taken infallibly.[23] In order better to understand the magnitude of *Ordinatio Sacerdotalis*, a close examination of this apostolic letter, the CDF's response, and the responses of scholars and theologians to the issue of infallibility is necessary.

Ordinatio Sacerdotalis is constructed around four points.[24] First, the pope states that priestly ordination in the Catholic Church has always been reserved for males alone. The reasons given in the 1976 declaration are reiterated: the indications in Scripture that Christ chose only male apostles, the constant practice of the church in imitating Christ, and the church's "living teaching authority," which holds that women's exclusion from the priesthood is in accordance with God's plan. Second, again referring to *Inter Insigniores*, the pope asserts that the church "does not consider herself authorized to admit women to priestly ordination." Further, he states: "Christ's way of acting did not proceed from sociological or cultural motives peculiar to his time"; rather, Christ established this particular "theological anthropology." The Gospels and the book of Acts, it is stated, support this claim. Third, we read that the presence and role of women remain essential to the church. The fact that the Virgin Mary received neither apostolic mission nor ministerial priesthood demonstrates that women's exclusion from priesthood is not discriminatory. And then, fourth, comes the much-talked-about finale: "Wherefore, in order that all doubt may be removed . . . I declare that the church has no authority whatsoever to confer priestly ordination on women and that this judgment is to be definitively held by all the church's faithful."

What precisely does this last statement mean? Here the response to *Ordinatio Sacerdotalis* by the CDF, made public November 18, 1994, must be addressed. In this document,[25] the question is raised whether the 1994 apostolic letter is to be understood as belonging to the "deposit of the faith." I quote the answer in full:

> This teaching requires definitive assent, since, founded on the written word of God and from the beginning constantly preserved and applied in the tradition of the church, it has been set forth infallibly by the ordinary and universal magisterium. . . . Thus, in the present circumstances, the Roman pontiff, exercising his proper office of confirming the brethren (cf. Lk. 22:32), has handed on this same teaching by a formal declaration, explicitly stating what is to be held always, everywhere and by all as belonging to the deposit of the faith.[26]

The letter, signed by Cardinal Joseph Ratzinger, states, moreover, that the pope "approved this reply" and "ordered it to be published."

Upon release of the CDF's statement, Bishop Anthony Pilla, president of the National Conference of Catholic Bishops, issued a response asking "all in the church in the United States, especially theologians and pastors who instruct and form our Catholic people in the faith, reverently to receive this teaching as definitive."[27]

Further, Bishop Pilla admonished: "To those who have questioned this teaching in the past, I ask you now prayerfully to allow the Holy Spirit to fill you with the wisdom and understanding that will enable you to accept it."[28]

Despite the CDF's declaration, there does not seem to be scholarly agreement on whether the apostolic letter is in fact an "infallible" document. At this point, some discussion on the notion of papal infallibility will clarify precisely what is being asserted. Contrary to popular understanding, papal infallibility does not mean that *all* of the pope's enunciations are without error. As the council of Vatican I (1870) makes clear, it concerns only those declarations made "ex cathedra": "The Roman pontiff, when he speaks *ex cathedra*, . . . defines a doctrine regarding faith or morals to be held by the universal church, by the divine assistance promised to him in blessed Peter, is possessed of that infallibility with which the divine Redeemer willed that His church should be endowed."[29] Vatican II further affirms infallibility as follows: "The whole body of the faithful who have an anointing that comes from the holy one (cf. 1 John 2:20 and 27) cannot err in matters of belief. This characteristic is shown in the supernatural appreciation of the faith (*sensus fidei*) of the whole people, when, 'from the bishops to the last of the faithful,' they manifest a universal consent in matters of faith and morals."[30] As historian of religion Huston Smith explains, this doctrine does not assert that the pope is free from sin, cannot make mistakes, or is endowed with superhuman intelligence.[31] Only in the spheres of faith and morals can the pope speak infallibly, and only after expert consultation is it believed that the Holy Spirit protects him from the possibility of error.[32]

Now that we have some understanding of what infallibility means in a Catholic context, we must ask this question: Does *Ordinatio Sacerdotalis* meet the requirements for an infallible doctrine? Two important issues have surfaced in this regard: (1) Was the pope speaking on an issue of faith and morals, and (2) did he seek all available assistance from expert consultants? In response to the first question, division exists over whether the issue of women priests is a matter of doctrine or of church order. If the latter, then infallibility would not apply. Catholic scholar Edward Schillebeeckx has stated publicly that the infallibility of this statement is "dogmatically impossible," because it is a matter of church order, "not the core of our faith."[33] Three criteria drawn from canon law and recent papal teaching suggest how an infallible doctrine might be recognized: (1) consultation with all of the bishops, (2) universal and constant consensus of Catholic theologians, and (3) common adherence of the faithful.[34] Father David Knight believes that the word *infallible* is misleading in this case. The CDF's official *opinion* (not infallible) is that women can never be ordained. It is also the CDF's opinion that this teaching has been believed in the church for so long that it must be accepted as belonging to the "deposit of the faith."[35] In Knight's view, because the pope's interpretation that women cannot be ordained was *not* an infallible clarifying definition, it does not have to be accepted by Catholics as a doctrine of faith.[36] Knight himself cannot accept the teaching as "definitive" as requested by Bishop Pilla, for, as he states, "it has not been declared definitive infallibly, and no convincing reasons have been offered to prove that this ever has been, in fact, a doctrine taught in the church as a revealed truth of faith."[37]

One might query whether it is possible, through an act of ordinary magisterium, to declare that a tradition is irreformable when the issues surrounding the tradition are still the subject of theological discussion.[38] As John Wright explains: "They [the pope and bishops] . . . bear authentic witness to the faith of the whole church. . . . They do not appeal to some special, unique revelation unavailable to the rest of the faithful."[39] We do not know, argues Wright, whether Pope John Paul II consulted the bishops of the world before issuing *Ordinatio Sacerdotalis*, but it would truly remove all doubt if he were to inform the faithful how he sought out the movement of the Holy Spirit throughout the Catholic Church.[40] At the least, it is apparent that the pope overlooked the U.S. bishops, for in a draft of the June 1995 U.S. Bishops Statement "Calling the Vatican to Collegiality," they report: "The questions now being raised by women, theologians, ecumenists, and many of the faithful as a result of this new apostolic letter present an immense pastoral problem that might have been prevented had there been more regular and open communication from us to Rome."[41]

In conclusion, *Ordinatio Sacerdotalis* neither advances new arguments to support women's exclusion from priesthood nor responds to critiques generated by the 1976 declaration. Nor are Catholic scholars universally convinced of the letter's infallibility. Discussion on the issue is therefore likely to continue. As Canadian bishop Bertrand Blanchet states concerning the response by theologians, "They will no doubt present the arguments *pro* and *contra*, just as St. Thomas Aquinas did when he was trying to understand more deeply the teachings of the Church."[42] In the meantime, the schism between those who argue that women's ordination is an issue of rights versus those who argue that it is an issue of theology continues to widen.

Now that the primary Vatican documents against women's ordination have been presented, we must turn to a careful examination of the arguments of natural resemblance and bridegroom imagery as found in these documents, paying particular attention to the expression of gender reversal in each. First, however, some attention needs to be given to the argument from tradition, as it is the most commonly voiced objection to women's ordination.

The Argument Against Women Priests from Tradition

In the Catholic Church, two sources of "revelation" or knowledge about God are accepted. Both Protestants and Catholics accept Scripture as a primary source of revelation. In addition, Catholics rely upon an "unwritten source" embodied in tradition, which most Protestants do not. This difference is to be attributed to the sixteenth-century Protestant reformer Martin Luther, who questioned much of Catholic unwritten revelation and argued for a return to *sola scriptura*, or scripture alone.

The argument against women priests from tradition runs that there have been no women disciples, apostles, or priests in Catholic heritage. Yet, historically, there is much evidence to show that women were indeed involved in the early ministries of the church. Jesus is presented in the Gospels as treating men and women in an egalitarian fashion. After his death, numerous women functioned as apostles.[43] The Gospels testify, for example, that women were the first witnesses to the resurrection (Mark 16, Matthew 28, Luke 24, John 20). The fact that no women were among the twelve disciples or apostles listed in the Gospels or Acts reflects the Jewish tradition of naming only men to be public witnesses, twelve being the number of tribes of Israel. There are many cited occasions, the Last Supper among them, in which women are not mentioned, yet there is no proof of their absence.

Feminist biblical scholars have argued that in the early church, women very likely functioned in the capacities of apostles, missionaries, and prophets. Women also probably blessed the bread at the Eucharist, as part of their leadership functions in early Christian "house churches."[44] In house churches, women participated as widows, deaconesses, and teachers. As noted by New Testament scholar Elisabeth Schüssler Fiorenza, women were able to take on leadership roles in the early church because of the egalitarian nature of Jesus' message.[45]

Schüssler Fiorenza's research brings into question the legitimacy of the argument made against women clergy from tradition. The Vatican is also incorrect in its claim that there have been no women priests. Giorgio Otranto, for example, has uncovered evidence that women of the first Christian centuries were in fact ordained into the diaconate, receiving ordination by a prescribed ritual. His research shows that women were both priests and bishops in southern Italy and Sicily at least through the fourth century.[46]

Finally, the discovery that married men and women priests were ordained in the 1970s in Czechoslovakia surely raises issues concerning what is normative for Catholic tradition. Certain sources indicate that during extreme Communist oppression, up to four hundred married men and some women were ordained in the clandestine Catholic Church. The Vatican apparently knew about women priests and deacons in Czechoslovakia years before it issued the 1976 declaration forbidding women's ordination.[47] Hence, the church cannot in truth claim that there were no women disciples, apostles, or priests, in either the recent or the remote past.

As mentioned, the reasons given against women's ordination in the 1976 declaration are reiterated in the 1994 apostolic letter, particularly that of tradition. I will emphasize a few points that have emerged in recent discussions of *Ordinatio Sacerdotalis*. The church will never deny that it wishes to be faithful to Jesus' action and example. But what exactly were these? The magnitude of the contemporary women's ordination issue has been compared with that of the early controversy over whether Gentiles could be accepted into the church.[48] This controversy centered around a debate between Peter and Paul over whether Jesus intended the church to be open to Gentiles, who did not follow Jewish law, or restricted only to Jews. The debate was resolved in favor of accepting Gentiles. Paul believed that Christ's death was salvific and superseded the need to obey Jewish law. According to the book of Acts, Peter had a dream that convinced him that Paul's belief was divinely inspired. I find this to be an interesting comparison because it highlights the fact that there have been other deeply divisive controversies that were decided in favor of greater inclusion.

The case of Gentile baptism illustrates that the church has never understood faithfulness to Christ in a fundamentalist way.[49] It is significant that the 1976 Pontifical Biblical Commission (i.e., one appointed by the pope) voted 17–0 that the New Testament does *not* settle the question of women's ordination. The commission also voted 12–5 that neither Scripture nor Christ's plan alone excluded the possibility.[50] The critical question seems to be, In what areas does the church have the authority to do what Christ did *not* do? If racial prejudice had been worldwide and universal, would the church say that it has "no authority whatsoever" to ordain black men because Jesus never did?[51] If women were not at the Last Supper, why are they even permitted to receive communion?[52]

GENDER REVERSAL IN TWO PRIMARY VATICAN ARGUMENTS AGAINST WOMEN'S ORDINATION

Natural Resemblance

As outlined, the 1976 declaration puts forth that when Christ's role in the Eucharist is to be expressed sacramentally, there would not be a "natural resemblance" between Christ and the minister if the role of Christ were not taken by a man. The natural resemblance argument is also found in three of the four pastoral drafts issued on the women's ordination debate. As it appears in the declaration:

> The Christian priesthood is . . . of a sacramental nature: the priest is a sign, the supernatural effectiveness of which comes from the ordination received, but a sign that must be perceptible with ease. . . . The same natural resemblance is required for persons as for things: when Christ's role in the Eucharist is to be expressed sacramentally, there would not be this "natural resemblance" which must exist between Christ and his minister if the role of Christ were not taken by a man.[53]

The document states that the incarnation took place in the form of the male sex and that this fact cannot be disassociated from the doctrine of salvation. Fundamentally, the argument runs, Christ cannot be symbolized as a woman because the historical Jesus was not a woman.

Scholars have found the natural resemblance argument flawed in at least two ways. One flaw concerns the doctrine of salvation that it conveys and the second, the identification of the priest with Christ. Claiming that the eucharistic celebrant must be of the same gender as Christ denies the universality of Christ's redemption. It also implies that Jesus' maleness is a necessary factor for the meaning of the incarnation, a notion that many scholars do not accept. For R. A. Norris, for example, conflating maleness with the incarnation subjects the divine to the limitations of the created world. In his view, because both men and women were baptized by Christ, both sexes were saved by Christ, and it follows that both men and women are capable of representing Christ in the role of the priest.[54] The women's ordination movement has long used this slogan: "Either ordain women or stop baptizing them."

The natural resemblance argument raises the issue of whether Jesus, as divine incarnation, *could* have been a woman. When I have asked undergraduate theology students this question, many have responded, "Well, Jesus could have been a woman, but she wouldn't have been accepted by the people." Was Jesus the man accepted by the people? One student suggested to me that maybe Jesus *was* a woman but was transformed into a man by recorded history. While most scholars do not seriously consider this to be an option, his answer points to the tendency of some to make Jesus into whoever they want him to be.

Interestingly, the Vatican objection to women priests on the grounds of identity borders on equating the eucharistic celebrant with Christ[55] and raises the issue of how Christ is present and active in the person of the presider. Contemporary Catholic theology teaches not that the priest actually becomes Christ during the moment of consecration but that Christ becomes present to the believer through the elements of bread and wine. The theological problem with natural resemblance is not that the priestly ordination configures one to Christ and that the priest acts *in persona Christi* (in the person of Christ). The problem is the leap from asserting that because Christ was male, the priest representing him to the community must also be male.[56] This assertion raises tricky theological questions, such as whether Christ's maleness is essential to the story of salvation. Why would not other characteristics, such as his Jewishness or his blood type, also be essential? His Jewishness was clearly more important to his religious vision than his gender was. The Vatican picks out one feature of Jesus to the exclusion of all others, making it central to his mission but failing to give a rational explanation for choosing this particular characteristic. As a woman Episcopal priest explained to me, natural resemblance implies that there is a sacramental presence to maleness and that Jesus' holiness derives from his maleness.

Inter Insigniores and the later pastoral drafts draw heavily upon the theology of medieval theologian Thomas Aquinas in their adherence to the natural resemblance argument. Aquinas's theology has had a major influence on the development of contemporary Catholic thought. Aquinas articulated that "sacramental signs" represent what they signify by natural resemblance. In his view, "because the female sex cannot signify eminence of rank—women being in a state of subjection—it follows that she cannot receive the sacrament of orders."[57] The "natural superiority" of men over women was at the core of Aquinas's argument against women priests. Ironically, while the Vatican insists that women are equal to men, the Thomistic notion of natural resemblance continues to be upheld.

Bridegroom Imagery

In three of the four pastoral drafts reference is made to the importance of gender in fully expressing "bridegroom" imagery. Like the natural resemblance argument, this argument against women clergy is rooted in the thinking of Aquinas, in particular in his biological determinism. The idea is most clearly expressed in the 1988 pastoral letter "On the Dignity and Vocation of Women." Stating that the sacrament of the Eucharist enacts a uniting of "masculine" and "feminine," the letter indicates that it is necessary for the priest to be male in order for Christ to be viewed as the "bridegroom" and the church as the "bride":

> The eucharist is the sacrament of our redemption. It is the sacrament of the bridegroom and the bride. . . . Since Christ in instituting the eucharist linked it in such an explicit way to the priestly service of the apostles, it is legitimate to conclude that he thereby wished to express the relationship between man and woman, between what is "feminine" and what is "masculine." . . . It is the eucharist above all which expresses the redemptive act of Christ, the bridegroom, toward the church, the bride. This is clear and unambiguous when the sacramental ministry of the eucharist, in which the priest acts *in persona Christi*, is performed by a man.[58]

I find it interesting that this imagery is similar to that used by psychologist Carl Jung in his efforts to point out what he saw as a universal archetypal theme. In his essay "Transformation Symbolism in the Mass," Jung assigns masculine and feminine imagery to the symbols of the elements. The ritual of the Eucharist, for Jung, unites masculine and feminine energies, and in doing so achieves wholeness or totality.[59] For Jung, however, it is the elements themselves that represent masculine and feminine energies, not the priest and the church, respectively. In addition, he never states that only men can represent masculinity, or vice versa.

The church has traditionally been considered by theologians to be feminine, as the body of Christ. This notion repeats a familiar dualistic motif of associating women with matter and men with spirit. Dualistic thinking, or splitting of reality into an absolute good and an absolute bad, has done much to contribute to doctrines of women's inferiority in Christian heritage. Such a perspective is also found in the Vatican notion of *complementarity*, although women's lesser position is not immediately obvious. Complementarity refers to the idea that men and women have different roles to perform within church and society, originating from innate, predetermined functions. In this "two nature" vision of humanity, men and women are ordained to complement one another, leading to a division of male and female roles, which are not interchangeable.[60]

The Vatican asserts that the concept of two human natures has a clear basis in the book of Genesis, chapters 2 and 3, i.e., that men's and women's roles are determined by the "revealed order of creation" as found in the Bible. Yet, liberal scholarly consensus suggests that Genesis 2 and 3 contain a *myth* of creation, one that should not be taken as literally as the daily newspaper. Feminist theologians further assert that the Hebrew creation myth found therein originated to reduce the power of women in a society struggling to affirm patriarchy.[61]

Taking Genesis 2 and 3 as a model for civilization, as the Vatican continues to do, is a thinly veiled rationalization for the continuation of male dominance. Regarding women's ordination, the declaration asserts that women's contemporary role manifests itself in either virginity or motherhood. If women are called to the latter, their place resides in the home. If to the former, they are permitted to perform "helping" functions—such as ministering to the sick, engaging in missionary work, and assisting men in their functions as priests. Men's role in church and society, on the other hand, expresses itself in terms of "headship." Headship allows men to take leadership roles in the church and includes such ecclesial positions as priest, bishop, cardinal, and pope.

Anachronistically, this document was written in the 1970s, not the 1950s. At that time many women were single-handedly raising children and working full-time to support them. Fortunately, much of this androcentric-patriarchal ideology was omitted in later pastoral drafts. Notwithstanding these changes, bridegroom imagery, supported by the notion of complementarity, implies that women are unqualified for the priesthood *because* of their femaleness. Pope John Paul II, for example, expresses in his 1988 pastoral letter his fear that women in their struggle for equality may become too "masculinized" and thus overstep their created nature:

> Consequently, even the rightful opposition of women to what is expressed in the biblical words "he shall rule over you" (Gn. 3:16) must not under any condition lead to the masculinization of women. In the name of liberation from male "domination," women must not appropriate to themselves male characteristics contrary to their own feminine "originality."[62]

Feminist scholars are in turn suspicious that women should be *prohibited* from priesthood because of their distinctive resources. On the contrary, in Christian denominations that do ordain women, women's traditional relational and caretaking roles have provided enormous benefits to church ministries.

Concerning bridegroom symbolism, there is no reason women could not image a bridegroom if they so desired. Symbolically, both male and female celibates are "feminine" or "brides" in relation to Christ, the "bridegroom." While it is assumed that Christ as bridegroom is necessarily a "masculine" symbol that can be represented only by males, no one questions whether men can be symbolic "brides of Christ." In fact, the pope frees the bride metaphor from sexual stereotyping when he writes: "In the Church every human being—male and female—is the 'bride,' by accepting the gift of the love of Christ the redeemer, and by responding with the gift of self."[63] According to Catholic teaching, the feminine is a symbol of both the church and each of her members, male and female.[64]

With respect to nuptial symbolism, a recent focus of discussion has been the significance of "gendered loving"—or the idea that men and women express love differently—for representations of Christ. Gendered loving is viewed in the context of the two roles of the priest, who acts both *in persona Christi* (as Christ) and *in persona ecclesiae* (as the church). Sara Butler, for example, argues that the masculine symbol of bridegroom better represents the human aspect of divine love that God has for the church. The analogy of bridegroom/bride is helpful, in her view, for understanding the two roles of the priest. To support her position, Butler draws upon the pope's view of love and sexuality: he states that a "masculine mode of loving" is characterized by "self-donation," while a corresponding "feminine mode" is marked by "active receptivity."[65] Other theologians also support women's exclusion from priesthood through the concept of gendered loving. Theologian Hans Urs von Balthasar, for example, states: "The man, as sexual being, merely represents what he is not and transmits what he does not really possess and so is simultaneously more and less, than himself. The woman, however, reposes in herself and is entirely her own being, namely, the total reality of a created being facing God as his partner, receiving, retaining, and nurturing his seed and his Spirit."[66] Sexual difference, according to this view, requires that woman be assigned "being" and man, "representation."[67] Butler argues that gender symbolism serves to represent the relational dimension characterized by masculine self-donation—i.e., Christ " 'given for us' "—which marks Christ's presence and activity.[68] The priest, for Butler, acting *in persona ecclesiae*, is a sign of the communion of Christ and church, but only because he first acts *in persona Christi*.[69] It is Christ, in her view, who unites the church with himself in the action of the liturgy.

The literature reflects a disagreement over whether the priest first and foremost acts in the role of Christ or in the role of the church. This makes a difference for views on nuptial symbolism and, by extension, on women's ordination. On the one hand, those who argue that the priest acts first *in persona Christi* also maintain that only men can be priests. On the other, theologians and scholars who admonish that the priest acts initially *in persona ecclesiae* tend to encourage dialogue concerning women's ordination. A contrary position to Butler's, for example, is held by such Catholic scholars as David Power and David Coffey.[70] Their views offer a needed alternative perspective.

For David Power, *in persona Christi* refers to "the recapitulation of the renewed human, in which from one point of view male and female together constitute the *one*, and in which from another 'there is neither male nor female.' " [71] It is within the context of the unity of the church (*in persona ecclesiae*), according to Power, that the role of the ordained minister is made most clear.[72] Power's argument implies that restricting priesthood to men perpetuates rigid gender roles *not* to be found in the eschatological or "saved" community, because in the future Christ will be united with *all* of humanity. It also suggests that the Vatican is taking the metaphors "bride" and "bridegroom" more literally than intended by biblical writers.

Metaphors generally convey greater depth than analogies (e.g., "God is like a mother" is an analogy; "God is love" is a metaphor); however, they begin to break down when taken as concrete realities. There is a difference between "representing another" and "impersonating" that individual, and it has been suggested that the Vatican's use of bridegroom imagery borders on impersonation. Acting in the person of Christ is traditionally understood in the context of serving as an ambassador, as Paul declares himself an ambassador of Christ in 2 Corinthians 5:20. In this sense, bridegroom imagery is meant to convey the fidelity and devotion of a spouse, not sex.[73]

David Coffey in turn maintains that the priest's primary and direct representation is of the earthly church (*in persona ecclesiae*). Because the personal symbol of the earthly church is a woman—Mary—a woman can better represent the church than a man can.[74] Coffey is less strongly convinced that a woman can equally represent Christ "the head."[75] He concludes that either a man or a woman can represent Christ and the church, although neither does so perfectly.[76]

Since the publication of *Ordinatio Sacerdotalis*, even more attention has been given to the issue of nuptial symbolism. Scholars and theologians in support of the 1994 apostolic letter draw upon the natural resemblance argument and bridegroom imagery as elaborated in *Inter Insigniores*. Much of the reasoning is the same, yet a few new nuances have emerged. Two final examples serve to illustrate recent arguments using bridegroom imagery.

Philip Lyndon Reynolds asserts that the most serious obstacle to women's ordination is a "gendered, hierarchical and partly nuptial symbol system which provides a way of understanding what God is and how his people and his creation are related to him."[77] Using the thought of Bonaventure, Reynolds explains that the ordained person represents Christ-as-mediator: "The mediator must act as someone between the people and God, and to this end the people must be able to look up to him as someone higher than themselves albeit lower than God."[78] He leaves open the notion that women cannot be ordained for the reason that men would not look up to them as they would to a man, and he implies that a man is a more appropriate symbol for Christ-as-mediator than a woman is.

John McDade uses opposite reasoning to arrive at the same conclusion—that women should not be ordained. For McDade, the apostolic office of priesthood is deliberately tied to maleness as a *reversal* of typical patterns of male domination: as priests, men are to exemplify the pattern of Christ, who was sent as a servant.[79] In defense of the male hierarchy, he states: "That dialectical tie between authority, service and maleness—and not some patriarchal *droits de seigneur*—is, I suggest, why maleness may be part of the meaning of that office within the Church, and may be part of the symbolic self-understanding preserved by the Pope's ruling."[80]

In sum, while McDade argues that women should be prohibited from taking on a servant role in the form of priesthood, Reynolds implies that women should not be ordained *because* they represent servants. Thus, the reasoning behind the use of nuptial symbolism to support the exclusion of women from the priesthood lacks clear consensus.

Gender Reversal in the Natural Resemblance and Bridegroom Imagery Arguments

We have seen that the natural resemblance argument suffers from several serious flaws, among them the doctrine of salvation conveyed and the identification of the priest with Christ. In addition, we observed that its corollary argument—that the priest must be male in order for Christ to be viewed as a "bridegroom"—makes no sense when at the same time male celibates can be understood to be symbolic "brides of Christ." Yet the Vatican continues to use these arguments to bar women from priesthood. Further analysis of the arguments of natural resemblance and bridegroom imagery demonstrates the five aspects of gender reversal stated earlier.

French ecclesiologist Yves Congar stated in an interview: "If it were a woman [who celebrated the Eucharist] there would be something somewhat disturbing."[81] The author of the interview, Richard Beauchesne, speculates on why Congar might feel this way:

> Might this "something somewhat disturbing" be (for Congar) the female/female (rather than the male/female correspondence) that would "disturb" the spousal analogy especially at Mass . . . were a woman priest to preside? The analogy then would be that of Christ/wife (rather than Christ/husband) and church/wife. In other words, there would exist "on each side" of the altar a female signification.[82]

Beauchesne points out that taking the spousal analogy literally would lead to understanding the ritual of the Eucharist, if women became priests, in terms of a lesbian relationship. I in turn suggest that taking the spousal analogy literally—at least on the side of the husband—is a screen for gender reversal in the Eucharist, which is expressed in several ways.

The Hiding of Jesus' Feminine Qualities and the Appropriation of These Qualities by the Priestly Role

Natural resemblance and bridegroom imagery function to camouflage Jesus' feminine qualities. In doing so, they provide a rationalization for the appropriation of women's functions by celibate male priests and the concomitant barring of women from maternal representations of Jesus. Feminist scholars have shown that Christ *has* been represented theologically and iconographically in feminine terms, in both the patristic and the medieval periods. Moreover, imaging divinity as feminine has strong biblical roots.

Biblical symbols of divinity illustrate that female symbolism for deity is indeed present in Christian heritage. A brief survey of Jewish and Christian scriptures suggests that God is portrayed primarily in masculine terms. Particularly in the Hebrew Bible, God is Lord, king, warrior, and vanquisher. A closer look, however, reveals that this male God also possesses maternal qualities, which include birthing, suckling, and caregiving. Several examples suffice to illustrate that the imagery is indeed present. In Deuteronomy 32:11–12 (RSV), for example, an analogy is made between God's protection and that of a mother eagle watching over her nest:

> Like an eagle that stirs up its nest,
> that flutters over its young,
> spreading out its wings, catching them,
> bearing them on its pinions,
> the Lord alone did lead him,
> and there was no foreign god with him.

Second Isaiah on several occasions also uses maternal imagery to refer to God. See, for example, Isaiah 49:14–15, where he tells of the comfort he gains in the fact that, like a mother who will not forsake her child, God will not forget him:

> But Zion said, "The Lord has forsaken me,
> my Lord has forgotten me."
> "Can anyone forget her suckling child,
> that she should have no compassion
> on the son of her womb?"
> Even these may forget,
> yet I will not forget you.

In the New Testament, maternal imagery is applied to Jesus, the apostles, and the early church. In Matthew 23:37, for example, Jesus is compared to a mother hen who longs to gather her chicks under her wing:

> O Jerusalem, Jerusalem, killing the prophets and stoning those who are sent to you! How often would I have gathered your children together as a hen gathers her brood under her wings, and you would not!

Throughout much of the Gospels, Jesus is depicted as having traditionally feminine qualities—such as meekness, lowliness, and humility. In addition, he fed his people, had disciples who followed him around the way children might, and generally was thought to be very nurturing and compassionate. How ironic is the Vatican's insistence that women cannot represent him.

Patristic scholar Elaine Pagels argues that much of the feminine language for God was preserved in heretical Christian movements such as Gnosticism.[83] An exception to the orthodox pattern of describing God as male, she states, occurs in the writings of Clement of Alexandria, who characterizes God in both masculine and feminine terms as follows: "To those infants who seek the Word, the Father's loving breasts supply milk."[84] Maternal images of Christ can also be found in patristic times. It has been suggested, for example, that Jesus was first thought of as the final emissary of female Wisdom or Sophia.[85] Catholic theologian Elizabeth Johnson asserts that Jesus probably understood himself as the prophet and child of Sophia, or the Hebrew female personification of God's own being in creative and saving involvement with the world. Johnson maintains that Christian reflection before the Gospel of John had not found it difficult to associate Jesus with Sophia.[86] Associating Jesus with Sophia or Hebrew wisdom has been very fruitful for feminist Christology.

In sum, Christ's gender has at periods in Christian history been viewed as female. Caroline Walker Bynum's work also illustrates ways in which Jesus' gender has been symbolized as female.[87] While Bynum's research is focused on medieval spirituality, she observes that the theme of Jesus as mother has roots in the biblical and patristic periods and notes that the Greek fathers, particularly those influenced by Gnosticism, seem to have been more comfortable with maternal metaphors: "The Latin translator of the Acts of Peter suppressed 'mother' in his list of titles for Christ, and the passing references to Christ's maternal love in Augustine and Ambrose in no way compare to the elaborate and lengthy passages that Clement of Alexandria devotes to the nursing Christ."[88] In her book *Jesus as Mother*, Bynum gives six examples of twelfth-century authors who use the notion of motherhood to talk about figures—Jesus among them—usually described in "male" language. Saint Anselm, for example, speaks of both Paul and Jesus as mother to the individual soul and suggests that "mother Jesus" revives the soul at her breast. Bernard of Clairvaux makes the most extensive use of maternal imagery for male figures, and it is almost always elaborated in terms of nurturing, particularly suckling. Another example, William of St. Thierry, extends the references to breasts in the Song of Songs as descriptions of Christ feeding and instructing the individual soul. He also includes references to "Christ nursing his children, to the fostering wings of Jesus, and references (perhaps with womb over-tones) to the soul entering the side of Christ."[89] Guerric, abbot of Igny, uses "motherhood" to explain the relationship of Christ, Peter, and Paul and "maternity" to describe the birth or incorpora-tion of Christ in the individual soul. This abbot speaks at length about the soul hiding in the wounds and heart of Christ. Bynum explains that the most frequent meaning of the mother-Jesus to twelfth-century Cistercians is compassion, nurturing, and union, and suggests that maternal imagery satisfied the need to supplement their image of authority with an image of love and nurture.[90]

Bynum also discusses ways in which Christ's body was imaged *sexually* as female during the medieval period. This information ren-ders doubtful the Vatican claim that Jesus expressed a solely "mas-culine" mode of loving. Taking issue with the view that Jesus' penis was a focal point of many medieval artistic depictions, Bynum argues that Jesus was also depicted as female—as lactating and giv-ing birth. It is significant that even Christ's bleeding was seen, in a certain strand of medieval theology, to depict femaleness:

Not only was Christ enfleshed with flesh from a woman; his own flesh did womanly things: it bled, it bled food and it gave birth. Moreover, in certain bizarre events of the late Middle Ages, there is further support for the argument that bleeding food and giving life through flesh were seen as par-ticularly female activities.[91]

Jesus' wound was correlated both with breast and womb imagery. Significantly, medieval stigmatic women saw themselves as imitating Christ's bleeding flesh: Christ's similar bleeding and feeding body was understood as analogous to theirs.[92] Bynum posits that equating Jesus with female imagery highlighted his humanity—his bleeding/lactating flesh was an example of the "humanation" of God and equated the humanity of Christ with the humanity of us all.[93] These women, it can be said, were acting *in persona Christi*.

Christ symbolized as female, however, was not free from sexist connotations by contemporary standards. For patristic and medieval theologians, women symbolized reproduction and nurture. Women also represented sin, carnality, and lust. Increasingly, only the asexual woman—the virgin—could be of special spiritual service to God. I doubt if the average peasant woman viewed Jesus as female, for to be female was to be depraved. The writers quoted by Bynum in all likelihood viewed a feminine Jesus much the same way as they viewed Mary—washed clean of original sin, asexual, nonmenstrual, and giving birth without impurity. Yet they did use feminine imagery, thus suggesting that these theologians may have ascribed to Jesus a feminine gender identity.

Clearly, this explicit feminine imagery for Christ flies in the face of the natural resemblance argument and bridegroom imagery. Since Christ has not always been represented as male, why must he be so in the contemporary Eucharist? Jesus' feminine qualities are hidden and appropriated by men, under the guise of natural resemblance. The insistence that Jesus the bridegroom be seen as a masculine symbol also serves to cloak feminine symbolism. The emphasis on Jesus' genitality obscures the fact that he has been imaged as both feminine and masculine by Catholic theologians. If women were to be ordained, the Vatican would have to admit the fact that in acting *in persona Christi*, male priests have been performing traditionally female functions; in effect, they have been imitating women.

The Cloaking of Feminine Symbolism in the Bridegroom Symbol and a False Emphasis on Jesus' Genitals

Gender reversal in the Eucharist is also found in the argument that the priest must be male in order to act *in persona Christi*. I find it interesting that there is no biblical distinction, particularly in the writings of Paul, between acting *in persona Christi* and acting *in per-*

sona ecclesiae. Paul demonstrates that the notion "body of Christ" is both a feminine metaphor associated with the church and a signifier of the sacramental presence of Jesus. Scripturally, the body of Christ as eucharistic presence (*in persona Christi*) and the body of Christ as symbolic of church (*in persona ecclesiae*) are not viewed as separate. Yet Vatican documents cloak this knowledge by presenting a litany of male disciples, apostles, and priests, insisting that only men can preside at the Eucharist. In doing so, they create a false emphasis on male genitality, appropriate spiritual nurturing and community in a male priesthood, and restrict women from symbolizing a feminine church.

While the Vatican argument against women priests from tradition is based on a long line of male disciples, apostles, and priests, I wish to emphasize that the important "tradition" of the early Eucharist is in Jewish meal fellowship, especially in the meals Jesus shared with his disciples and others. It has been argued, for example, that table fellowship with Jesus constituted the offer of a share in future eschatological blessings.[94] Jesus frequently used meal imagery in his teaching, a favorite theme being that of the heavenly wedding banquet.[95] In essence, Jesus' table fellowship with all— regardless of whether they be saint or sinner—was a way of proclaiming God's universal forgiveness.

The inspiration for all Christian eucharistic rites, of course, is the "meal of meals," or the Last Supper, the farewell meal that Jesus held with his disciples on the night before he died. Four accounts of the Last Supper (Mark 14:22–24, Matthew 26:26–28, Luke 22:19–20, and 1 Corinthians 11:23–25) describe what the church believes to be the institution of the Eucharist. While all of the Gospel renditions of the Last Supper place it on the night before Jesus' death, disagreement exists about the date. According to the Synoptics (the first three Gospels), the Last Supper is a Passover meal and takes place on the first evening of Passover. In John's account, however, the Last Supper is held a day earlier. Jerome Kodell maintains that the most convincing evidence is that the Last Supper was not a Passover meal but a meal organized by Jesus when he recognized that he might be prevented from celebrating the Passover meal with his disciples the following night.[96] Even if it was not a Passover meal, what is most important for this discussion is the general scholarly agreement that the Last Supper was in the tradition of the Jewish festive meal.

In all Jewish meals, a special blessing is recited at the breaking of the bread by the head of the household or host at the beginning of the meal. Festive meals began with the customary breaking of the bread and had two formal cups of wine, but on especially significant occasions provided a third cup, the "cup of blessing," shared by the participants.[97] A special blessing was also recited over the wine cup at the conclusion of the meal. The New Testament accounts of the Last Supper illustrate that Jesus was repeating customs and reciting table blessings familiar to every Jew.[98] What was different was the interpretation he gave to his actions. Jesus gave a new meaning to the familiar Jewish family ritual when, acting as a host, he said a blessing over the bread, followed by the words "This is my body." After the main meal, in blessing the wine he identified it with his blood. As Kodell puts it, the disciples understood that Jesus was sharing himself with them in an intimate way through this gesture.[99]

The identification of Jesus' blood with the wine and his body with the bread occurs in all four of the Last Supper accounts. The account in 1 Corinthians 11:23–25, most likely the oldest, reads as follows:

> For I received from the Lord what I also delivered to you, that the Lord Jesus on the night when he was betrayed took bread, and when he had given thanks, he broke it, and said, "This is my body which is for you. Do this in remembrance of me." In the same way also the cup, after supper, saying, "This cup is the new covenant in my blood. Do this, as often as you drink it, in remembrance of me."

Paul's understanding of "body," and of Christ's body in particular, is significant, for it influenced developing theology of both the nature of church and the Eucharist. This theology then became tradition.

Paul uses the metaphor of body on several other occasions in 1 Corinthians. In 1 Corinthians 10:17, he writes, "Because there is one bread, we who are many are one body, for we all partake of the one bread." In 1 Corinthians 12:12–13, he states, "For just as the body is one and has many members, and all the members of the body, though many, are one body, so it is with Christ. For by one Spirit we were all baptized into one body—Jews or Greeks, slaves or free—and all were made to drink of one Spirit." At the conclusion of this chapter we again find Paul's belief that Christians are members of the body of Christ: "Now you are the body of Christ and individually members of it" (1 Corinthians 12:27). He draws this analogy in other places in his letters as well (e.g., 1 Corinthians 6:15).

The members of the body of Christ constitute the church. Paul was the first to develop the notion of the church as body of Christ in writing to the Corinthian community, which was deeply divided at the Eucharist. The point of the image was the unity of Christians in the local church.[100] It has been suggested that in Ephesians and Colossians, the body of Christ represents the church universal, whereas in Romans and 1 Corinthians, this metaphor refers to the local church community.[101] As stated in 1 Corinthians 12:13, through baptism into Christ, the members of the church become members of the one body of Christ.

According to Paul, those who partake of the Eucharist become bound to one another and to Christ. In 1 Corinthians 10:1–4, Paul draws a parallel between the eucharistic bread and wine and spiritual food and drink. The cup of blessing is a "koinonia" of the blood of Christ, and the bread is a "koinonia" of the body of Christ. *Koinonia* can be translated as "fellowship," "communion," or "sharing." Paul affirms in 1 Corinthians 10:17 that those sharing bread and cup are bound together: "The many are made one by partaking of the one loaf."[102] As 1 Corinthians 10:16 ff. articulates, when the Christian eats the bread of the Eucharist he or she shares in the body of Christ. Christians become one body, which is the body of Christ—for there is one bread and one body. The instructions of 1 Corinthians 11:17–33 disclose that the Eucharist was united with a meal taken in common by all the members of the Church, the agape or love feast. The Eucharist is thus an effective sign of Christian unity.[103] In sum, for Paul in 1 Corinthians, the three New

Testament uses of "body"—the human body of the historical Jesus, his sacramental presence in the Eucharist, and his body that is the church—are united to form one total symbol.[104] Significantly, the "blood of Christ" is never used as a way to name the church, most likely because in the Jewish tradition blood was defiling.

We have seen that in Paul and in the later Catholic tradition, the Eucharist is a particular point of emphasis for application of body imagery to a spiritual reality.[105] It is significant that the church in the Catholic tradition is thought of as both body of Christ and "bride" of Christ. While the argument is made that Christ cannot be represented by a woman, there is no problem with using feminine imagery to symbolize the church. Yet, as found in 1 Corinthians, the ecclesial body of Christ and the eucharistic body of Christ are not separated.[106]

Thus, the body of Christ as manifested in the Eucharist represents the church and the church (or *ecclesiae*) is symbolized as feminine. In prohibiting women from acting *in persona Christi* in the Eucharist, Vatican officials are also preventing them from acting *in persona ecclesiae*, or from representing the church as Christ's body. We must ask why women, who have signified "body" for centuries of Catholic church tradition, are excluded from doing so in this context of ritual leadership? In prohibiting women from celebrating the Eucharist, the Vatican appropriates bodily metaphors of nurture and mystical unity in the context of a male priesthood, offering the false reasoning that in terms of body, it is Jesus' genitals that really matter, and that "tradition" is preserved by privileging those who emulate Jesus' anatomy.

A defender of the Vatican position might respond that only a man can represent Christ as "head" of the body. For example, Ephesians 5:21–23 expounds: "Be subject to one another out of reverence for Christ. Wives, be subject to your husbands, as to the Lord. For the husband is the head of the wife as Christ is the head of the church, his body, and is himself its Savior." This passage has caused Christian feminists much difficulty and has been used to reinforce women's subordination to men for centuries. Its power is diffused when one realizes that (1) Jesus did not say this, (2) in all likelihood neither did Paul, and (3) the passage reflects the androcentric-patriarchal worldview of the time.[107] In addition, it has been suggested that Christ's headship is not meant as authoritarian but that Christ fills his body with his own spirit.[108] In the Greek sense, there is no "essence" apart from the body.[109] The priest and congregation are an organic sign of the whole Christ.[110] A second biblical metaphor used to describe the relationship between Christ and church is that of the vine and the branches (John 15:5). This metaphor conveys the sense of mutual reciprocity among all members of the church: there is no greater authority implied in the image of vine than in that of the branches.

I have chosen to explore gender reversal as expressed through natural resemblance and bridegroom imagery because these two arguments reveal the hiding of Jesus' feminine qualities, the appropriation of these qualities by male priests, and the barring of women from maternal representations in the Eucharist. By means of a false emphasis on Jesus' genitality, the Vatican arguments against women priests incorrectly locate church tradition in the preservation of a male hierarchy instead of in biblical understandings of the Last Supper. We have seen that while Jesus has been represented as feminine in Christian heritage, this dimension is cloaked by the argument of natural resemblance. I have also shown that Jesus' feminine qualities have been appropriated by the priestly role. Because male priests act in the person of Christ (*in persona Christi*), they function as spiritual feeders and nurturers, roles traditionally associated with women. Yet women are prohibited from representing the body of Christ in the Eucharist under the guise that they cannot represent a bridegroom. In consequence, only male celibate priests are permitted to symbolize community and the union of believers in Christ (*in persona ecclesiae*).

The Restriction of Representations of Birth and Feeding to Celibate Male Priests

We have seen that historically, female reproductive functions are also associated with Jesus. Whereas Jesus was symbolized as lactating and giving birth in the medieval period, in the contemporary Eucharist these functions are restricted to a celibate male priesthood. Catholic scholar Christine Gudorf suggests that since all of the Catholic sacraments (excepting Holy Orders) are celebrations of values inherent in the processes of sustaining life, they are overwhelmingly female activities.[111] Gudorf explains:

> For Baptism, Reconciliation, Anointing, and Eucharist, the human activities they imitate are clearly female activities. Only women give birth. Throughout history women have been and continue to be the chief gatherers, preparers, and servers of food. Similarly, women have historically been designated the round-the clock caretakers of the sick and dying and the preparers of bodies for burial.[112]

Gudorf states that the Eucharist—as the "bread of life"—manifests men's need via priests to likewise claim the ability to nurture life.[113] This need has caused the church to deny women's significance in the activities on which the Eucharist is modeled, leading to the phenomenon of gender reversal.

Continuing in this vein, it should be noted that other, "unofficial," reasons against women priests have periodically surfaced. In the context of the Episcopal women's ordination debate, one male priest objected to women clergy on the grounds that if men could not be mothers, women should not be allowed to be priests.[114] Another issue raised was, What if the priest is pregnant? Can she still celebrate the Eucharist? Underlying this concern is an implicit questioning of the relationship between sexuality and priesthood, and the "fitness" of women—because of their biology—for the office. A woman Episcopal priest whom I interviewed was told by a bishop that she was "inferior matter," for example, and therefore unordainable. Still another source of anxiety in the context of Episcopal women's ordination was the symbolic implications of female celebrants for images of divinity. Episcopal bishop C. Kilmer Myers, for example, argued that "such ordination and consecration [of women] flies against fundamental imagery of Holy Scripture." His objection entailed "basically a theological question pertaining to the Christian doctrine of God."[115] A male Episcopal priest I spoke with argued that women clergy "foul up the symbolism of the uniqueness of the incarnation." These objections suggest that the reasons of tradition, natural resemblance, and bridegroom imagery are not sufficient to account for the depth of resistance to women clergy in the Catholic Church—which to some extent still remains in the Episcopal Church as well. Rather, male resistance to women priests has more to do with women's capacities to be mothers, to become pregnant—and as sexual beings who *can* become pregnant and be mothers—to represent Christ at the altar.

I believe that gender reversal in the Eucharist extends far deeper than the dimensions addressed thus far. It is manifested in the eucharistic prayer, for example, in which celibate men have the ability to turn bread and wine into Christ's body and blood, despite the fact that only women give birth to new life and only women turn blood into milk. The quotation at the outset of the chapter reveals that since women make food within their bodies, they truly embody both earthly and eschatological feeding. Gender reversal is certainly expressed when men alone are allowed to take on the role of the "feeder" in the Eucharist (a reenactment of the Last Supper). In addition, to perpetuate an exclusively male priesthood upholds the denial of women as the "body of Christ." Instead, men, acting *in persona Christi*, become the ones who provide sustenance. The church thus conveys the assumption that feeding and nurturing (i.e., bodiliness) are sacred activities when performed by men, but merely ordinary—even profane—when ritualized by women. As we will explore more fully in the next chapter, the depth of male appropriation of women's functions goes beyond meals and feeding, extending to women's capacities to give forth and sustain life. Gender reversal in the Eucharist, in its most fundamental sense, is about male appropriation of female reproductive roles.

3

MATERNAL ENVY

It is all about mirroring, and one mirrors the mother.
—*Episcopal laywoman*

I'm already acting like my mother—I run around on Sundays
in this dress. How do I know who I am as a man if you can
do this?
—*Male Episcopal priest*

What is behind gender reversal in the Eucharist? It is obvious to a casual observer that the mass is a powerful ritual fueled by deeply evocative symbols. The ritual of a priest reciting the words of institution—"This is my body," "This is my blood"—not only is rooted in a long established tradition but also calls out for psychological analysis. Since it has been suggested that the Vatican arguments from natural resemblance and bridegroom imagery mask men's appropriation of female roles, the next question is why? What other reasons could the male hierarchy have for claiming that women cannot represent Christ or that Christ's body can never be viewed as feminine? The following discussion suggests that maternal themes run even deeper, to the theology of the Eucharist itself. The Eucharist is not only a supper ritual in which believers are "fed" the body and blood of Christ. In addition, psychologically the mass expresses pre-Oedipal issues concerning the infant-mother relationship. I will argue that gender reversal in the Eucharist is deeply rooted in unconscious envy and fear of the archaic mother figure.

As stated earlier, the psychological schools of thought most useful for this study are Freudian, object relations, and French feminist.

Discussion of French feminism will be reserved for chapter 6. First, a basic overview of the first two approaches is offered, with particular attention to issues of gender identity. Also evaluated are such general psychoanalytic notions as the unconscious and defense mechanisms. For the reader who is unfamiliar with the methodology, this introductory section is intended to clarify the strengths and weaknesses of a psychoanalytic approach.

Some background in ritual studies will provide further foundation for the arguments made here. Since the Eucharist is the central ritual of Catholicism, an overview of the nature and function of ritual activity helps to situate it within a larger context. As a field, ritual studies offers theories of why and how people engage in ritual behavior. Particular attention is paid to the power of ritual to transform individuals and social institutions. Subsequent discussions of the theology and psychology of the Eucharist furnish a basis for exploring male gender identity issues in terms of maternal envy and the desire for feminine identification.

USES AND CRITIQUES OF PSYCHOANALYSIS

In recent years psychoanalysis has become quite popular as a method of inquiry in the humanities and in social sciences fields. It is possible to buy books on psychoanalytic interpretations of historical figures, social movements, classic works of literature, and even film and other media genres. Terms such as *repression, defense mechanisms,* and *Oedipus complex* have become mainstream vocabulary words. Increasingly, feminists in the humanities and social sciences need to be knowledgeable about psychoanalytic theory if they are to keep up in their respective fields. This is a shift from the position of earlier feminist theorists, who tended to regard all psychoanalytic methods with suspicion. In this section I offer a synopsis of Freudian and object relations theories as well as answer a series of objections to them. By doing so I demonstrate the value of psychoanalytic theory as an analytic tool, especially for those interested in feminist theory and religious studies.

Freud

Psychoanalysis began with Sigmund Freud, a Viennese physician who lived from 1856 to 1939. Freud was trained in neurophysiology, and his first research was in the treatment of nervous disorders. He became interested in the study of the mind primarily through the influence of the famous French hypnotist J. M. Charcot. While Charcot viewed his interests in hysteria and hypnotism in terms of branches of neuropathology, for Freud they were the first investigations into the human psyche.

In his 1920 essay "Beyond the Pleasure Principle," Freud explains that psychoanalysis was "first and foremost an art of interpreting." Since interpretation alone did not "cure" the patient, a second goal emerged, that of forcing the patient to confirm the analyst's interpretation through memory. Here the chief aim was to uncover the patient's resistances, point them out to the patient, and induce him or her to abandon them.[1] For Freud, early psychoanalysis was concerned chiefly with uncovering unconscious material, and later evolved into a technique that included exposing defenses against repressed memories.

After the publication of *Studies on Hysteria* (1895) Freud underwent a period of intense self-analysis, consisting in large part of his own dream interpretation. He discovered that dreams, like neurotic symptoms, were the product of a conflict and a compromise between the "primary" unconscious impulses and the "secondary" ones. With this he uncovered the distinction between primary and secondary processes. His period of self-analysis led to his abandonment of the trauma theory of hysteria[2] and to the recognition of infantile sexuality and the Oedipus complex. These theories are presented in *The Interpretation of Dreams* (1900). In this seminal work, Freud offers the first full account of his dynamic view of mental processes, of the unconscious, and of the dominance of the "pleasure principle." He also makes it clear that his concepts apply not only to pathological states but also to normal mental life.

The Oedipus complex is of primary importance to understanding Freud's theory of the construction of gender identity, so it will be reviewed here. In *The Interpretation of Dreams* Freud refers to the well-known myth of Oedipus, in which King Oedipus slays his father, Laius, and marries his mother, Jocasta. Freud states: "It is the fate of all of us, perhaps, to direct our first sexual impulse towards our mother and our first hatred and our first murderous wish against our father. Our dreams convince us that that is so."[3] While Freud believed dreams were the "royal road to the unconscious," in waking life these sexual and murderous impulses remained sublimated or repressed.

Freud outlines his theory of the Oedipus complex more fully in "The Dissolution of the Oedipus Complex (1924)," "Some Psychical Consequences of the Anatomical Distinction Between the Sexes (1925)," and "Female Sexuality (1931)." He argued that both males and females initially take their mother as love-object. Boys retain the mother as love-object throughout the Oedipus complex. During the phallic phase of development, the boy's sexual wishes in regard to his mother become more intense and his interest in his genitals increases, which he betrays by manipulating them more frequently. The threat of castration by his father does not become a real danger to the boy, however, until he inadvertently observes his mother's or sister's already castrated state. The Oedipus complex offers the boy two ways of satisfaction: putting himself in his father's place and having intercourse with his mother or taking the place of his mother and being loved by his father. The boy's identification with his father begins to take on hostile tones, expressing itself as a wish to get rid of his father in order to take his place with his mother.

The recognition of his own potential castration and women's lack of a penis puts an end to both of the above fantasies. As a result, the object-cathexes of feminine identification and feminine attraction must be given up and masculine identification adopted. Freud states: "The authority of the father or the parents is introjected into the ego, and there it forms the nucleus of the super-ego, which takes over the severity of the father and perpetuates his prohibitions against incest, and so secures the ego from the return of the libidinal object-cathexis."[4] Hence, while the castration complex initiates the destruction of the Oedipus complex, the resolution of the Oedipus complex results in establishment of the superego and repression of the boy's mother as love-object.

Freud initially developed his theories of the Oedipus complex in terms of male psychology and only later attempted to explain what the phenomenon might mean for girls. He rejected the term "Electra complex," which Carl Jung used to describe the female correlate to the boy's Oedipus complex. He purportedly found women's psychology enigmatic, referring to adult women's sexual life as a "dark continent."[5] Not surprisingly, his theories of female Oedipal development have come under heavy fire from feminists, as have his theories of Oedipal development.

While boys must give up their mother for their father, girls, for Freud, must undergo a twofold change: a change in the leading sexual organ and a change in the sexual object. Like boys, for girls the mother is the original love-object. Freud asks: "But how does it happen that girls abandon it and instead take their father as an object?"[6] Penis envy is the key to his answer. Penis envy is also an integral concept to Freud's understanding of women's psychological development. Penis envy dates to the time a girl first observes her parents *in coitus*, or sees the penis of a brother or playmate and decides she wants a penis herself. While boys resolve the Oedipus complex *by means of* the castration complex, girls enter into the Oedipus complex *via* the castration complex.

Freud writes that the girl's recognition of the anatomical distinction between the sexes leads to a new position—the "equation of 'penis child.'" The girl then abandons her wish for a penis and takes her father as a love-object. For Freud, renunciation of the penis is not tolerated without some attempt at compensation, which becomes expressed in a desire to receive a baby from her father—to bear him a child. As well, her mother becomes the object of her jealousy. Freud states that the girl's Oedipus complex "seldom goes beyond that of taking her mother's place and the adopting of a feminine attitude toward her father."[7] For Freud, the girl's Oedipus complex is then gradually given up, because the wish for a baby from her father remains unfulfilled. The desires to possess a penis and a child remain strongly cathected in the unconscious, however, and prepare the girl for her future feminine role.

To summarize, a psychoanalytic approach looks at the unconscious material of individuals and groups, and does so through
uncovering the familial or societal past. Freud put immense importance on the relationship the child has with his or her parents, particularly the father. He believed that the child's initial relationship
with the father laid the foundation for relationships with all later
male figures, especially authority figures. Because he believed childhood conflicts with the father were not always resolved, Freud felt
that neurotic expressions of the child-father relationship were often
retained in adult life. Freud's strengths lie in the exploration of the
unconscious roots of individual and societal behavior and the illu-
mination of the construction of gender identity in unconscious
dynamics. Much popular literature and film illustrate strong
Freudian themes, such as unconscious conflicts, repressed memories and desires, and the effects of early childhood traumas. In the
film *Ordinary People*, for example, Conrad blocks out the memory
of his brother's drowning to avoid feelings of anxiety and guilt as a
result of the trauma. Because he will not let himself feel, however,
he lives without affect or purpose. Through establishing a transference, Conrad's psychiatrist breaks through his denial and is able to
facilitate emergence of the repressed memories. This experience is
cathartic for Conrad. *The Edible Woman*, by Margaret Atwood,
illustrates Freudian themes of displacement and aggression. The
main character becomes engaged to a man who she perceives is suf-
focating her, and she gradually is able to eat fewer and fewer types
of food. The story comes to climax when she symbolically offers a
cake, baked and decorated in the shape of herself, to her fiancé for
his consumption.

Because the unconscious is where notions of gender identity
originally develop, a psychoanalytic understanding of unconscious
processes is necessary for studies of gender. As Jane Flax writes,
"Psychoanalysis provides essential insights into the problem of differentiation. . . . Since gender identity develops originally and most
deeply through pre-verbal and nonrational experience, an understanding of unconscious processes is crucial for feminist theory."[8]
Particularly through exploring early patterns of childrearing, psy-

choanalytic theory can illuminate the construction of what has traditionally been considered "feminine" identity. Object relations theory, to be discussed next, is especially useful in this regard.

Freud's major weaknesses lie in the method by which he arrived at his conclusions and in his confusion of biology with social normativity. A primary criticism is that his theories are difficult to validate. He pieced together his research from his own behavior, the behavior of a limited number of neurotic patients, and events in the world at large. Freud did very few child analyses, so his theory of the Oedipus complex, for example, is based primarily on his analysis of adults. He has also been faulted for accepting his patients' verbalizations without attempting to verify them through outside resources. This criticism has in recent years been leveled against contemporary psychotherapists under the name "false memory syndrome."

As psychologist of religion Diane Jonte-Pace articulates, scholars in women's studies have pointed out three types of androcentrism in Freud's work: "the premise that the male is the human norm; an exclusion of women or womanlessness expressed in the assumption that the crucial cultural and psychological relation is between father and son; and the insistence on female moral and intellectual inferiority."[9] In the 1970s feminists such as Betty Friedan, Shulamith Firestone, and Kate Millett made Freud a common target for criticism, accusing him of using a male model by which women were found deficient. In particular, they argued against his aphorism "anatomy is destiny"—the notion that a woman's reproductive role, gender identity, and sexual preference are determined by her lack of a penis. These feminists asserted that women's social position and her subordination to men had little to do with female biology and everything to do with the social construction of femininity.[10]

Two feminists who address feminist criticisms of psychoanalysis, yet also point out the virtues of Freud's theories, are Simone de Beauvoir and Juliet Mitchell. While French existentialist de Beauvoir underscores Freud's misogyny in his claims of biological innateness and the primacy of the Oedipus complex,[11] she also highlights the importance of body and sexuality in Freud's theories and in women's alienated condition. Freud takes into account the importance of physicality to humans' sense of who they are and their place in society. He acknowledges gender identity issues. American feminist Juliet Mitchell in turn criticizes Freud for his failure to be attentive to the social character of his theories. For Mitchell, the Oedipus complex is a patriarchal myth, reflecting the entry of humanity into culture through the exogamous incest taboo, the role of the father, the exchange of women, and the consequent difference between the sexes. Yet Freud's theories give the beginning of an explanation of the inferiorized psychology of women under patriarchy—defined by Mitchell as the "law of the father."[12] It is not on account of women's "natural" procreative abilities but on account of their cultural civilization as exchange objects that women acquire their feminine definition.[13] Extending Mitchell's interpretation, until patriarchy is overthrown, we need an explanation of how the family constellation affects the psychological development of the sexes.

I believe the Oedipus complex correctly highlights the important role of the familial father to maintaining patriarchal social structures. In addition, as Jonte-Pace points out, women are not entirely absent from the Oedipal scenario. In theory, the child's incestuous desire for the mother is the catalyst for the Oedipal struggle, a fact that Freud ignores or deemphasizes.[14] Thus, Freud's Oedipus complex also casts light on the notion of envy, a dynamic of enormous importance in gender reversal.

Some of the directions that post-Freudian psychoanalysts have taken are object relations theory, ego psychology, Kohutian self psychology, and Lacanian psychoanalysis. All of these have generally adhered to Freud's original emphasis on uncovering unconscious motivations for behavior and on exposing resistances to repressed material. They do not all share his understanding of the importance of the Oedipus complex, however, or of biology as prescriptive for identity. Two schools of thought that pay special attention to women's psychology are object relations theory and feminist psychoanalytic theory as it has emerged from France. Both of these psychoanalytic schools offer necessary correctives to Freud's misogynism.

Object Relations Theory

Object relations theorists have in general been much more systematic in their methods than Freud was—that is, they did not use themselves as patients, and they made repeated observations on infants before theorizing about childhood issues. Object relations theory originated in Britain and developed under the auspices of such analysts as W. D. Fairbairn, Michael Balint, Karen Horney, and D. W. Winnicott. In contrast to Freud's emphasis on instincts, object relations thought begins with the idea that infant development originates in relation to other human beings rather than in relation to the vicissitudes of their drives.[15] In addition, this school of thought focuses on an earlier period of childhood than did Freud. While Freud rarely worked with children, object relations theory is replete with clinical examples of infant research.

As such, it gives more emphasis to the child's relationship with her or his mother than does classical Freudian analysis. While Freud focused on the Oedipus complex, object relations theorists concentrate on the pre-Oedipal period. One major distinction that psychoanalysts generally make between the Oedipal and pre-Oedipal periods is that the mother is formative for development during the pre-Oedipal stage, and the father during the Oedipal one. Object relations theorists claim that the pre-Oedipal period, and the mother-infant relationship, is formative for and underlies the Oedipal stage. One of the most important pre-Oedipal issues is the infant's sense of connection to and differentiation from her or his mother.

Object relations theory is useful for feminist research for at least four reasons. One is its critique of Freud's misogynism, particularly by Melanie Klein and Karen Horney. A second is its focus on social interactions rather then biological drives. A third is the concern with the pre-Oedipal period of development and maternal influences. A fourth reason is its use by feminist scholars to gain insight into early gender differentiation. A brief introduction to the theories of Karen Horney, D. W. Winnicott, Melanie Klein,[16] Dorothy Dinnerstein, and Nancy Chodorow follows, for their work is important to our later discussion.

Karen Horney was a contemporary of Freud. Janet Sayers observes that her work is particularly useful for feminists because of its rejection of Freudian phallocentrism and its attention to psychological causes and effects of sexual inequality.[17] Horney questioned some of Freud's formulations of psychosexual development, particularly in relation to women. For example, she attacked his overemphasis on penis envy, his neglect of womb envy, and his lack of attention to cultural factors that shape women's psychology. On the other hand, some feminists find limitations in certain of Horney's theories, such as the notion that women's psychology is determined by inherent identification with the mother. In addition, Horney has been accused of adhering to a position of innate heterosexuality, a stance that was influential in the writings of Klein.[18] Horney offers important correctives to Freud, however, for the following reasons. She argued that women's feelings of subordination originate not in castration anxiety but in social subordination. She augmented Freud's notion of penis envy with breast and womb envy. While Horney made use of Freudian concepts, she located them in a social rather than a biological explanation. "Femininity" was, for Horney, not innate but a defensive adaptation to male domination.

Melanie Klein was also a contemporary of Freud. Klein is well known for developing the first play therapy with children. Her results led her to take issue indirectly with some of Freud's theories on childhood development. For example, Klein argued that the Oedipal phase develops much earlier than Freud had supposed and that initially it describes the infant's relationship with her or his mother. In addition, Klein argued that the mother, not the father, is seen by the child as the first castrator.[19]

Klein hypothesized that an infant comes into the world with feelings of both love and hate toward the mother, or the "object" of its first attentions. She believed these feelings were innate; she argued, however, that they are exacerbated by the infant's experiences of frustration and deprivation at the breast. The infant's hostility toward its mother expresses itself in terms of sadistic and persecutory phantasies.[20] In particular, the infant's world is dominated by a "breast" and a "belly": the breast, which is the source of nurturance or deprivation, and the belly from which it came. In Klein's view, these two body parts are both dangerous to the infant and are endangered by it. As a result, the infant has sadistic oral and tactile impulses directed toward the mother's breast and belly.

Klein states that at approximately six months of age, the infant reaches the "paranoid-schizoid" position. At this stage, the internalized breast is split into "good" and "bad" objects—the nurturing breast and the depriving breast. Later, at about eighteen months of age, the infant begins to be able to integrate the breast as a whole object. At this point in development, the infant also begins to view the mother as a whole object rather than as just a breast. Klein calls this stage the "depressive position." The depressive position is marked by guilt for what the infant fears it has done to the mother in phantasy, and by its attempt to make "reparation" to her through love and good deeds for possible inflicted harm. This shift is necessary for healthy childhood development.

Klein acknowledges that splitting and paranoid-schizoid and depressive positions are also found in adults. Her work is important for its attention to the overwhelming power of the mother figure in the infant's psyche, breast envy, and internalization of good and bad objects. Weaknesses in Klein are that she adheres very closely to Freudian notions of castration anxiety as well as to innate drives of love and hate.

D. W. Winnicott shared terrain with other English analysts such as W. D. Fairbairn and Harry Guntrip. He is important for his notions of transitional objects and transitional experience, and for his location of the origins of cultural phenomena in the early infant-mother relationship. Winnicott explores the very earliest playful mother-infant communications. He writes, for example, that the first "play at the breast enables the baby to find the mother and to communicate with her."[21] Without this interaction, baby and mother would remain strangers. Playful interaction between baby and mother paves the way for the infant's development of "transitional objects," as well as for adult creative behavior.

According to Winnicott, transitional objects originate and develop as follows. In the theoretical "first feed," the creative potential of the infant causes it to hallucinate the "would-be-breast," in response to which the mother provides the breast "more or less in the right place in and the right time." Much repeated, this ritual initiates the infant's ability to form illusions. At eight to ten to twelve months, a particular object—the transitional object—comes to replace the infant's illusions.[22] Thumbs, blankets, and teddy bears are frequent choices for transitional objects. Transitional objects involve what Winnicott calls an "intermediate" area of experiencing, which he equates with the infant's being lost in the activity of play.

Play and transitional objects are later important to cultural experience. Winnicott asserts that cultural experience is the adult continuity of the childhood experience of play and is an extension of transitional phenomena. An inability to play early in life, because of loss of the mother or her failure to be dependable, results in the loss of meaningful cultural symbols in adulthood.[23]

Winnicott has been criticized for his prescription of the "good enough" mother. While he may have meant that the good enough mother need not *always* be there for her child—only most of the time—his work has been interpreted to mean that the mother must slavishly wait on the child, suppressing her own needs and desires. Jonte-Pace makes note of this in her critique of object relations theory:

> First, the mother remains an object of service whose desire is shaped by the child's need and whose subjectivity remains unexamined. Second, there is an underlying idealization and romanticization of motherhood. . . . third, in the literature on pathology, we seem to find a reversal of this set of assumptions in a position that might be characterized as "blaming the mother."[24]

While the tendency to view motherhood as an ideal state—and the pre-Oedipal period as a paradisaical period in childhood development—is not particular to Winnicott, he exemplifies this perspective. His theory of symbol formation, however, has been important for scholars in religious studies in understanding the genesis of religious symbols.

The work of Dorothy Dinnerstein and Nancy Chodorow contributes to an understanding of male dominance in Western cultures from a feminist psychoanalytic perspective. Psychologist Dinnerstein utilizes object relations theory, particularly Klein's work, to argue that the female monopoly over child care results in male domination of society. Dinnerstein implies that because women mother, children are less likely to move out of the paranoid-schizoid position and into the depressive position. As such, they permanently sidestep the task of working through persecutory and depressive anxieties. Because of female mothering, children view the father as good and the mother as, at best, ambivalent. As adults, individuals retain their infantile sense of the mother figure as "engulfing" and "nebulously overwhelming." Dinnerstein explains that the ambivalence toward the parent who is first representative of "nature" consists not only of unstable, conflicting feelings but of unstable, conflicting perceptions of her sentience. Woman's anomalous image fluctuates between "omniscient goddess" and "dumb bitch."[25]

According to Dinnerstein, girls and boys deal with this situation in different ways. In order to avoid the pain involved in separating from their mothers, girls grow up to be dependent on men. They choose not to undergo the process of forging a separate feminine identity; instead they, like their mothers, accept the reign of male authority. Dinnerstein states: "Positive feelings toward the mother are normally split off from negative ones in early life in order to preserve the possibility of feeling, at least sometimes, a sense of unqualified oneness with this central source of all that is good."[26] These positive feelings are largely transferred to the father. Boys grow up, on the other hand, to feel vindictive toward women, and in turn they seek vengeance for being subject to the female will in childhood. Male vengeance, according to Dinnerstein, is expressed in patriarchal tyranny and authoritativeness.[27] Men attempt to overcome the fact that they were at one time absolutely dependent on their mothers by exerting absolute control over both women and nature.

Dinnerstein proposes dual parenting as a solution to maternal ambivalence. If both parents were equally involved in child care, good and bad objects could not as easily be assigned to father and mother, respectively, and children would be forced to deal with the parents as whole people. While Dinnerstein's theory is compelling, as Jean Bethke Elshtain points out, lack of a thorough political analysis makes dual parenting seem something of a cure-all, a panacea for centuries of female subordination.[28] Moreover, Dinnerstein does not take into account the diverse forms that the family takes, both interculturally and intraculturally.[29] Nevertheless, her theory deserves attention for its focus on the family and early childhood relationships as factors in the perpetuation of male domination of women.

Sociologist Nancy Chodorow concentrates on why women continue to mother despite an expansion of women's roles in contemporary society. Dismissing the idea that mothering is innate, Chodorow concludes that it has to do with unconscious desires originating in the pre-Oedipal period of development. She states that the model of mother as primary caretaker involves a woman in a double identification, with her own mother and with her child, putting her in a situation of repeating her own mother-child history. One result of this set of circumstances is that mothers and daughters develop a stronger bond than do mothers and sons. Another result is a greater degree of infant-mother merging for girls than for boys. Chodorow maintains that because of this pattern of early bonding, girls develop more flexible ego boundaries than do boys, and that, as adults, women find a certain psychological security in feeling interconnected with other women. This pattern also creates the conditions for the perpetuation of women's mothering and their subordination to men.

Chodorow's theory of mothering involves differences in the development of core male and female gender identity. She states that while children of both sexes are originally part of the mother, a mother unconsciously and often consciously experiences her son as "more of an 'other'" than her daughter. The development of male gender identity, as a result, becomes based on a greater "fixed 'me'—'not me' distinction." In contrast, formation of the female self involves less dichotomizing into "me"—"not me" distinctions.[30] While girls grow up with a sense of continuity and a relational connection to the world, for boys, separateness and difference are important components of differentiation. The separation process between mothers and sons is further promoted by boys' repudiating their first object relation—their mother—in the course of forging a masculine identity. Boys grow up fearing connection, and instead model their masculine gender identity on roles occupied by men in society. Because of early-developed, conflictual core gender identity problems, men find it important to have a clear sense of gender difference and to maintain rigid boundaries between what is masculine and what is feminine. As Chodorow explains: "Thus, because of a primary oneness and identification with his mother, a primary femaleness, a boy's and a man's core gender identity itself—the seemingly unproblematic cognitive sense of being male—is an issue. A boy must learn his gender identity as being not-female, or not-mother."[31]

Thus, for Chodorow, women's mothering perpetuates traditional gender roles for men and women in modern society. Like Dinnerstein, Chodorow in her early work argues for the desirability of dual parenting.[32] In *The Reproduction of Mothering: Psychoanalysis and the Sociology of Gender*, Chodorow, like Dinnerstein, puts too much emphasis on dual parenting as a solution to the human malaise, and one is left wondering how equal parenting would leave persons of both genders with the positive capacities that each has, but without the destructive extremes of each.[33] This emphasis on dual parenting is not present in her later work, which also takes into account differences in race, class, and sexual orientation.[34] Her theory offers a compelling analysis of women's tendency toward connection and relationality, and men's toward separateness and autonomy, and the origins of these tendencies in early mother-infant relationships.

Ellyn Kaschak offers a critique of Chodorow's assumption that the nuclear family is normative, even in white, middle-class settings. By pointing out that the majority of children who grow up in non-nuclear family settings do not differ in gender-related attributes from those who do, Kaschak raises questions of whether female "mothering" per se—or a culture that attributes certain meanings to females and males—is, in actuality, responsible for observed gender differences.[35] Kaschak also suggests that the propensity for girls to grow up more relationally oriented is increased rather than decreased when the father is the more dominant parent.[36] To

respond to these criticisms, Chodorow would not likely differentiate between the cultural meanings Kaschak refers to and the mothering she describes. In defense of *The Reproduction of Mothering*, for
example, Chodorow indicates that the book can be read as much as
an account of how psyches produce social and cultural forms as vice
versa. Her discovery, she explains, was that unconscious processes
"contributed to the reproduction of mothering and to other aspects
of the ideology and organization of gender. . . . But this is not the
same thing as claiming that gender ideologies are directly internalized, that society and culture precede individual pscyhological creativity."[37] She acknowledges that for all the women she has worked
with in pscyhoanalysis, perceived paternal power and paternal
appreciation were important contributions to the sense of self and
gender.[38]

Before turning to women's ordination and the Eucharist, a few
words need to be said about the psychoanalytic notion of the
"unconscious." What makes dynamics "unconscious" versus "conscious"? Popular media have recently entertained discussion over
whether there in fact *is* an unconscious.[39] Whether or not the
unconscious exists as a separate entity of the mind, there is no doubt
that persons are not consciously and rationally aware of the entire-
ty of dynamics involved in their actions. In this sense, latent dynamics can be called "unconscious" ones. Thus, in a general sense one
may view the unconscious as the untapped aspects of mental functioning. Given this definition, much of human action can be said to
be driven by unconscious motivation, motivation that may or may
not surface into consciousness. I will argue that the roots of gender
reversal in the Eucharist lie in general and long-standing tendencies
in male psychological development, which are not easily overcome
by education or the desire to be fair.

One must also take note of what are known psychologically as
defense mechanisms, particularly repression. Defense mechanisms
are methods employed by the ego to shield the conscious mind from
psychic anxiety resulting from threat or danger. As such, they deny,
distort, or falsify reality in some fashion. The most basic of these is
repression. In repression, the ego excludes from consciousness that
which it cannot accept—undesirable or unpleasant impulses,
thoughts, feelings, or memories. Repression may prevent a person

from seeing something that is in plain view or may distort or falsify the information coming in from the sense organs in order to protect the ego from anxiety. For example, a person who has trouble with boundaries may make an inappropriate pass at a coworker and then, when confronted, claim there was no such intent and that the problem is with the coworker. Similarly, memories or ideas may be repressed. Repressed cathexes in turn may exist unchanged in the personality, may force their way to consciousness, or may find expression by displacement. Repression is lifted when the source of the threat disappears, rendering the repression no longer necessary.[40] In the case above, if this individual through therapy is able to see that she has trouble with boundaries because of childhood abuse, she can be made aware of her own tendency to violate boundaries without being as defensive about it.

To reiterate, much of human behavior is driven by unconscious motivation. This unconscious motivation need not always be viewed in a pejorative fashion, however. Unconscious dynamics also hold enormous power to transform individuals and institutions. I believe that unconscious elements are an integral aspect of ritual activity. Next we will turn to an examination of fundamental issues in ritual studies, focusing on the Eucharist in particular, followed by a look at important unconscious psychological themes underlying the Eucharist. By gaining knowledge about what ritual is and how it functions, we can begin to explore what difference women priests would make as ritual celebrants.

THE TRANSFORMING POWER OF RITUAL

As stated, an introduction to the field of ritual studies assists us in understanding the nature of the Eucharist as the central rite of Catholicism. It also supports claims made in subsequent chapters about the power of ritual to effect individual and social transformation. Ritual studies as a discipline has grown significantly since the early eighties, in large part because of the pioneering work of two religious studies scholars, Ronald Grimes and Catherine Bell. Previously the field had been almost exclusively defined by Victor Turner, an anthropologist whose work still remains highly influential. Four basic questions provide a framework for a general discussion of ritual. First, how is *ritual* to be defined? Are there features common to all ritual activity? Second, why do people ritualize? What social and psychological functions do rituals serve? Third, what is the relationship between ritual and power? Does ritualization preserve the status quo, or can it also be subversive? And fourth, how does gender affect ritual activity? In other words, do women ritualize differently than men? This last question, of course, sets the stage for investigating the significance of women clergy for the Eucharist. Answering these questions will provide a context for later psychological arguments.

How does one define the term *ritual*? I have mentioned the importance of the Eucharist to Catholic belief and practice, but to what larger category of activity does it belong? Most discussions of the nature of ritual make reference to Turner's definition, so we will begin there. For Turner, ritual is defined as "prescribed formal behavior for occasions not given over to technological routine, having reference to beliefs in mystical beings or powers."[41] In the case of the Eucharist, the "formal behavior" includes the prayers and actions of the priest during mass, such as the consecration of the bread and wine and their distribution among the people. While many scholars accept Turner's definition, Grimes finds it inadequate for the following reasons: (1) rituals are not always "formal," (2) ritual cannot be definitively separated from technology, and (3) not all rituals refer to mystical beings or powers.[42] Grimes prefers the term *ritualization*, which he defines "softly" as follows: "Ritualizing transpires as animated persons enact formative gestures in the face of receptivity during crucial times in founded places."[43] "Formative gestures" here refers to the consecration and distribution mentioned earlier. In the case of the Eucharist, "crucial times in founded places" points to the reenactment of the Last Supper ritual by the early Christians shortly after Jesus' death. In a later work, Grimes posits that ritual refers to the general idea of which a "rite" is a specific instance. "Ritualizing," in his view, conveys the activity of deliberately cultivating rites.[44] In other words, ritualizing is the process out of which rites emerge.

Several other definitions of *ritual* are worthy of note. Bruce

Lincoln suggests that ritual is a "coherent set of symbolic actions that has a real, transformative effect on individuals and social groups."[45] In this definition, the terms *symbolic* and *transformative* are important—symbols are the building blocks of ritual, and they effect change in people's lives. As will be discussed in subsequent sections, the priest, the bread, and the wine are the building blocks of the Eucharist. Emile Durkheim in turn posits that ritual consists of "rules of conduct which prescribe how a man should comport himself in the presence of these sacred objects."[46] "Rules of conduct" suggest how one must behave around the priest, bread, and wine. A consecrated host, for example, must not be dropped or thrown away. Finally, Bell articulates that ritualization is a way of acting designed to distinguish and privilege what is being done in comparison to other, more ordinary activities.[47] More specifically, for Bell ritualization establishes a "privileged contrast," differentiating its way of acting as more important or powerful than others. In other words, eating bread and drinking wine are not in themselves considered sacred, but these actions become holy when carried out in the context of an altar and a priest. For Bell, ritualization is fundamentally meant to give the impression that its practices are distinct and its associations special.[48]

From the above discussion, one can see that the nature of ritual does not enjoy scholarly agreement. One reason for controversy seems to be that what some call ritual, others call "liturgy." Grimes, for example, notes six modes of ritual sensibility: ritualization, decorum, ceremony, liturgy, magic, and celebration.[49] Liturgy, he states, is "any ritual action with an ultimate frame of reference and the doing of which is felt to be of cosmic necessity."[50] In other words, liturgy is in some way centered around the divine, whereas other forms of ritual may not be. Bell explains that *liturgy*—derived from the Greek *leitourgia*—means an act of public service or ministry. Christian scholars generally have preferred this term when talking about their own rites and ritual tradition, and the Eucharist is often referred to in this context.[51] Hence, liturgy implies ritual enacted in an ecclesial or church setting. One may create a "church setting," however, without necessarily being in a church—the presence of priest, bread, and wine does not require a building. Scholars also

disagree with Lincoln's claim that ritual is transformative, a controversy that I will address in due course. Most, however, would support his position that symbol is the basic building block of ritual.
For example, the fundamental unit of ritual for Grimes is "gesture,"
defined analogously as a "dynamic symbolic act."[52]

Defining ritual becomes only slightly easier as characteristics of
ritual are investigated. First we must ask, Are there universal features of ritual activity? Arnold Van Gennep, for example, discerned
three stages in rites of passage: separation, liminality, and reaggregation or reincorporation. In the course of a ritual, an individual is in
some way separated from his or her normal reality, has an experience
of being at the threshold of another reality, and then becomes part
of that new reality. The traditional understanding of the ritual of
marriage, for example, is that two people—who before marriage
were separate individuals—are in the course of the ceremony (the
liminal stage) bound together forever. Turner focused on the middle stage of liminality, adding his own twist. The bonds that are
formed during liminality, according to Turner, are "anti-structural,
undifferentiated, nonrational, I–Thou."[53] Liminality, for Turner, is
an "in-between" state, in which individuals are not bound by the
constraints of their old reality. The function of liminality, in
Turner's view, is to provide a smooth segue into the final reaggregation stage, where the individual prepares to enter structure once
again. Through the "interstices" or breaks in structure in liminality,
"communitas" occurs. Turner defines *communitas* as "a relational
quality of full unmediated communication, even communion,
between definite and determinate identities which arises sponta-
neously in all kinds of group situations and circumstances."[54]
Communitas is that quality to which I will later refer as "relationality" or "communion." Communitas enables persons to bond together, and it is a central feature of eucharistic theology and experience.

While communitas and liminality have been fundamental to
much theological discussion of ritual, they have also been seen as
problematic.[55] Grimes lists more than forty "family characteristics"
of ritual, insisting that no single quality is unique or definitive.[56]
Bell, on the other hand, names three central features: formality, fix-
ity, and repetition. A fourth characteristic, in her view, is the inter-

action of a "social body" with a "temporal and spatial environment": "the strategies of ritualization are particularly rooted in the body."[57] In the context of the Eucharist, the social body can be said to refer to the congregation, and the temporal and spatial environment mark the space and time of each particular eucharistic ritual.

In sum, while there seems to be little scholarly consensus on features common to ritual, Grimes's forty family characteristics include the descriptors "performed," "repetitive," and "collective." Rituals are not merely thought or said, they are not ordinary in the sense of being unnoticeable or unadorned, and they are usually enacted within the context of a community. These three descriptors encompass Bell's notion of social body and one of her characteristics of ritual—repetition. So perhaps we can proceed with these two generally common features of ritual in mind—repetitive and communal. The Eucharist certainly meets these two criteria. As stated, it originated as a reenactment of the Last Supper, and in a theological sense the Last Supper is "repeated" each time the Eucharist is performed. The Last Supper was also held on behalf of a community, namely, Jesus' disciples. Later the Eucharist was celebrated for the benefit of the community of Christian believers.

Answers to the question of why people ritualize vary. Anthropology would suggest that it is "in our nature" to do so. Ritualization seems basic to human existence. Grimes, for example, states that ritualization is a human necessity, arising out of the rhythms and structures of our bodies and psyches: "Coming together and pushing apart—intimacy and aggression, symbiosis and isolation—are the most basic rhythms of which ritualization is constructed."[58] Shortly I will offer a psychological explanation of why people ritualize. Tom Driver, a theologian, suggests that like other animals, human beings engage in rituals to communicate and to give stability to behavior. In primates, ritualizations appear to "result from an interaction between genetic codes, group processes, the environment, and individual learning."[59] Driver explains that ritualized behaviors, because they are patterned and repetitive, have been used both as signaling devices and as a means of transmitting and storing information across time and generations. He speculates that they were the first means for doing this.[60]

This brings us to the question of what social functions rituals serve. We have just learned that one function is communication. But communication in what sense? Turner posits that through repetitiveness and constancy of form, ritual serves to reinforce cognitive patterns. In doing so, the ritual participant learns to take as axiomatic the ideals, values, and norms that are overtly expressed or symbolized in the ritual. In this way, then, ritual serves to communicate the status quo. To return to the example of marriage, Turner's theory would suggest that marriage rituals generally reinforce such values as monogamy, lifelong partnership, and heterosexuality. Bell observes that Turner initially described ritual in terms of the affirmation of communal identity, in contrast to the frictions, constraints, and competitiveness of social organization. Marriage is meant to bond the community together to support the newly-wedded couple.

Turner subsequently portrayed ritual as embodying aspects of both structure and "anti-structure."[61] In other words, he suggested that ritual can perpetuate the societal status quo while at the same time effecting individual change within an accepted social structure. For example, a male-dominated Eucharist perpetuates women's subordination in the Catholic Church while simultaneously functioning to mediate grace, and therefore forgiveness, to parishioners—thus changing their status before God. One could argue also that marriage rituals generally attempt to control threats to social unity that polygamous sexual relationships or homosexual unions present. Perhaps this is why the blessing of homosexual unions is so controversial, even in liberal Protestant traditions today. At the same time, for monogamous heterosexuals, marriage functions to affirm their love for and commitment to one another in the context of a supportive community. As stated, the two become bound together before God, and the individual status of each is changed.

Here the question of ritual and power becomes apropos. To what extent do rituals perpetuate the status quo, and to what extent are they transformative, as suggested by Lincoln? Interestingly, Turner argues that a proper definition of *ritual* is in terms of social transition. He states: "Ritual is not necessarily a bastion of social conservatism; its symbols do not merely condense cherished sociocultural values. Rather, through its liminal processes, it holds the generating source of culture and structure. Hence, by definition ritual is associated with social *transitions*."[62]

It would seem that ritual serves different functions in different contexts. Sometimes ritualization works to perpetuate the status quo, at other times (or perhaps simultaneously) ritual effects individual transitions, and at others it fosters social change. I have offered examples of the way in which marriage and the Eucharist both perpetuate the status quo and bring about individual change. I believe that the advent of women celebrants would further illustrate the function of ritual to advance social change.

It has been suggested that ritual can be important to the forces of political change precisely because of its conservative properties. As David Kertzer points out, by borrowing legitimacy from old ritual forms, new political systems redirect them to new purposes.[63] Emphasizing eucharistic sacrifice, for example, has been used to deepen national commitments during a time of war. In the case of women priests, I will argue that while they may speak the same words as the male priests, what they are *doing* is perceived by parishioners as different.

Marjorie Procter-Smith's work on feminist ritualizing further aids our understanding of the relationship between ritual and social change. Historically, she states, liturgy has preserved and ritualized patriarchal memory. Through restriction of ritual acts to men and barring of women from sacred places, a "liturgical anamnesis" has taken place, in which women have lost the use of their bodies to communicate sacredness. Yet at the heart of liturgy, argues Procter-Smith, should be *metanoia*, conversion, transformation. Because genuine liturgy, in her view, involves dialogue with God, an inevitable result of the encounter is change.[64] As I have stated, women priests would bring about change in the church even when they do not alter the words of the liturgy, because their very presence at the altar leads to a different understanding of these words.

I believe that Driver best encapsulates the relationship of ritual to power in suggesting that ritual has a tripartite function: order, community, and transformation. Rituals establish and maintain various kinds of social and cosmic order, they bring people together both physically and emotionally, and they effect various kinds of transformation. Driver writes: "Rituals generate, maintain, and celebrate order; but they do so in a peculiar way, by grounding the sense of order in something that is other than itself, something fundamentally at odds with order—namely, participation in an undifferentiated core of life."[65] In ensuing chapters I offer a psychological interpretation of his notion of an "undifferentiated core of life" in terms of the early infant-mother relationship. In a theological context, the notion of communitas or union with God expresses this idea.[66]

Finally, what is the significance of gender for ritual activity? Is women's ritualizing significantly different from men's? Turner has been criticized for positing a universal theory of ritual when his research is based upon solely male rituals. It has been argued, for example, that women's rituals of the European Middle Ages do not display liminal features as described by Turner.[67] Also, Lincoln's study of women's initiation rituals suggests that they do not conform to Van Gennep's three-part pattern of separation, liminality, and reaggregation; instead they manifest an alternative tripartite structure of enclosure, metamorphosis, and emergence. Lincoln concludes that women's initiation rituals do not function to change women's status the way that men's initiation rituals do, but rather to address ontological concerns—questions of being. Changes to women's being include an expansion of powers, capabilities, and experiences.[68]

In a recent book titled *Ritualizing Women*, Lesley Northup outlines major ways in which women ritualize, offering as emerging patterns the ritual images of the circle, horizontality (abolishing dualisms), nature, the body, childrearing and mothering, the ordinary, women's crafts, community, memory, insight, the shaman, the teacher, and empowerment. Common characteristics of women's rituals, according to Northup, include spontaneity and informality, deemphasis of formal leadership, enhanced roles for older women, ecumenicity, and nonreliance on texts.[69] Women who engage in ritual, she states, overwhelmingly favor a vision of indwelling divinity—i.e., the numinous is thought of as immanent rather than transcendent.[70] In addition, in women's rituals the body is a primary source for ritual metaphors and a channel of revelation and sacredness. In emphasizing ordinary activities, women's rituals celebrate the worldly rather than the transcendent and recognize sacredness in everyday tasks.

The end goal of women's ritual activity, for Northup, is empowerment. She explains: "Finding ritual in their traditional religions impervious to change—even in such matters as inclusive language—and suspecting that existing ritual presents a distorted model of and for authentic relationship, they [women] are exploring instead the power of ritual to enable, accelerate, and even create new social constructs."[71] In investigating feminist liturgies, Procter-Smith finds that women explicitly reject hierarchical forms of liturgical leadership and are correspondingly committed to shared leadership. She states that the three values of contextuality, commitment to process, and experimentality give feminist liturgical events a distinctive character.[72] We will find that the sacramental ministries of Episcopal women priests generally support Procter-Smith's findings.

I now turn to explore a specific ritual, the Catholic Eucharist, utilizing the analytical methods offered by theology and psychology. The above background on ritual studies has alerted us to the fact that ritual is basic to human activity. Moreover, ritual can be characterized as both repetitive and communal. We learned that ritualizing is an evolving process, subject to change. Rituals can perpetuate the status quo, effect individual change, and/or foster social change. We found that gender holds great potentiality to bring about social transformation in the context of ritual. Significant attention will be given in the next three chapters to the transformative power of female symbols. Because symbols are integral to ritual action, they are the key to the relationship between gender and power.

THE THEOLOGY OF THE EUCHARIST

As mentioned, unconscious psychological dynamics are fundamentally embedded in the sacrament of the Eucharist. A brief discussion of eucharistic theology will provide a context for uncovering its psychological roots. The literature on the Eucharist is extensive, so I will limit my discussion to an overview of prominent themes. An extremely helpful resource in this regard is David Power's *The Eucharistic Mystery: Revitalizing the Tradition.*[73]

Power argues that amid cultural diversity, the Eucharist continues to function as the Catholic Church's central confession of faith and the pivotal ritual expressing the presence of Christ. The Eucharist is always celebrated and understood in reference to Christ's death and the church's witness to his death in the Gospels. Traditional Catholic teaching emphasizes sacrifice, presence, transubstantiation, and priesthood. Yet the contemporary Eucharist, in his view, has lost its power to offer an overarching vision of the world. Through an exploration of eucharistic theology and practice from New Testament times to the present day, Power endeavors to offer measures by which the Eucharist can be rejuvenated.

First, Power focuses on the Eucharist as an account of church life as illustrated in the New Testament texts. The rites of shared bread and cup, he states, with their respective blessings, must be understood in relation to a sense of unity brought about by "shared word, mutual service, crossing of social barriers, shared goods, and shared meals" (p. 30). Shared meals were an expression of communion and unity. The New Testament texts also offer insight into the nature of the Eucharist as memorial action: "Facing death at the supper, obedience and prophetic narration coincide with a recasting of eschatological expectation when Jesus is said to look forward to the kingdom, to drinking the fruit of the vine in the kingdom. This indicates that he anticipates what lies beyond his betrayal and death and that he sees in that future the fulfilment of the covenant promises regarding the final establishment of God's reign" (p. 50). Power indicates that more attention today needs to be given to the liberating power of the memorial of Christ's suffering. The memorial of Christ should speak to all human tragedy and loss.

Drawing from the eucharistic theology of the pre-Nicene church (i.e., before the Council of Nicea in 325 C.E.), Power reiterates the inextricable link between culture and remembrance. Liturgy makes use of Scripture in a cultural milieu, utilizing whatever approaches to history and text are fostered by that milieu (p. 132). After Nicea and before the Middle Ages, the language of eucharistic prayers shifted from gift and offering to cultic service and sacrifice. Power admonishes that today this language needs to be demythologized, stating: "Redemption is not wrought by violent action that invites violent retribution, but by nonviolent justice that witnesses in face of rejection to the power of communion" (p. 323).

Power next analyzes the eucharistic theology of the Middle Ages, particularly that of Thomas Aquinas. In Aquinas's vision, the presence of Christ himself was central to the efficacy of the sacrament as communion and representation. Aquinas utilized Aristotelian categories of "substance" and "accidents" to develop his ontology of the Eucharist, known as transubstantiation. According to this doctrine, while the accidents (whatever touches the senses) of bread and wine do not change, the substance (the core reality) is transformed into the body and blood of Christ when the priest repeats Jesus' words at the Last Supper. Christ's presence in the sacrament causes the believer to be one with the mystical body of Christ. Aquinas's theology, for Power, provided a model of cultural integration for developments in the mass system and in nonliturgical eucharistic devotion. At the same time, however, it did not allow for renewed devotionalism or for nonhierarchical movements in the church (pp. 237, 240).

Power explains that today there is no dominant theological or cultural perspective at work in eucharistic practice. He points out that in a time calling for greater sensitivity to suffering, a theology that lifts up the Eucharist as memorial is needed. Of primary importance, in his view, is the communion table as the central act of the liturgy: "In the gift given at the table, the self-gift of Christ on the cross is mediated and the life of the Spirit is shared in communion with the risen Lord. It is by way of the quadruple reference to supper, cross, resurrection, and eschatological hope that the meaning of eucharistic communion is expressed" (p. 293). Points that must be considered in a contemporary eucharistic theology are the communion table, the nature of Eucharist as ecclesial sacrament and communion in the Spirit, memorial, representation, sacrifice, and ontology (p. 326). For the purposes of ecumenical dialogue, Power explains, the main eucharistic themes generally emphasized are (1) thanksgiving, (2) anamnesis or memorial, (3) invocation of the Spirit, (4) communion of the faithful, and (5) meal of the kingdom (p. 265).

Since theologian Edward Kilmartin assigns these same five meanings to the Eucharist, they provide a helpful framework for discussion.[74] All five meanings are found in the eucharistic prayer, considered to be the central prayer of the eucharistic liturgy. Theologically, the Eucharist is thought to be a meal of the people of God that originates from the Christ event. It is considered to be the ongoing, repeated sign of intimate communion with Christ and of the individual's dedication of his or her life to God.[75] Sacramentally, it is believed to be the proclamation and application of the redemption given to humankind once and for all through the death and resurrection of Christ made present in sensible signs. As a sacrament, the Eucharist is a means of mediating the reality and presence of God through sensible signs. The word *eucharist* means "thanksgiving." As Emminghaus states, the basic form of the mass is a "eucharist," that is, a "blessing" or prayer of praise over bread and wine . . . in this case a meal in which the eating is symbolic and sacramental."[76]

The Eucharist as a meal of the kingdom has already been discussed. As stated, the origins of the Eucharist have a biblical foundation in the Last Supper ritual described in the Gospels. However, whether or not the Last Supper took place on Passover remains uncertain.[77] Historically, the Eucharist developed from a Jewish supper ritual, probably the Kiddush, which was basically a ceremony of sanctification, usually recited on the Sabbath or on a festival day. Upon the benediction over the wine and the sanctification of the day, those present partook of bread and wine.[78]

The third and fourth meanings of the Eucharist given above are best addressed together. By means of the offering of bread and wine, the mass becomes a communal celebration. In the ritual of the Eucharist, persons are thought to become one body with Christ through the power of his Spirit. As George Worgul observes, "In the eucharistic meal, in the eating and drinking of the bread and wine, Christ grants communion with himself. God himself acts, giving life to the body of Christ and renewing each member."[79]

Communion with Christ in the Eucharist presupposes his true presence in the species of bread and wine.

The second meaning, memorial, is effected whenever the central block of the eucharistic prayer is recited. The memorial, or *anamnesis*, is considered to be an "active" or "effective" memorial. This means that in remembering a past event, the believers make it present again to themselves. Hence, memorial entails both representation and anticipation of the passion, death, resurrection, and ascension of Christ. The memorial action that Christ orders the church to repeat is the blessing that transforms the bread and wine into his body and blood by the power of the Holy Spirit, and the reception of these gifts.[80]

The memorial involves a sacrifice, a making present of Christ in the sacrifice, and the union of believers with Christ through means of the sacrifice. The Eucharist is believed to reenact Christ's sacrifice at Calvary.[81] While sacrifice is a predominant motif in much of contemporary Catholic theology, it is the notion of sacrifice as offering rather than sacrifice as immolation. As Power puts it, the preferred Catholic explanation of sacrificial language consists in "relating a self-offering by the church to the sacramental representation of Christ's sacrifice, so that the church can be said to either offer itself along with Christ or even indeed to offer Christ."[82]

In order to present a more comprehensive psychological interpretation of the mass, the significance of important symbols must be addressed as well. Prominent symbols in the Eucharist are the priest, who acts *in persona Christi*, and the elements of bread and wine. One could also analyze the altar, the chalice, the special arrangement of utensils, and so on. While these may vary from parish to parish, mass cannot be celebrated without the central and constant symbols of priest, bread, and wine.

According to Catholic theologians, the Eucharist and the priesthood are integrally entwined. The priest fulfills his principal mission and is manifested in all his fullness when he celebrates the Eucharist.[83] The Eucharist, concomitantly, is the principal and central raison d'être of the sacrament of priesthood. In this role the priest represents Christ. Theologically speaking, the priest re-presents the sacrifice of Christ's offering himself once and for all to

God as a spotless victim.[84] By the anointing of the Holy Spirit, priests are configured to Christ the Priest in such a way that they can act in the person of Christ the Head. Through the Holy Spirit, then, the priest is marked with an indelible character, making him a "living image" of Christ.[85]

Historically, the precise relationship between the priest and Christ has been a matter of theological debate. While it is not believed that the priest becomes Christ during the moment of consecration, how exactly the priest acts *in persona Christi* during the Eucharist is not universally agreed upon. Power, for example, observes that the "sacramental relation of the priest to Christ in this act is that he is almost the same person as Christ, the eternal high priest."[86] Kilmartin in turn asserts that the minister is personally united to Christ by the Holy Spirit when acting in Christ's name: the minister and Christ form one "mystical person."[87] Alternatively, the antihierarchical strain of Catholic thinking adheres more to the notion that in acting *in persona Christi*, the priest acts as Christ the "representative human," serving as a representative of the congregation. It is important to note that in both views, the priest—in acting *in persona Christi*—communicates something important about God incarnate, i.e., God-in-the-flesh. As Power states, the Catholic position is that the priest mediates a participation in the sacrifice of Christ, and ushers in the benefits of Christ's death for the believer who has faith.[88]

The theology of the symbols of bread and wine is less controversial than that of the priest, but only if one remains within Catholic tradition. For Catholics, the doctrine of transubstantiation as developed by Aquinas fundamentally informs the meaning of these symbols. As stated, the species of the bread and wine are changed—Christ becomes present instead—while physically remaining the same. As Kilmartin explains, an ontological change takes place within the earthly bread and wine. They become sacramental signs of Christ's self-offering, while remaining subject to the earthly laws of corporeality: the physical magnitude remains, while the anthropological magnitude changes.[89] In the Western tradition, this change is thought to be effected in the moment of consecration. The consecration in turn happens during the institutional narrative, when the priest acting *in persona Christi* says: "This is my body, which will be offered up for you. . . . This is the cup of my blood, the blood of the new and everlasting Covenant. . . . It will be shed for you and for all for the forgiveness of sins."[90] In most Protestant traditions, "memorialism" rather than transubstantiation is the generally accepted view. According to this perspective, no ontological change in the elements of bread and wine occurs. They are partaken of in memorial of Christ's death, but Christ is not thought to become "present" in a bodily sense, as is believed in the Catholic tradition. This theological divergence is responsible for the practice of "closed" communion in Catholic parishes—Protestants are not supposed to take mass from a Catholic priest, because of conflicting understandings of what happens during the ritual.

According to Catholic tradition, the transubstantiation of bread and wine points to the Eucharist as a sacrament—that is, an occasion in which transcendence becomes symbolized and mediated through sensible realities.[91] It is during the rite of the Eucharist that the "word" becomes "flesh." The bread and wine are obvious symbols of spiritual and physical nourishment. Through eating, it is believed, the worshiper is forgiven by and sustained in Christ. Bread and wine also signify the relationship between the earth and human productivity, i.e., the agrarian cycle and the human labor necessary to transform grain and grapes into bread and wine.[92] In sum, the bread and wine express Christ's presence, nourishment on divine and physical levels, and human connectedness with the earth.

TOWARD A PSYCHOLOGY OF THE EUCHARIST

Now that a general understanding of the theology of the Eucharist has been provided, we can turn to its underlying psychology. I believe that object relations theory provides a more comprehensive psychological theory of the Eucharist than does a Freudian one based on Oedipal dynamics. Most psychologists, however, have understood the Eucharist primarily in terms of Oedipal or paternal characteristics, not in terms of pre-Oedipal or maternal features. An important exception is the approach taken by Mary Ellen Ross and

Cheryl Linn Ross in their 1983 article "Mothers, Infants, and the Psychoanalytic Study of Ritual," which offers a psychoanalytic interpretation of ritual that includes the pre-Oedipal period when the mother is critical.[93] They write of the ritual of the Catholic mass:

> The mass is not only an oedipal ceremony of fathers and sons but also a ritual of mothers and infants. That Father, Son, and Holy Spirit are referred to as males may obscure the presence of the maternal image; nevertheless many of the themes and issues raised during the mass have relevance to the preoedipal period when the interaction between mother and infant is central.[94]

Ross and Ross conclude that the mass exhibits as strong a connection to pre-Oedipal issues as it does to Oedipal ones. Beneath Oedipal dynamics in the Eucharist are found themes of play, creativity, and liminality—anthropologist Victor Turner's term designating loss of status and an "in-between" state.[95] The presence of these themes, for Ross and Ross, flows from what is essentially an experience of God as mother.

I shall build upon Ross and Ross's notion that Catholic eucharistic theology reveals underlying unconscious pre-Oedipal features. First, however, Freud's Oedipal theory of the Eucharist deserves some attention.[96] Freud was one of the first to offer a psychological interpretation of the Catholic mass and of ritual in general. For Freud, all religious rituals are attempts to replay and resolve the Oedipus complex. The Christian Eucharist, in his view, is an expression of aggressive Oedipal impulses toward the father, in which Christ the Son becomes a substitute for God the Father.

Freud argues that the Eucharist originally developed from an ancient totem meal, during which the totem animal was ceremonially killed and eaten.[97] This argument is considered ahistorical by most scholars today, and indeed exemplifies the weakness mentioned earlier—that Freud's theories are very difficult to validate. Yet his notion that the Eucharist is grounded in a hostile act, a murder, clearly is correct. Is the Eucharist therefore expressive of sublimated aggression?[98] While I would not trace the Eucharist back to cannibalism in any anthropological sense, Jesus' death on a cross is considered a sacrifice, an event that generally has violent connotations. As has been mentioned, this aggressive component of the Eucharist is often downplayed in theological discussions.

A strictly Freudian interpretation, however, fails to take into account additional aspects of eucharistic theology, such as the making present of Christ in the eucharistic sacrifice and the union of believers with Christ through means of that sacrifice. In addition, while a Freudian understanding of the Eucharist does offer an explanation of the notion of memorial—the events around Christ's death are actively replayed in much the same way that a childhood issue is reenacted in the psyche of an adult—it does not address Catholic theology as it has developed since Christ's death. In particular, it does not allow for the Eucharist to be interpreted as the invocation of the Spirit or communion of the faithful. A comprehensive psychological understanding of the Eucharist must address these theological views as well.

The notion of communion or union is inordinately underrepresented in most psychological interpretations of the Eucharist. Instead of using an Oedipal model focusing on sublimated aggression, I will show that, psychologically, the Eucharist expresses events that take place before the development of the superego. By exploring the Eucharist's pre-Oedipal components, we can expand our earlier discussion of ritual. In such a pre-Oedipal paradigm, ritual is the attempt to (1) re-attain union with the early mother, (2) separate from her, and (3) repair a relationship with her. Using object relations theory, the Eucharist becomes a reenactment of the early relationship between mother and infant, a period in which communion is prominent.

First, ritual is the attempt to re-attain union with the maternal matrix. As psychoanalyst Michael Balint asserts, the first and most traumatic disturbance of a newborn's life is separation from the womb. The individual tries to re-create that early harmonious environment in various ways throughout life.[99] This oceanic and all-nurturing intimacy with the mother is thought to be a goal of much religious striving. "Communitas" re-creates the original sense of unity, which, Balint argues, originates with the early infant-mother relationship. It is significant that the bonds of communitas are described by Turner as "undifferentiated, egalitarian, direct, non-rational"[100]—adjectives also used to connote the earliest infant-mother relationship.

Second, ritual is the attempt to separate from the early mother. Psychologically, D. W. Winnicott's notions of transitional space and transitional experience illustrate this theme. According to Winnicott, the infant initially perceives himself or herself as merged with the mother. Separation takes place gradually, through a series of "illusions," in which the infant imaginatively re-creates the mother's presence. As stated, these illusions take place in a "transitional space" between mother and infant, and eventually result in the formation of transitional objects. Transitional objects in turn represent the infant's attempts to separate "me" from "not me."

Third, ritual is the attempt to repair the relationship with the early mother. Psychologically, reparation can best be understood using Klein's concept of the move from the paranoid-schizoid to the depressive position. As discussed, during the paranoid-schizoid position the infant feels hostility toward the mother for failing to fulfill his or her needs. This hostility is expressed in terms of fantasies of hurting and destroying her. Later, during the depressive position, the infant learns that the "bad mother" is also the "good mother," the one who supplies his or her needs for nurture, warmth, and so on, and responds by wanting to make reparation. The obvious equivalent to reparation in the Jewish and Christian traditions is atonement, which consists of redress for past inadequacies in the effort to achieve right relationship with God.

Using the categories outlined above—union, separation, and reparation—the Eucharist expresses the unconscious desire for union with the early mother, the wish to separate from her in the process of forming a self, and the desire to make reparation to her for harm. Union with the early mother manifests itself theologically in the notions of communion and meal. It is through blood from her womb, and later milk from her breast, that union with the mother is first experienced. The body and blood of Christ represent the body and blood of the first caretaker, the first provider of nourishment. The body and blood of Christ also function transitionally, as an "illusion" in the psychological sense, allowing a union/separation dialectic between Christ and believer. The absent Christ becomes present once again in the elements of bread and wine. Reparation is evidenced in the function of the Eucharist as a sacrament of grace. Through the invocation of the Spirit, persons become one with the body of Christ through the forgiveness of sins.

The reappearance of Christ in the elements of bread and wine is of interesting psychological significance in the context of mourning. Psychologically, mourning is a reaction to the loss of a loved person or to the loss of an abstraction that has taken the place of a loved person.[101] Klein, for example, emphasized the complexity of the inner world in which the lost person is eventually restored as an "internal good object." In Klein's view, the first object mourned is the mother's breast, and what the breast stands for—love, goodness, and security.[102] Kleinian theory suggests that the believer obtains great comfort in reinstating the crucified Christ as an internalized good object and that at a deep level what is being reinstated is also the archaic mother figure.

What happens, then, is that in the context of the mass Christ becomes present again in the psyche of the believer, as well as through the ontological change of elements of bread and wine. In the mass, the eucharistic prayer serves to abolish the internal sense of separation and loss regarding Jesus' death and to once again effect Christ's presence. Christ, the loved object, is mourned but is "resurrected," mediated by the priest who consecrates bread and wine. Psychologically, the process of reinstating lost loved objects in the ego is called "internalization." Briefly, this process has origins in the mother-child matrix, and involves separation—i.e., relinquishment of external objects—and their restitution within psychic structure as a whole. Psychoanalyst Hans Loewald notes how internalization is symbolically expressed in Christianity in the figure of Christ. He explains that Christianity initiated "the greatest intensification of internalization in Western civilization" in the death of God as incarnated in Christ: "Christ is not only the ultimate love object, which the believer loses as an external object and regains by identification with Him as an ego ideal."[103] The figure of Christ, through his passion and death, also exemplifies the internalization and sublimation of all earthly relationships.[104] In other words, believers partake of the mass out of a desire to feel loved and accepted by Christ, to be forgiven of their faults, and to be assured a future with Christ—just as they want these things from those persons they love. On the other hand, believers may choose not to partake of the Eucharist out of feelings of unworthiness, just as they may have difficulty approaching someone they have wronged to ask forgiveness.[105] In transference, both positive and negative feelings are evoked.

I have discussed the way in which bread and wine serve to mediate Christ's presence, but what about the priest? As we have seen, theologically it is believed that the priest acts *in persona Christi* during the consecration of the elements—the priest is a "living image" of Christ. I submit that the priest symbolically represents Christ on a theological level, while on a psychological level the priest functions—through transference—to manifest parental figures. Hence, much the same way as the analyst in the analytic situation, the priest is a figure for transference and projection of internalized objects. This comparison would suggest that analysis and the Eucharist have a common basis. Psychologist of religion Robert Moore has made this connection in his correlation between ritual space and psychotherapeutic space. Moore argues that in psychotherapy, the individual is offered an opportunity "temporarily to surrender autonomy, to submit to a total process which has an autonomy of its own and which can enable the individual to maintain needed orientation and structure during this time of deconstruction."[106]

While there are many obvious differences between analysis and the Eucharist, psychologically it can be said that the symbols of priest and analyst in some ways function similarly. Both priest and analyst represent authority figures, and both provide a ritual context for transformation. One main difference, in the case of the Eucharist, is that the priest is a template not only for internalized figures of mother, father, lover, and so on, but also for projection of religious symbols such as Christ and God. Thus, the priest does symbolize Christ, but he or she also serves as a template for the believer's internalized representation of God. The figure of the priest cannot be reduced to the internalized mother or father but must be viewed within the religious context in which he or she functions. Thus, we can conclude that while perceptions of the priest are influenced by parental and other authority figures, the priest also symbolizes the community of the faithful, Christ the high priest, a Christ-like person, Christ as both human and divine.

It has been shown that Christ's presence in the elements of bread and wine elucidates the transitional function of these symbols. Bread and wine serve to mediate Christ's presence to the believer. I must reiterate that it is not only Christ's presence that is mediated through these symbols but also the figure of the early mother. As stated, the body and blood of Christ represent the body and blood of the first caretaker, the first provider of nourishment. Hence, we return to Ross and Ross's observation—that underlying the male-oriented symbolism of the mass are deeply rooted feminine components. My use of Catholic theology to support psychological theory mitigates a criticism that has been leveled against Ross and Ross—namely, that they overlook the reception of ritual in the experience of various individuals.[107] While theology does not substitute for personal interviews, it does reflect the beliefs of a faith community for many generations.

We have seen that an object relations perspective more fully encompasses the Catholic understanding of the mass than does an Oedipal interpretation: object relations theory provides a more comprehensive psychological rubric for the Eucharist as sacrifice, memorial, communion, and meal than does Freud. This leads us to ask, If the Eucharist expresses early issues concerning the relationship between mother and infant, would it not make sense to have women as well as men involved in the psychological and symbolic replaying of these events? Yes, in my opinion, it would. Second, would not women celebrants make more explicit the underlying pre-Oedipal themes in the Eucharist? This is precisely what I believe would occur if women were ordained to the priesthood.

Just as unconscious dynamics underlie the theology of the Eucharist, it can be shown that unconscious factors are fueling the Vatican's strong resistances to women priests. A dialectic exists between psychic dynamics and contemporary cultural symbolism, pointing to a deeper reason for the perpetuation of a solely male priesthood than those issued by the Vatican. Since the Eucharist expresses unconscious pre-Oedipal features, the Vatican's insistence that only men can preside at the altar reflects a conflict between conscious expression and unconscious origin. I believe that gender reversal in the Eucharist finds its cause in deeply rooted psychological factors, in particular issues having to do with male gender identity.

MALE GENDER IDENTITY ISSUES

Let us now return to the question raised at the outset of the discussion: What is behind gender reversal in the Eucharist? Up to this point, I have shown that maternal themes underlie the Vatican arguments from natural resemblance and bridegroom imagery, and that these themes extend to the theology of the Eucharist itself. I believe the reasons for male appropriation of female roles can be found through an exploration of male gender identity issues. In particular, gender reversal is rooted in maternal envy and the male desire for feminine identification.

Surely a male-dominated institution that prohibits women from celebrating a ritual of mothers and infants signals the existence of male gender identity issues. These issues are expressed in other areas of contemporary culture as well, and in part have to do with preserving a "masculine" identity in the face of the perceived "feminization" of society. Recently, for example, conservative Christian-based groups such as the Promisekeepers have stressed that men "take back their place" in the home. "Real men" do not permit women to function as "heads" of households. Southern Baptist leaders voted in 1998 that women are to be "graciously submissive" to their husbands. In the case of the Catholic Eucharist, men enact a feminine role yet prohibit women from acting in that same role. Are men afraid that the Eucharist will become too "feminized" if they allow women priests to celebrate it? Or are they afraid their own femininity will be exposed? In order to begin to answer these questions, I turn first to several examples from the Episcopal tradition.

A male Episcopal priest suggested to me that for those opposed to women's ordination, "essence" and "ontology" issues are involved. According to this view, the "essence" of Jesus was male, and all the rest of the priesthood is to stand within that essence. But what does "essence" really mean in this context other than identity? Continuing this line of thought, the argument becomes that because Jesus' identity was male, women clergy representing him would confuse it. But whose identity would they confuse: Jesus' or that of male priests who have represented him for centuries?

Another male Episcopal priest told a woman I interviewed that she could not be ordained because it would be demeaning for her to wear men's clothes. When she replied, "What are you talking about?" he said, "You know, the vestments of the liturgy." She promptly responded that they were dresses, to which he answered, "When you come up with some decent vestment designs, then we'll talk about it." This argument against women's ordination also points to issues of male gender identity. This same woman priest had another confrontation with a male priest, who told her:

> I cannot stand it if you are ordained, because it calls into question everything I'm doing with my life. Because if you can do it, then what does it mean that I as a man can do it? If you as a woman can do it, then what does it mean? I'm already taking care of people all day long. I'm already acting like my mother—I run around on Sundays in this dress. How do I know who I am as a man if you can do this?

My interviewee said that as long as this male priest could prevent women from being ordained, he did not have to confront the terrifying subject of who he was. Misogyny, she told me, is about women's power: "It's connected with the ability to bear life, the ability to survive, and mind/body dualisms, where the body is outrageous, uncontrolled—women represent that." When I contacted her again in 1998, she said that she still had substantially the same response, but acknowledged that much of the attention and controversy had shifted into other gender-related areas, such as homosexuality. Many men, she explained, are afraid that all women priests are lesbians. As another clergywoman confirmed, those conservatives who feared in the 1970s that ordaining women would bring homosexuality into the arena were quite right. Women's very presence at the altar raises issues of gender identity.

Psychological theory further illustrates that gender reversal in the Eucharist is rooted in deep-seated concerns about masculinity and femininity. In North American society, men must dis-identify[108] from the mother and in turn identify with the father in order to achieve a "healthy" sense of maleness. Women, on the other hand, are allowed to retain their feminine identification as well as to behave in a "masculine" manner—for example, women can dress like men and are allowed to compete for most jobs that traditionally were restricted to men. Androgyny is more acceptable in women than in men.

If men have to dis-identify with the mother, they must renounce all ties to her, as well as all attachments to what they consider femininity. Yet their feminine identification does not disappear; it merely remains at an unconscious level of awareness. As mentioned, Chodorow argues that while men attempt to deny attachment to the mother, they retain their pre-Oedipal attachment to her on an unconscious level. She posits that underlying core male gender identity is an "early, non-verbal, unconscious, almost somatic sense" of primary oneness with the mother. This underlying sense of femaleness continually and insistently challenges and undermines the sense of maleness. According to Chodorow, the primary oneness with the mother—a primary femaleness—results in gender identity issues for the boy. A boy must learn to view his gender identity as "not-female," or "not-mother."[109] Gender identity thus becomes an issue for men because of their underlying feminine attachment to the mother.

Hence, if at a conscious level men are not allowed to express femininity, yet they retain an unconscious pre-Oedipal maternal attachment, conditions are ripe for gender reversal—appropriation of women's functions while denying those same functions to women. In the case of the Eucharist, recognition of underlying maternal-infant themes would pose a tremendous threat to masculine gender identity. Otherwise, why not let women co-celebrate with men?

Notwithstanding unconscious desire for feminine identification, we still have not unearthed the full complement of reasons against women's officiating at the Eucharist. An additional dynamic at work in gender reversal in the Eucharist is maternal envy. Male fear and envy of female reproductive and nurturing capacities and the consequent wish to be feminine are unconsciously fueling the strong resistances to women priests. The following psychoanalytic exploration of the notion of envy gives credence to this claim.

Since much of Freud's writing about women is misogynistic, one would not expect to find reference in his work to fear and envy of female reproductive capacities in men, or to a resultant male wish to be feminine. And one does not. For example, Freud gives only peripheral attention to Hans's desire to have children in "Analysis of a Phobia in a Five-Year-Old Boy (1909)":

> **I (Hans's father):** You'd like to have a little girl.
>
> **Hans:** Yes, next year I'm going to have one, and she'll be called Hanna too.
>
> **I:** But why isn't Mummy to have a little girl?
>
> **Hans:** Because *I* want to have a little girl for once.
>
> **I:** But you can't have a little girl.
>
> **Hans:** Oh yes, boys have girls and girls have boys.
>
> **I:** Boys don't have children. Only women, only Mummies have children.
>
> **Hans:** But why shouldn't I?
>
> **I:** Because God's arranged it like that.
>
> **Hans:** But why don't *you* have one? Oh yes, you'll have one all right. Just you wait.[110]

While clearly it can be seen from the above dialogue that Hans is quite interested in being able to have children the way his mother does, Freud dismisses this piece of clinical data with a flourish: "There is no necessity on this account to assume in Hans the presence of a feminine strain or a desire for having children."[111]

Another occasion on which Freud seems to overlook a desire for gender reversal in men is found in the case of Senatspräsident Schreber. One aspect of Schreber's illness consisted of delusions that he had a mission to redeem the world. This mission was to be preceded, in Schreber's view, by his "transformation into a woman." Freud records the way in which Schreber believed this change would come about: "By means of what he calls 'drawing' (that is, by calling up visual images), he is able to give both himself and the rays an impression that his body is fitted with female breasts and genitals."[112] "The rays" refers to divine rays that Schreber imagined would impregnate him, "to the end that a new race of men might be created."[113] Freud's explanation of this bizarre fantasy does not include the possibility that Schreber might have had secret wishes to possess women's functions. Instead, he adamantly proclaims: "It is not to be supposed that he *wishes* to be transformed into a woman; it is rather a question of a 'must,' based upon the Order of Things, which there is no possibility of his evading, much as he would personally prefer to remain in his own honourable and masculine station in life."[114]

Interestingly, Hanna Lerman argues that Freud does acknowledge in a rudimentary way the existence of male wishes to bear children. She observes, however, that he does not extend his thinking to the possibility of male envy of childbearing, or to potential ramifications of these wishes for his psychological theories.[115] Instead, as we have seen, Freud focuses inordinate attention on female penis envy and on the consequences of this envy for women's psychological development. While Freud seems unwilling to acknowledge a corresponding envy in men of breasts or wombs, it is logical to suggest that all children to some degree are jealous of anatomical parts they do not possess. Just as girls see penises and desire them, boys see breasts and vaginas and exhibit a similar desire. For this reason, Freud's notion of envy should not be discarded but should be explored as an potentially important dynamic. Male envy of female reproductive anatomy has a much larger role in men's psychology than Freud acknowledged.

While Freud dismissed men's envy of childbearing and other reproductive functions, other psychoanalysts give the idea more serious attention. G. Bose, for example, founder of the Indian Psychoanalytic Society, is recorded to have written the following statement to Freud: "My Indian patients do not exhibit castration symptoms to the same degree as my European cases. The desire to be female is more easily unearthed in Indian male patients than in European."[116] One might argue on the basis of this anecdote that perhaps Indian male patients express a desire to be female while men in other cultures do not. Yet the work of Bruno Bettelheim and Karen Horney leads to a different conclusion. Bettelheim's psychological study of male puberty rites in traditional cultures demonstrates the cultural expression of male envy of female functions. Bettelheim became interested in puberty rites in traditional cultures from his work with emotionally disturbed children. These children, he observed, exhibited extreme envy of the other sex's reproductive organs. For example, some of the boys were obsessed with the idea of possessing a vagina. Others expressed aggressive desires to cut off and tear out breasts and vaginas. Bettelheim concluded from his observations that it is natural for each sex to envy anatomical parts it does not possess. Through studying traditional cultures Bettelheim further came to believe that many male puberty rites are in fact imitations of female fertility rites—such as girls' initiation into menstruation. Hypothesizing that rituals of cutting, circumcision, and subincision represent men's attempt to "bleed" the way women bleed, he suggested several reasons for the phenomenon. One is that boys feel they need to compensate for their lack of one specific physiological and hormonal change—such as menstruation in girls—in the transition from adolescence to adulthood. Another possible reason, in his view, is men's desire to participate in women's procreative ability. He describes a ritual of birthing performed by men, called the *couvade*:

> The woman works as usual up until a few hours before birth; she goes to the forest with some women, and there the birth takes place. In a few hours she is up and at work. . . . As soon as the child is born, the *father takes to his hammock* [emphasis mine], and abstains from work, from meat and all food but weak gruel, from smoking, from washing himself, and above all, from touching weapons of any sort, and is nursed and cared for by the women of the place. . . . This custom goes on for days, sometimes for weeks.[117]

The couvade demonstrates men's desire to participate and experience birth, and also illustrates men's attempt to detract from women's importance in the birthing process.

Similarly, Horney takes issue with Freud's emphasis on penis envy in girls, arguing that there is a corresponding envy in men of female functions. Her studies indicate that men feel extreme envy toward female processes of pregnancy, childbirth, and motherhood, as well as of breasts and suckling. Horney posits that men's envy of women is expressed in several ways. One is resentment toward women. Another is the tendency to devalue functions such as pregnancy and childbirth while at the same time overemphasizing male genitality. A third way is to sublimate the envy into cultural values such as productivity and creative work. She asserts: "Is not the tremendous strength in men of the impulse to creative work in every field precisely due to their feeling of playing a relatively small role in the creation of living beings, which constantly impels them to an overcompensation in achievement?"[118]

Horney's argument is persuasive in its attempt to redress an imbalance—that envy is exclusive to women. The film *Junior*, in which Arnold Schwarzenegger plays an emotionally frigid scientist who gets pregnant to further the cause of research, suggests that male envy of childbearing is not to be summarily dismissed. Emma Thompson in turn poses as an absentminded scientist who has frozen her own eggs. In an experiment to test the effects of a drug designed to simulate pregnancy, Danny De Vito, an enterprising M.D., unknowingly takes her egg and injects it into Schwarzenegger's perineal cavity. Schwarzenegger is scheduled to stop taking the drug after six weeks, but discovers that he likes being pregnant and wants to have "his baby." While the consequent feminization of his character—he now worries about clothes and whether Danny will be home in time for dinner—is unrealistic and unfair to women, his softening into a more nurturing, humane human being as a result of being pregnant sends an important message to viewers about a male wistfulness to be more traditionally "feminine." The film also makes it clear that the desire to be pregnant exists at least in the realm of male fantasy.

If the desire to be pregnant, suckle, or have children remained at the level of male heterosexual fantasy, it would not be of much concern. Both men and women, however, tend to act out their fantasies on some level. The phenomenon of transsexuality, for example, suggests that members of both sexes can have a desire for the other's reproductive capacities, which some choose to actualize surgically. In Ralph Greenson's study of one hundred cases of transsexuals, between two-thirds and three-fourths were men hoping to become women. In addition, Greenson lifts up the fact that transvestitism—or cross-dressing—is almost exclusively a male behavior.[119] These statistics suggest not that more men want to become women than women do men but, as mentioned, that it is more socially acceptable for women to act like men without the need for surgery. Women already cross-dress.

Robert Stoller, who has written widely in the field of transsexuality and transvestism, differentiates between male primary transsexuals and male secondary transsexuals. The former, according to his definition, present a history of wishing to dress and live exclusively as females since early childhood. The latter most commonly progress to transsexualism over a period of years, during which the "patient feels himself to be a homosexual, with a slant toward the feminine or effeminate side and with, in time, a sense that he would do better if female."[120] Stoller attributes boyhood femininity to a prolonged, mutually pleasurable period of mother-infant son symbiosis, without qualitative and quantitative interruption by the father. Much like Chodorow, he explains that for masculinity to develop, the infant boy must erect intrapsychic barriers warding off the desire to maintain the "blissful sense of being one with the mother."[121] While Stoller's theory has been contested, most researchers in the field seem to agree that as children male transsexuals lack self-confidence that they are "real boys."[122] Male transsexuals themselves attest to the sense of being "in the wrong body" before taking up life as a woman.[123]

Janice Raymond offers a critical feminist perspective on transsexualism, attributing the phenomenon to male recognition of female power by means of possession of "artifactual female organs." In Raymond's view, this power—evident in giving birth—cannot be reduced to procreation and includes the many levels of creativity that women have exercised in the history of civilization.[124] Male transsexuals, or "male-to-constructed-females," according to

Raymond, are the result of a patriarchal society and its socially prescribed definitions of masculinity and femininity.[125] Studies have
indeed suggested that (1) most transsexuals have exceedingly rigid
views on gender roles, (2) more transsexuals seek consultation in
societies that are more gender-role-rigid and anti-homosexual than
in societies that are less so, and (3) most transsexuals are from work-
ing-class environments in which gender roles tend to be more rigid
and well defined.[126] It must be pointed out, however, that regardless
of the causes of transsexualism, a substantial group of transsexuals
studied present no form of psychiatric disorder—many have stable
ego strengths and an intact sense of reality.[127] Transsexuality can
thus be viewed as one form of male appropriation of female capacities, yet it need not be viewed as necessarily pathological, nor,
despite Raymond's critique, as destructive to women.

Transsexuality is not the only form in which male fantasies of
being a woman are manifested. Male homosexuals, for example, are
often seen as more traditionally feminine than are heterosexual
males. Richard Friedman's review of the literature on homosexuality indicates a strong correlation between a feminine or nonmascu-
line concept of self during childhood and expression of male homosexuality in adulthood.[128] As with transsexuality, however, this correlation need not be viewed as pathological. It has been noted that
apart from sexual orientation, homosexual and heterosexual individuals do not differ significantly in their psychological adjustment
and behavior. One could say that there is no gender identity "disorder" involved in homosexuality, for the identity of homosexuals is
compatible with their anatomy.[129] This view signifies a turn away
from earlier homophobic discourse in psychoanalysis. The most
recent work on homosexuality takes the striving for same-sex libidinal objects as a given, in much the same way as the search for cross-
sex objects is.[130] Contemporary research also suggests that homosexuals tend to be androgynous rather than masculine- or feminine-
identified.[131] Psychoanalyst Beverly Burch, for example, posits that
lesbians lean more toward "androgyny" than masculinity, and that,
for lesbians, the gendered sense of self may be more fluid than for
heterosexual women.[132]

All male sexual behaviors—heterosexual, homosexual, bisexual—can be viewed as being on a continuum of appropriation of female capacities. Yet, as illustrated by male homosexuality and transsexuality, not all male sexual behaviors are harmful to women or express gender reversal. While heterosexual male desire for feminine identification *may* be expressed in damaging ways, such behavior is not inherent to a feminine identification in males. I will give a few examples of the type of heterosexual male appropriative behaviors with which we do need to be concerned.

Research on fetishistic behavior and on latent homosexual tendencies in heterosexual men highlights some of the ways in which male fantasies of possessing female capacities can be expressed pathologically. Angela Moorjani, for example, describes what she calls male "matric fetishism," in which the "missing childbearing powers of the father result in the child's feelings of guilt for having caused this partial and damaged state by mutilating wishes against the phantasmatic father-mother."[133] In matric fetishism, heterosexual male rage is directed at the mother-father's deliberate deprivation of his female body parts. Fueling this rage, according to Moorjani, is male envy of the mother's procreative abilities. Moorjani asserts that male matric fetishism expresses itself in male womb fantasies, female masquerades, and rivalry with women. She gives examples from literary and artistic works, such as German surrealist artist Hans Bellmer, who constructed life-size "child-woman" dolls and Samuel Beckett's *Molloy*, which posits a male persona "seeking in vain to give birth (and death) to a self through words."[134] Another example of heterosexual male envy of female capacities is expressed in the "vagina-man"—the counterpart of the phallic woman. The vagina-man, as put forth by Adam Limentani, harbors a secret wish to be a woman, associated with profound envy of everything female. Vagina-men often become involved with masculine, intellectually powerful women, forming identifications with these women in order to escape from threats of homosexuality. In many cases, their femininity is well integrated and only faintly noticeable to others. There is evidence, according to Limentani, of a masculine, if not a phallic, mother, who often "treated her child as a phallus"[135]—in other words, she treated her son as an object for satisfaction of her desires.

Just as fantasies generally do not remain solely within the realm of the human psyche, their enactment does not restrict itself to the individual level. One could argue that Senatspräsident Schreber's fantasies of being impregnated by God may have prevented him from living a normal life but that they did not affect anyone outside his immediate family. Horney is correct, however, to suggest that heterosexual male envy of women's functions is expressed on a cultural level. She is also right to insist that such envy can manifest itself in ways that are destructive to and devaluing of women. This is where the notion of gender reversal becomes important. In the case of gender reversal, men appropriate women's functions in a way that devalues or detracts from women's performing those functions. In gender reversal, while the fantasy centers around possessing feminine capacities such as birthing, bleeding, and lactating, concomitant with this fantasy is hostility toward women's having these capacities and men's not having them. As one woman priest told me regarding those opposed to women's ordination, "Some of them are just misogynists. They don't know that. They don't believe that. The Church is misogynist. Our culture is misogynist. It's so ingrained . . . so subtle and pervasive."

At this point, some exploration of the psychological roots of male hostility toward women will be helpful. Not only do men at an unconscious level desire to possess female reproductive capacities, but, in the case of gender reversal, they fear women *because* of the power these capacities engender. This fear originates in an early childhood scenario, in which women, as mothers, have absolute dominion over them. Ralph Greenson points out, for example, that envy as a male driving wish to be a woman originates in the early envy that all children feel toward the mother.[136] Early envy of the mother is best elucidated in the work of Klein, who, as discussed earlier, posited that an infant comes into the world with feelings of both love and hate toward the mother, or the "object" of its first affections. The first "object" to be envied is the breast, for "the infant feels that it possesses everything that he desires and that it has an unlimited flow of milk and love which it keeps for its own gratification."[137] Viewed in terms of the power of the breast to grant or withhold nurturance, the mother looms as an awesome and at times terrifying figure to her child. Klein asserts that when envy is excessive, the infant does not sufficiently build up a good object and is later unable to establish good objects in the inner world. Fundamentally, she states, envy is directed against creativeness, because breast and milk are the source of life.[138]

I do not accept Klein's notion that love and hate are innate impulses much like drives, but her idea that the mother is viewed with enormous power by the child seems intuitively correct. Do we not all harbor a certain degree of envy toward those more powerful than we are? Yet, as Greenson observes, her theory does not adequately address the *difference* in the envy of men and women.[139] If both boys and girls envy the breast, how is this played out as children of each gender develop physically and psychologically?

Klein briefly discusses gendered notions of envy, suggesting that in men excessive envy of the breast is likely to extend to all feminine attributes, in particular childbearing. It was left to Dinnerstein, however, to offer an explanation of men's greater degree of hostility toward the mother. As discussed earlier, Dinnerstein argues that in order to avoid the pain involved in separating from their mothers, girls forgo the process of forging a separate feminine identity and instead grow up to be dependent on men. Boys, on the other hand, grow up feeling vindictive and vengeful toward women. Male vengeance, for Dinnerstein, is expressed in adulthood through tyranny and authoritativeness over women. Dinnerstein's theory provides important insights into the inverse relation between female power in childhood and male power in adulthood. When her theory is supplemented with Chodorow's work on male gender identity issues, we can seen how men might wish to appropriate maternal capacities.

In this discussion I have suggested that the mass expresses pre-Oedipal issues concerning the infant-mother relationship. An object relations approach to ritual confirms Ross and Ross's viewpoint that eucharistic theology and psychology flow from what is essentially an experience of God as mother. We have seen that the body and blood of Christ also represent the body and blood of the first caretaker.

The priest, in turn, serves as a template for the believer's internalized representation of both God and archaic mother figure. Maternal envy and desire for feminine identification have been shown, psychologically, to be at the root of continued opposition to ordaining women to the Catholic priesthood. I have suggested that at an unconscious level of awareness, men harbor envy of women's birthing and nurturing abilities. Because Western society emphasizes male dis-identification from the mother, men cannot readily express feminine attachment or identification—hence its manifestation in gender reversal. I cannot comment on the dynamics of those societies in which the mother is not the primary caretaker; however, in most of the cultures in which Catholicism is practiced, women are primary caretakers of children. The dynamics of envy and the desire for feminine identification reside largely repressed in the unconscious. There are some men, however, who will admit to womb envy—most often when their partners or siblings become pregnant.

If women were to be ordained to the priesthood, the explicitly feminine imagery underlying the symbols of bread and wine would become apparent. Moreover, because the priest is a symbol of Christ, women priests would alter traditional symbolism for divinity. Symbols shape reality. Male symbols for God and Christ have shaped a largely oppressive ecclesial environment for women for centuries. Symbol and ritual also hold enormous power to change individuals and institutions. Next, I explore the transformative power of ritual in depth. Specifically, the ways in which feminine symbolism would influence eucharistic theology, Christology, and conceptions of God are more fully investigated. This exciting new ground shifts the debate on women clergy from "why they cannot be priests" to "what would be different if they were?" And this, I believe, is where our attention should be focused.

4

SACRIFICE

In whatever way a woman is representative of Christ, it's a whole different thing [to have a female celebrant]. Because it seems natural that a woman's body is broken. It doesn't seem natural for a man's body to be broken.
—*Episcopal laywoman*

I have particular gifts that center around nurturing, enabling—yes, *mothering*, but in an affirming, rather than protecting way. However, I believe it is possible for men to feel exactly the same way about their priesthood.
—*From John Morgan*, Women Priests

Now that an explanation has been offered for gender reversal in the Eucharist, we can turn our full attention to what difference women priests would make. Since underlying pre-Oedipal themes in the Eucharist would become more prominent if women were celebrants, women priests would challenge core dimensions of theology, as well as how parishioners experience the sacrament. One of the first issues raised by women celebrants would be their impact on eucharistic sacrifice. Of the major Christian traditions in North America, Roman Catholicism holds most strongly to the doctrine of the recurrent sacrifice of Christ in the mass. In the Eucharist, Christ's sacrifice is made "present" again for priest and worshiper through the consecration of the bread and the wine, which are transformed into the body and blood of Christ.[1] A fundamental question concerning women celebrants is, What does it mean to talk about women priests performing sacrifice? Are women merely participating in a ritual of male violence—as some feminist scholars would

argue—in blessing the bread and wine at the altar, or are they transforming it in some way? Many feminists advocate abolishing sacrificial theology on the grounds of its destructiveness to women. As a
feminist, I do not wish to see women participate in a ritual that
would perpetuate a "sacrificial mentality" of the ilk that women have
suffered from for centuries and still struggle to overcome. Yet I
believe that women priests celebrating mass would transform the
priesthood, theology, parishioners' experience, and the church in
important and positive ways.

First, however, some discussion of the primary psychoanalytic
theories and theorists utilized provides a vantage point for understanding how such a transformation would take place. Most psychological theories of sacrifice adhere to a Freudian interpretation,
one focusing on Oedipal aggression. A Freudian view of sacrifice is
not entirely misguided, but it does not allow room for pre-Oedipal
dynamics, which are also present. We have already seen that a pre-
Oedipal view of the Eucharist in many ways makes much more
sense than a strictly Oedipal one. Now we shall look at the ways in
which a pre-Oedipal view of sacrifice also "makes much more sense"
than one based solely on Freud. Evidence to support this perspective is offered by women Episcopal priests themselves, who indicate
that in celebrating the Eucharist they are in fact reclaiming female
reproductive functions and social roles.

MARGARET MAHLER, TRANSFERENCE, AND INTERNALIZATION

Object relations theorist Margaret Mahler's work is important to
my questioning of sacrifice as a ritual of male violence. In addition,
the psychoanalytic notions of transference and internalization, while
mentioned previously, deserve further elaboration at this juncture.
Mahler is best known for her theory of how the infant first establishes a sense of identity—how the concept "I" is initially formulated. Her early research was conducted with symbiotic psychotic children and their mothers and later extended to normal human development. Mahler postulated that the universal human condition

originates in a symbiotic state, followed by a separation-individuation process in normal development. Four subphases were later discerned in the separation-individuation phase of development, thought to occur between the second half of the first year and in the second year of infant life.[2]

Mahler identifies a stage of absolute primary narcissism, a state of undifferentiation between "I" and "not I," or of fusion with the mother, from which the infant first begins to differentiate the quality of experience. At some point the infant reaches a symbiotic stage of mother-child dual unity, during which she oscillates between perception of her mother as separate and as not separate. A series of gratification-frustration sequences promote structuralization of the ego, ideally gradually and from an optimal symbiotic state. In the further course of development, a unified object representation becomes demarcated from a unified self representation, establishing object constancy.[3] Yet a dialectic between self and other remains, evidenced in the continual need to establish connection and separateness throughout life. Mahler's phrase "separation-individuation process" refers to the "establishment of a sense of separateness from, and relation to, a world of reality, particularly with regard to the experiences of one's own body and to the principal representative of the world as the infant experiences it, the 'primary love object.'"[4] As stated, normal separation-individuation is the first crucial prerequisite for the development and maintenance of the sense of identity.[5]

Mahler's theory is important for its view that identity formulation begins to take place in the earliest stages of life, in the pre-Oedipal period of development, when the mother figure is primary. On the other hand, she has been criticized for paying too much attention to the self's struggle for independence from the mother and for her focus on development of an isolated individuality. As psychologist of religion James Jones points out, "How common in psychoanalytic theory is this single-minded focus on autonomy and the fear . . . that relationships must mean the loss of individuality."[6] Significantly, Mahler is important to my discussion of sacrifice precisely because she does focus on initial relationality with the mother as an aspect of the universal human condition.

Relationality is the essence of the psychoanalytic concept of transference. Simply put, transference refers to the tendency of the client to attach childhood emotions to the analyst. For example, the client may see the analyst as an authoritarian father, a passive mother, or a seductive lover. These transferences must be recognized if the client is to move forward in therapy. Transferences enable clients to reexperience early relationships from an adult vantage point and to resolve childhood issues more satisfactorily.[7] Recent models of transference use the image of "reciprocal interaction," in which neither the client nor the analyst is the primary focus of attention, but instead the relationship between them.[8] As Nancy Chodorow writes, this relationship is "emergent in the here-and-now of intrapsychic process."[9] Moreover, when contemporary psychoanalytic writers refer to the role of the past in transference, it is the "inner psychic past" rather than an objective history that concerns them. In other words, the client's creation of a subjective past, rather than what actually happened in a given situation, forms the basis for transference.[10] Because transference is the individual's most fundamental pattern of interaction and meaning-making,[11] it can be applied to the context of religion as well as personal analysis. Jones, for example, is interested in exploring ways in which an individual relationship with the sacred functions as a "transferential ground" of the self. This "affective bond with the sacred," as he calls it, "enacts and reenacts the transferential patterns present throughout a person's life."[12] For example, a woman with an authoritarian father may image a punitive God but may shift to a more forgiving and caring representation as she begins to work through shame issues in therapy.

The concept of internalization was discussed previously in the context of Christ becoming present to the believer through the elements of bread and wine. As explained, the process originates in the mother-child matrix, and it involves relinquishment of external objects and their restitution within psychic structure. Jesuit priest and psychoanalyst W. W. Meissner offers the following definition of internalization:

The processes by which the inner world arises are termed "internalizations" in the parlance of analytic thinking. The basic notion is that the inner world takes shape through the child's evolving developmental experience, whose course is shaped by the internalization of the child's relationships to specific objects. Thus the child's evolving psyche is formed under the influence of his [*sic*] object relationships and comes to bear their imprint.[13]

Psychoanalyst Roy Schafer defines internalization in terms of those processes "by which the subject transforms real or imagined regulatory interactions with his environment, and real or imagined characteristics of his environment, into inner regulations and characteristics."[14] We have seen that internalization is a useful concept in the context of mourning. A son, for example, may become more like his father after his father's death, appropriating characteristic gestures, temper, and affinities for nice clothes and gourmet cuisine.

Externalization is essentially the reverse of internalization. Under certain circumstances, such as analysis, formation of psychic structure is reversible to a degree. In these cases internalizations can be partially undone and replaced by relationships with an external object. In the above hypothetical example, if the son then goes into therapy and develops a father transference with his analyst, he begins to see qualities of his father to whatever degree they are present in the person of the analyst. He may anticipate the analyst's anger, for example, even if the latter is normally even-tempered. He may interpret the analyst's suit and tie as a penchant for nice clothing.

Religious ritual, like analysis, is a scenario in which externalization of internal objects can occur. It has been shown that Christ, God, mother, and father become present to the worshiper in the image of the priest in much the same way that internalized parental figures become "present" to the analysand in the image of the analyst during transference. A woman at the altar may evoke issues one has with one's mother, for example, just as a male celebrant may provoke father issues. These can be tinged emotionally either positively or negatively. An understanding of transference, internalization, and externalization is important to my discussion of what difference women priests would make to sacrificial theology.

SACRIFICE AS A RITUAL OF MALE VIOLENCE

"Women and sacrifice" for many feminist scholars is synonymous with "women and abuse" or "women and suffering." In 1973 Mary Daly wrote: "As the powerless victims of a scapegoat psychology, women are deprived of the 'credit' for sacrifice and the dignity of taking an active role. . . . Women, though encouraged to imitate the sacrificial love of Jesus, and thus willingly accept the victim's role, remain essentially identified with Eve and evil."[15] The context of this quotation is Daly's discussion of the implications of "Jesus and the scapegoat syndrome" for women. In order to imitate Jesus' lifestyle, states Daly, it is necessary to live "sacrificially." Daly argues that the qualities that Christianity idealizes, especially for women, are also those characteristic of a victim: sacrificial love, passive acceptance of suffering, humility, meekness. Since these are the qualities idealized in Jesus, who "died for our sins," his functioning as a model reinforces the scapegoat syndrome for women. While male priests have come to be understood as set apart to participate in Jesus' supreme sacrifice of himself on the cross, women universally have been excluded from this role.[16]

More than fifteen years later, Joanne Carlson Brown and Rebecca Parker argued that atonement theology encourages martyrdom and victimization, and that to claim that salvation can come only through the cross is to make God a "divine sadist and a divine child abuser."[17] In "For God So Loved the World?" Brown and Parker advocate a mass female exodus from Christian churches, maintaining that women who stay are as victimized and abused as any battered woman. The heart of their critique is atonement theology—the notion that Jesus' sacrificial death was salvific. In the view of Brown and Parker, Christianity is an abusive theology that glorifies suffering. They argue that Christianity has been a primary force in shaping women's acceptance of their own abuse, communicated in the theological message of redemptive sacrifice. The notion of imitating Christ sanctions selfless suffering, held before women daily in the image of the bloody Jesus hanging from a cross. Those theologians who stand critical of atonement theology, but who retain the cross as a symbol of liberation, are given little sympathy, for "to sanction the suffering and death of Jesus, even when calling it unjust, so that God can be active in the world only serves to perpetuate the acceptance of the very suffering against which one is struggling."[18] For Brown and Parker, Christian atonement cannot be redeemed.

These feminist theorists suggest that religious sacrifice promotes a scapegoat mentality of which women have frequently been the victims, and they maintain that women have given enough blood for the sake of humanity. Views to the contrary have had little support from anthropological, psychological, or sociological interpretations. Sacrifice is problematic also because there is no consensus on exactly how it should be defined. The term *sacrifice* conveys multivalent meanings, which include an act of offering to a deity, the killing of a victim at an altar, destruction or surrender of something for the sake of something else, something given up or lost. To expiate—defined as "to atone for," "to extinguish guilt incurred by," "to pay the penalty for"—is a component of nearly all prominent theories of sacrifice.

Popular definitions of sacrifice imply a "giving up" or "loss" of something valued. Views within the academy tend to share this connotation. For example, sacrifice as interpreted by the eminent sociologists Henri Hubert and Marcel Mauss set the tone for a number of its later treatments. For them the essential action of sacrifice is accomplished through an expiatory act of destruction: a victim is separated definitively from the profane world, consecrated, and reborn sacred.[19] The unifying feature of all types of sacrifice lies in one procedure: "establishing a means of communication between the sacred and the profane worlds through the mediation of a victim, that is, of a thing that in the course of the ceremony is destroyed."[20] The victim serves as an intermediary through which communication is established between sacred and profane worlds. This Durkheimian theory of sacrifice developed in a context of French nationalistic fervor, in which the Catholic intellectual minority linked eucharistic sacrifice with ultimate civic sacrifice and heroism.[21]

While the work of Hubert and Mauss is not in common use today, the sacrificial theory of René Girard is currently in widespread circulation. It exemplifies a virtually universal focus on expiation in academic discussions of sacrifice. *Sacrifice*, for Girard, refers to the complex phenomenon of the collective killing of a human victim, its mythic rationalization, and its ritualization. The scapegoating mechanism, emerging from "mimetic desire"—or the desire to be like the other—underlies Girard's notion of sacrifice as expiation. Mimetic rivalries and conflicts have no braking mechanism short of murder, achieved through the vehicle of a surrogate victim.[22]

Girard's theory of sacrifice presents several thorny issues concerning contemporary sacrifice and women and sacrifice. For one, notions of offering, communion, or thanksgiving are in his view reaction formations against their solely violent origins. That is, he offers no reading of eucharistic sacrifice that could highlight nonviolent elements of meaning. In addition, while his descriptions of sacrifice and scapegoating show women as common victims, Girard offers no corresponding gender analysis of historical incidents of scapegoating or of scapegoating mechanisms. Most theories of sacrifice that focus on expiation necessitate that a particular group of people serve as scapegoats. Those marginalized by society, such as women and minorities, become the victims.[23] Womanist theologian Delores Williams, for example, has pointed out the destructive implications for African American women of viewing Jesus as a surrogate figure.[24] Girard's theory of sacrifice neither challenges domination-submission dynamics in a given society nor offers a critique of the victim mentality that is common to women and others cast in the scapegoat role.[25]

Analysis of Girard's theory again raises the questions posed by Daly and Brown and Parker. If sacrifice is to be viewed in terms of scapegoating, as Girard would have it, then women become the victims. No better illustration of this is found than in the film *Breaking the Waves*. Here a young bride blames herself for her husband's paralysis and believes that God will heal him if she sacrifices her body through sex. Victimized by an authoritarian religious ideology and a "community" that shuns her in her time of need, the young woman confuses masochism with atonement and abuse with love. The ending is far from redemptive.

It is important to note that the overemphasis on violent separation in theories of sacrifice is also reflected in a one-sided psychological model, namely, that of Freud. Psychologically, the customary explanation of sacrifice is a Freudian one, and many contemporary theories of sacrifice still reflect a Freudian rubric. An examination of Freud's approach and that of those influenced by him will show that a Freudian-based model does not enable us to understand the role of gender in the specific practice of a sacrificial tradition. In addition, Freudian theory veils the pre-Oedipal elements in sacrificial rituals.

As summarized, for Freud the Eucharist is a sublimation of Oedipal aggression against the father, with Christ the Son serving as a substitute for God the Father. In Freud's view, Christ's sacrifice atoned for the original sin of patricide. The primal brothers killed the father out of desire for the mother, and the two fundamental societal taboos—murder and incest—were instituted from the resultant guilt. These two taboos correspond to the two repressed wishes of the Oedipus complex. Freud in turn relies upon earlier research, which postulates that the origins of sacrifice lie in totemism as found in traditional cultures. For Freud, the sacrificial animal is the totem animal, which is in reality a father substitute.[26]

Because they draw from a Freudian template, most psychologically oriented theories of sacrifice equate it with violence.[27] For example, while Girard observes differences between mimetic desire and Freud's Oedipus complex, both, in his view, involve the choice of a model—in Freud's case, identification with the father.[28] Girard praises Freud for being the first to maintain that all ritual practices have their origin in an actual murder, and yet he faults Freud for banishing mimesis from his later work.[29]

While a Freudian approach acknowledges themes of killing, guilt, and sublimation of aggression in sacrificial rituals, the role of gender is murky at best. In addition, what does not fit is that according to the founder of psychoanalysis, aggression is the root cause of Jesus' sacrifice. However, in Christian doctrine it is ostensibly love—identification with suffering humanity—that led Jesus to bleed.[30] In particular, pre-Oedipal themes surface upon examination of the sacrifice of Christ as seen in the Christian doctrine of atonement. "For God so loved the world that he gave his only Son," the Bible text reads (John 3:16). In this case, God the Father allows his beloved Son to be sacrificed out of love for those who killed him. I suggest that a psychological analysis along pre-Oedipal lines offers a more fruitful avenue for exploration than does Freud. Freud's theory hints at the pre-Oedipal dimension of sacrificial rituals, yet does not go far enough. Because Freud overlooks the pre-Oedipal components of sacrifice, he misses the component of gender as well.[31] Other psychologically oriented theorists who pay more attention to gender argue that repression of the maternal is at the root of ritual sacrifice. Yet, upon examination of their theories one concludes that sacrifice must be relegated to males.

ANOTHER LOOK AT GENDER AND SACRIFICE

The work of sociologist Nancy Jay on blood sacrifice has received increasing attention among feminist scholars of religion, and as such it provides a starting point for discussion of the issue of gender and sacrifice. In her 1992 award-winning book *Throughout Your Generations Forever: Sacrifice, Religion, and Paternity*, Jay demonstrates an overarching concern with gender in rituals of blood sacrifice in a variety of cultures. In particular, she illuminates the relationship between sacrifice and maintenance of a male-dominated social order. Her theory has significant implications for the status of female clergy in contemporary Catholic and Anglican traditions, for which eucharistic sacrifice is pivotal and the ordination of women a continuing controversy. Jay situates the sociological function of male blood sacrifice in a gender reversal. While I believe she is correct to do so, certain aspects of her theory remain sketchy, particularly concerning women performing sacrifice. Feminist psychology in turn has much to offer in the way of deepening and extending Jay's sociologically oriented theory.

Jay's groundbreaking work is focused on the social contexts of sacrificial rituals, and in particular on ways in which sacrifice affects family structures. Uncovering a symbolic opposition between sacrifice and childbirth, Jay argues that sacrifice creates a male social bond transcending women's physiological reproductive powers. Through creating and maintaining the social relations of reproduction—that is, a patrilineal line of descent—sacrifice functions as a remedy for biological reproduction or "having-been-born-of-woman." Jay effectively demonstrates the way in which sacrifice centralizes and makes exclusive a patrilineal link with transcendent powers that in turn legitimates a male-dominated social order.

Thus, for Jay, sacrifice is to be connected with kinship. In patrilineal societies, sacrifice maintains descent structures through fathers and sons, while in matrilineal or bilateral systems sacrifice may work in opposition to genealogical structures through the mother. Unrelated traditions exhibit a common feature: only adult males may perform sacrifice. Women as mothers are never recorded as enacting sacrifice, and women who do sacrifice always do so in specifically nonchildbearing roles such as virgins, consecrated married women, or postmenopausal women. Because sacrificing marks social and religious descent, rather than biological descent, it identifies membership in groups with no presumption of actual family descent—for example, the Catholic mass. Sacrifice thus "produces and reproduces forms of intergenerational continuity generated by males, transmitted through males, and transcending continuity through women."[32]

Jay does not offer an overall definition of sacrifice, stating that sacrifice can only be determined within the context of its own tradition (p. xxv). She does, however, offer a logic of sacrifice. Sacrifice is grounded in an opposition between communion and expiation. This point is central to my own analysis of sacrifice. Sacrifice joins people together in community and at the same time separates them from defilement, disease, and other dangers. As Jay writes:

> Communion sacrifice unites worshippers in one moral community and at the same time differentiates that community from the rest of the world. Expiatory sacrifice integrates by getting rid of countless different moral and organic undesirable conditions: sin, disease, drought, . . . blood guilt, incest, pollution of childbirth or of corpses, and so on and so on, all having in common only that they must be expiated. (p. 19)

The symbolic opposition between sacrifice and childbirth can be seen in terms of logical oppositions between the purifying power of sacrifice and the pollution of childbirth and menstruation. Sacrifice can thus simultaneously expiate the consequences of having been born of woman and integrate the pure and eternal patrilineage (p. 40).

A significant contribution of Jay's research to feminist scholarship is the notion that blood sacrifice expresses male appropriation of female reproductive capacities. She argues that taking place alongside the development of the Eucharist as a blood sacrifice was the restriction of childbearing women from performing the rite. One of the reasons for their exclusion was the male desire to keep separate the "involuntary, unclean, vulnerable" bringing of life into the world that takes place during childbirth from the voluntary "purifying" taking of life that occurs in the "sanctioned killing of sacrifice."[33] Jay shows how blood sacrifice enables men to both appropriate and transcend women's reproductive powers—it is "birth done better."

Two fundamental questions emerge from Jay's analysis. First, does she intend to make the claim that sacrifice is the prerogative only of men? And second, *can* women sacrifice? If the first question is answered affirmatively, then women should not be priests. The second question can be rephrased as follows: Episcopal women priests now can stand at an altar and recite special words, but is what they are doing considered sacrifice?

Most other prominent views of gender and sacrifice echo Jay's in affirming sacrifice as a ritual of male violence. While Jay disagrees with Girard on the grounds that he presents sacrifice in terms of a universal human nature (which includes gender relations determined by biologically given male violence),[34] she does not directly dispute the "male nature" of blood sacrifice. As a rule, theories that acknowledge gender share an interpretation of sacrifice in terms of violent separation. They also make explicit the repression of women associated with male-condoned violence. The theory of sacrifice advanced by psychologist of religion William Beers illustrates this viewpoint.

Beers draws from the work of psychoanalyst Heinz Kohut to develop his theory. In his view, ritual blood sacrifice embodies male and male-identified anxiety and men's symbolic efforts to control and acquire the experienced power of women. Beers explains that blood sacrifice is the religious symbol that psychologically express- es the male need for, resentment of, and envy of the omnipotent maternal self-object. Men envy and fear women, Beers suggests, because male identification with the maternal idealized self-object remains incomplete. "Unlike the idealized mother imago of the nar- cissistic period, the cultural self-object experience cannot adequate- ly mirror male grandiosity."[35] Sacrifice for Beers comprises four interrelated narcissistic self-object functions, which express: (1) the grandiose desire for merger with an idealized self-object, (2) the dread of such a merger through the act of separation, (3) the nar- cissistic rage and violence surrounding the disappointment in the merger with and separation from the self-object, and (4) the sym- bolic transfer and transformation of omnipotence from the idealized maternal self-object to the grandiose male self.[36] In sum, men sacri- fice in order to move closer to, gain distance from, or acquire the experience of power and perfection fantasized to reside in the mater- nal self-object. While Beers's theory of ritual sacrifice takes gender dynamics into account, and in particular acknowledges fear and envy of women as essential components of male sacrifice, it becomes problematic in its exclusion of women as sacrificers. Interestingly, while Beers indicates that his observations about the factors that lead to violence against women are completely culture bound, he reiterates that sacrifice is, with some "minor or recent exceptions," a male ritual.[37] Yet, is not sacrifice also culture-bound? If so, would not women sacrificers reflect the underlying psychology of the ritu- al? I believe the answer to both questions is yes. For Beers, howev- er, women as sacrificers remain an unaccounted-for anomaly, an exception to the rule.

This is also the belief of Jonte-Pace, who offers the following observation:

The existence of women as sacrificial officiants represents a *minor variation in a very stable pattern*. The stable pattern is precisely the one Nancy Jay described: sacrifice functions as a remedy for being born of woman. The same minor variation is that in today's Episcopal churches we allow a few women to perform these mother-remedying sacrifices. We let women act like men; we let women remedy or repudiate maternal birth; we let women participate in an intergenerational lineage independent of biological birth from biological mothers. Differentiating "being born of woman" from "being woman," we separate women as birthing mothers from women as sacrificial officiants functioning symbolically as women.[38]

I will return to Jonte-Pace's criticism after discussing my own view of how women priests would affect eucharistic sacrifice.

CAN WOMEN SACRIFICE?

Thus far, sacrifice has been based on some combination of male expiatory violence and female victimization. The theories have an internal coherence so long as the sacrificers are men and so long as women are routinely excluded from ritual participation. But here is where the slippage lies. What if the sacrificer herself is a woman? Jonte-Pace suggests that she is merely acting like a man: remedying or repudiating maternal birth. Have we separated in a new way "being born of woman" from "being woman"? If so, Episcopal women clergy would do well to reevaluate their function in the Eucharist, and those Catholic feminists pushing for women's ordination would be advised to step back for a moment. Maybe we haven't come so far after all.

My understanding of the phenomenon is as follows. Ritual sacrifice, while frequently expressed in terms of male violence, actually manifests elements of both expiation and communion as described by Jay. The views of sacrifice discussed to this point are not incorrect, but there is a lack of attention to the issue of women as sacrificers. Jay's theory does not take into account women priests because none of the societies she studied allowed them. Yet that does not mean that women cannot fit into a theory of sacrifice. Jay, for example, affirms that "without sacrifice there can be neither a hierarchical priesthood nor its institutionalized genealogy linking males in unilinial descent."[39] She does not suggest, however, that there can be no sacrifice if hierarchical priesthood and male descent are *not* present, which I argue is the case with Anglican women priests.

In Jay's view, communion and expiation are interdependent forces. She states that in a formal sense, communion is a kind of integration, and expiation is a kind of differentiation. Integration is not possible without some kind of differentiation from other things; conversely, differentiation cannot be done without a recognizable whole. In all traditions, communion sacrifice is alimentary. Jay observes that there is a common association of femaleness with what must be expiated.

While both communion and expiation are necessary elements of sacrificial systems, Jay admonishes that they need not be equally represented. For example, in early Israelite sacrifice communion was of primary importance, while in late Israelite sacrifice expiatory elements predominated (p. 24). As well, as a result of Vatican II and diminishing clerical-lay distinctions, notes Jay, the Christian eucharistic sacrifice became less expiatory, with a renewed emphasis on alimentary communion (p. 112).

Jay's views illustrate the tensions between communion and expiation as they have been expressed theologically in eucharistic sacrifice. At the outset of her chapter "Sacrifice and Social Structure in Christianity"(pp. 112–127), Jay claims that to question the eucharistic sacrifice has been to question the hierarchical social structure, and to reject the social organization has been to question the sacrificial practice. Parallels between changes in early eucharistic theology and changes in the social organization reveal that both the mass and the church hierarchy became controlled by males. In addition, both became patrilineal. The net result was that sacrificial theology became linked with apostolic succession and the institutionalization of a male priesthood.

In the contemporary eucharistic sacrifice, the priest is said to act supernaturally, *in persona Christi*, as a mediator between God and the faithful. The fundamental hierarchical distinction is between God and nature, ascent and descent. Jay maintains that as long as the church does not ordain women, control of the social relations of reproduction remains inseparable from control of the social order. The strictly patrilineal sacrificial line of descent is illustrated by the fact that precisely those traditions that practice the Eucharist as sacrifice also refuse to ordain women. Jay argues that the immovable barrier to Anglicans and Catholics sacrificing together is not a theological concern but a concern for purity of descent. Thus, women seeking ordination in the Catholic Church necessarily also seek a redefinition and restructuring of the church.[40]

I agree with Jay that if women were to be ordained to the Catholic priesthood, the result would be a redefinition and restructuring of the church. Yet, is sacrifice to be understood only in terms of apostolic succession and the institutionalization of a male priesthood? To return to Jonte-Pace, is sacrifice merely a remedy for being born of woman? We must ask this of Jay: if not sacrificing, what are Episcopal women priests in fact doing when they bless the bread and wine at the altar? Jay's research is not intended to address this question. She does, however, speak to the issue of Anglican sacrifice in the continuing controversy over the validity of Anglican orders in Vatican ecumenical dialogue. "The Anglicans say to Rome," writes Jay, "we have accepted sacrifice, why don't you accept our orders? And Rome responds, you say you accept sacrifice, but you ordain women; therefore it cannot be sacrifice as we understand it."[41] Jay has shown that for the Vatican, sacrifice remains hinged upon maintaining a male system of unilineal descent. Yet if Jay's earlier premise—that sacrifice is determined within the context of its own tradition—also is accepted, the issue of Anglican sacrifice cannot be dismissed so easily. Nor should we accept Beers's conclusion that "the male function of sacrifice psychologically precludes a woman from performing the act."[42] This claim serves only to perpetuate a gender reversal inverting female reproductive powers.

Another way to approach the issue is to ask whether Jay suggests that sacrifice is *only* the prerogative of men. Can only men sacrifice? She does not, in fact, make so bold a sociological claim. In discussing sacrifice in the Ashanti, a matrilineal society, Jay states that sacrificing has no regular relation to intergenerational continuity figured through women. Yet, she continues, there are problems in defining the place of sacrifice in matrilineal societies, because it may have "so peripheral a role that it is overlooked by ethnographers."[43] If undescribed, there is no way to recover an indigenous religion, nor sacrifice by women in this religion. As Jay observes, "Just because sacrifice is not mentioned does not prove its non-existence" (p. 62).

A danger arises if sacrifice is viewed solely in terms of a "male" ritual. Perhaps this is precisely what some men would have women think. I suggest that Jay's theory applies more directly to men as sacrificers than it does to women. Since all the societies she studied are patriarchal (although not all are patrilineal), Jay is describing how sacrifice functions in a situation of male dominance, but not how sacrifice always functions. To expand upon her theory, if male sacrifice is a means of taking away power and descent from the mother and ritually giving it to the father, then sacrifice also reflects hidden female abilities. Female functions have been appropriated by men and in the process disconnected from actual women. As has been shown, there is perhaps no better example of this type of gender reversal than the Eucharist. In the Eucharist, while acting in the person of a feminine Christ, male priests appropriate for themselves a rite whose origins lie in feeding, nourishment, and meals, and in the process emulate women's ability to bleed without dying and to give forth new life. As has been suggested, envy of and desire for maternal capacities provide unconscious motivations for men's co-optation of female functions in the Eucharist. While outwardly voicing more "rational" reasons for prohibiting women clergy, Vatican officials preserve a male line of descent through transcending women's reproductive powers in the perpetuation of blood sacrifice.

A PRE-OEDIPAL UNDERSTANDING OF SACRIFICE

Margaret Mahler's research is useful in extending Jay's theory. In a pre-Oedipal view, sacrifice expresses the separation-individuation process for both women and men. I believe that a pre-Oedipal reading of sacrifice—a reading in terms of "birthing"—fills a gap in the traditional Oedipal view of sacrifice as killing. This more balanced view of sacrifice can be seen in Ross and Ross's reading of the

Catholic mass, which focuses on the creative, playful, and liminal elements of the ritual—expressive of pre-Oedipal issues in addition to Oedipal ones.

While ritual sacrifice has generally been viewed to be about death, ironically, a deeper reading renders it to concern life—both physical and psychological life-giving from the mother. I submit that this is what has been missing in most theories of sacrifice, and yet is present in real sacrificial rituals. In order to illustrate the theme of birthing in the context of sacrifice, I examine a situation in which it is least expected to surface: father-son sacrifice. Abraham's sacrifice of Isaac and Jesus' sacrifice serve as examples.

It is significant that in both Abraham's sacrifice of Isaac and the sacrifice of Jesus, the son is not really killed, or at least does not remain permanently dead. In fact, in both cases the son lives on to establish or reconfirm a covenant, either through his person or through his lineage. In these two examples of father-son sacrifice, the son is "reborn": Isaac's life is spared, and Jesus regains his through the resurrection. A consequence of Isaac's "rebirth" is the continuance of the male lineage begun with Abraham, leading to the genesis of the people of Israel. A result of Jesus *redivivus* is the continuance of the human lineage for eternity—humanity is saved from the wages of sin and death. The resurrection also initiates another lineage—an apostolic one of male popes, bishops, and priests. The end result in these examples is the reverse of termination—the male line lives on to develop a special relationship with God. We can see that while killing is a component in these two examples of sacrifice, the sacrifice *results* in the rebirth of the son. In those cases in the ancient Near East in which the son was actually sacrificed, the ritual was thought to effect better relations between God and humanity for the coming generations, thus also ensuring the continuance of the male lineage. Therefore, we must also explore the concept of covenant. For covenant is what is involved in the rebirth of the son.

The binding of Isaac takes place after Yahweh (or God) makes a covenant with Abraham, described in Genesis 12 and 17. According to the covenant, Yahweh is to favor Abraham with land and progeny. Biblical scholar Jon Levenson has observed that the second address in Genesis 22 (verses 15–18) makes Abraham's binding of Isaac into a basis for the renewal of the covenantal promise of nation, land, and blessing.[44] Here God is reported as saying: "By myself I have sworn, says the LORD, because you have done this, and have not withheld your son, your only son, I will indeed multiply your descendants as the stars of heaven and as the sand which is on the seashore" (RSV). The passage infers that Abraham will have his multitudes of descendants only because he was willing to sacrifice the son who is destined to beget them (p. 13). Levenson's reading of this passage suggests that the greatness of the Israelite nation rests on Abraham's surrender of Isaac for sacrifice to Yahweh. Abraham's son later becomes identified with the paschal lamb, also a symbol of the covenant (pp. 182, 184). Rabbinic midrash, in Levenson's view, makes the binding of Isaac into an archetype of redemption and thus a foreshadowing of eschatological deliverance, the new Exodus (p. 183).

In the case of Jesus, all we have to do is look to Christian theology to find support for the motif of covenant and its connection to rebirth. It is easy to understand why Christians have viewed the sacrifice of Isaac as a typology of the sacrifice of Christ. Christ, the lamb of God, is also seen as voluntarily led to the slaughter and is also a symbol of a covenant—a new covenant of faith rather than of law (Romans 3). The doctrine of atonement holds that Jesus' death was a sacrifice enabling reconciliation between God and humanity. This reconciliation enabled forgiveness of sins and eternal life—or birth into a spiritual realm. As such, the meaning of the cross took on at least three connotations for the developing Christian community—representation, substitution, and participation. Jesus was understood to be the covenant representative of humanity: Christ, through his obedience upon the cross, represents the covenant people. Jesus also substituted for humanity: in offering himself on the cross in place of everyone, Jesus took humanity's guilt upon himself. Lastly, those who have faith in Christ as risen savior were thought to participate in the benefits that his death conferred—forgiveness of sins and eternal life. Hence, it is thought that through faith, believers come to stand within the covenant between God and humanity.[46] In this fashion, the Christian community believed that the covenant of law was superseded by the covenant of faith, typified by Abraham's faith in Genesis and made possible by the crucifixion of Christ.

As stated, theories of sacrifice do not usually stress the components of covenant or continuance of a lineage. I have suggested that the reason for this omission is that most theories of sacrifice draw from an Oedipal model focusing primarily on aggression and guilt. Yet covenant and continuity are central to the examples I have been discussing. We have seen that both the sacrifice of Isaac and Jesus' crucifixion speak to the issue of birth—to the rebirth of individuals and to the initiation of new communities. As such, they beg for a pre-Oedipal in addition to an Oedipal analysis.

The pre-Oedipal elements, which Freud left out of much of his theorizing, include maternal identification, maternal love, maternal nurturing, maternal idealization, and maternal hostility. The most primordial pre-Oedipal component is the phenomenon of birth itself. While most psychoanalytic theorists writing about the pre-Oedipal period do not discuss the significance of birth,[47] they do discuss its inevitable consequences—what Margaret Mahler labels the infant-mother separation-individuation process. From the infant's perspective, birth and its aftermath concern the process of becoming separate from the mother—first physically and later psychologically.

Object relations theory offers a theory of sacrifice in terms of infant-mother differentiation that is experienced by *both* girls and boys. Mahler, for example, states that the relatively normal adult takes for granted the experience of being both fully "in" and simultaneously "separate" from the external world: "Consciousness of self and absorption without awareness of self are the two polarities between which we move, with varying ease and with varying degrees of alternation or simultaneity."[48] Her portrayal of the struggle against both fusion and isolation discussed earlier parallels the opposition between communion and expiation described by Jay in her logic of rituals of sacrifice. The separation-individuation phase, for example, is explained as a "kind of second birth experience," a "hatching from the symbiotic mother-child common membrane."[49]

I believe a push-pull dynamic—expressing the need for community while at the same time warding off the taboo—heralds the fundamental function of sacrifice to express the separation-individuation process for both women and men. If sacrifice reflected only male differentiation, there would be no instances of women sacrificing. Documentation exists, however, indicating that fish, eagles, dogs, and other animals were sacrificed to the goddess during the Neolithic period, an age when a queen priestess presided over agriculture and religious life.[50] From this research, it can be inferred that women were involved in blood sacrifices. The contemporary phenomenon of women priests in the Episcopal Church also suggests that women sacrifice—if sacrifice is to be reenvisioned in the way I am suggesting.

Mahler's pre-Oedipal stage of absolute primary narcissism, in which "I" and "not I" are not differentiated, points to the psychological root of union-separation dynamics, such as is found in ritual sacrifice, in early separation-individuation. Similarly, Balint's notion of "primary love," or the sense of primary relationship or merging with the environment, harkens back to the relationship between the fetus and the womb, in which environment and individual interpenetrate one another in a "harmonious mixup."[51] "The aim of all human striving," he writes, "is to establish—or, probably re-establish—an all-embracing harmony with one's environment, to be able to love in peace."[52] Winnicott concurs with Mahler and Balint that the infant's sense of self is completely merged with that of the mother at the beginning of life. For Winnicott, the infant's first "not me" possessions, or transitional objects, are perceived to be in an "intermediate area of experiencing" to which inner reality and external life both contribute. In adult life, transitional objects are symbolically expressed in religion and art.[53]

Merging is ritually expressed as union or "communion." If expiation is destruction or surrender of something for the sake of something else, communion is mutual participation, intimate fellowship or rapport, an act or instance of sharing. Pre-Oedipal merging-separation issues later become overlaid with Oedipal concerns such as aggression, guilt, and scapegoating. Although separation is an element of both pre-Oedipal interactions and the Oedipal triangle, it is by no means the sole dynamic of either.

As suggested, what interests me about Mahler's description of the separation-individuation process is that it parallels the opposition between communion and expiation described by Jay in her

logic of rituals of sacrifice. Sacrifice, Jay has informed us, joins people together in community as well as separates them from an "other."
For Mahler, the separation-individuation process constitutes the
child's efforts, as a relational being, to form a distinct identity from
mother as "other." Mahler explains that separation-individuation
generally entails four subphases: differentiation, practicing, rapprochement, and "on the way to libidinal object constancy."[54] The
period of rapprochement is particularly important in finding the balance between union and separation and reflects the child's anxiety
around separation from the mother as he or she becomes more indi-
viduated from her.

In sum, a pre-Oedipal theory of sacrifice applies to both sexes,
allowing for women as well as men sacrificers. In addition, sacrifice
need not always emphasize violent expiation; sometimes sacrifice is
more about communion, or about finding "right relation"[55]—exemplified through covenant—as a balance of separation and communion dynamics. To extend Ross and Ross's perspective, in the
Catholic Eucharist sacramental union can be seen as analogous to
pre-Oedipal primary love or mother-child symbiosis. The individual who becomes one with the body of Christ through partaking
bread and wine is at a deep level restoring this primal harmony.
Union between God and believer is effected through incorporating
Christ's body and blood, just as infant-mother union is initially
obtained through blood from the mother's body. It has been shown
that the Eucharist, with its theology of transubstantiation, functions
transitionally to make present what is absent, to transform bread
and wine into Christ's body and blood.[56] The bread and wine function multivalently, symbolizing Christ but also symbolizing the
archaic mother and her body and blood. The mediation that takes
place during eucharistic sacrifice expresses the transitional object's
ability to overcome infant-mother separation, to once again attain a
stage of mother-child dual unity.

SACRIFICE AND MATERNAL TRANSFERENCES

Because the symbolism of the celebrant is multilayered, women at
the altar would evoke a variety of images, not only pre-Oedipal

ones. I suggest, however, that psychologically, the internalized connection with the early mother is reestablished when women sacrifice. In addition, women performing eucharistic sacrifice express pre-Oedipal themes of communion to a greater extent than do men performing eucharistic sacrifice. This happens through the process of externalization of internalized maternal imagoes.

Earlier when externalization was discussed in the context of analysis, I explained that the priest functions similarly to the analyst as a slate for transference of maternal and paternal imagoes. Some research on the significance of the gender of the analyst indicates that maternal transferences may happen more frequently when the analyst is female. As psychoanalyst Eva Lester puts it, the "affective tone and regressive potential in the pre-oedipal, dyadic transferences are stronger than in analyses with male analysts."[57] In other words, women analysts evoke pre-Oedipal issues more strongly in their clients than do men analysts. This finding leads one to speculate that pre-Oedipal transferences would also be more common and more deeply emotionally tinged with women celebrants than with men celebrants. Similarly, a female priest would allow for the possibility of recovering access to the mother's body in a more profound way than a male priest would. I will explain.

While Freud's notion of sacrifice involved replaying relationships with paternal objects and their externalization in Christianity onto the figure of Christ, in a pre-Oedipal understanding of sacrifice, the ego itself is the focus of investigation. In a pre-Oedipal framework, the way in which the self is constructed becomes a paradigm for understanding sacrificial dynamics. As Chodorow has suggested, the central core of the self is, internally, a "relational ego."[58] The formation of a self takes place in relation to the mother and affirms the earliest sense of self-in-connection, or the "self-in-good-relationship."[59] If the female priest allows more easily for externalization of the internalized mother, she is also more effective in strengthening this sense of self-in-good-relationship. The male priest could also represent the internalized mother; however, the association of maleness with separateness and splits in the internal object world make this possibility more difficult.

Thus, through the process of externalization, I believe that women priests would facilitate greater emergence of pre-Oedipal issues. In particular, a woman celebrant would make external the underlying primary oneness with the mother that is part of both core gender identities. The theological notion of mystical union with Christ, expressed psychologically in the restoration of infant-mother dual unity, would become apparent when women enact the eucharistic sacrifice. Any issues with the separation-individuation process would also surface, including maternal envy and hostility.

Examples from my interviews illustrate the Eucharist as a ritual of birthing and nurturing, charged with maternal transference issues.

First, one woman Episcopal priest related that she has experienced a number of "female" moments in her history of celebrating the Eucharist. She spelled out three such moments that she viewed as symbolic of the types of female experiences she had had. The first took place at a house blessing. She celebrated the Eucharist on the coffee table, which required her to look down upon the elements from where she was standing. As she prepared to lift up the chalice to say the words of institution, she saw her face perfectly reflected on the surface of the chalice. This amazed her, and she moved the chalice around to see her reflection changing (she realized that "yes, it is me in here, and yes, I dissolve"). When she lifted up the chalice to say the words, at that moment the movement broke the surface of the wine, and she thought to herself: "That's what is happening. Whatever is distinctly 'me' (my ego) is really to be drowned in this given moment, and that's really what it is about—this giving of self to be food and drink for everyone else."

The second experience occurred at a baptism. The infant fell asleep against her shoulder. She explained that she had an instinct, which she obeyed, to keep that child with her while she celebrated. It felt wonderful, and she could feel the whole congregation watching her. "Even the old crusty types commented on it." After that occasion it became the tradition whenever possible to have babies baptized just before the Eucharist and to have the priest hold the newly baptized baby while she celebrated. She observed that while there may be male priests who would do this also, the picture is not the same. People in the congregation saw themselves as a baby being fed and the Eucharist as feeding. This priest explained that the experience pointed out to her that the Eucharist is really about baptism. The last experience took place at a funeral service for a baby. The woman priest stated that at the time she was very conscious of the relationship between embryonic life and a mature adult life. The group did a eucharistic thanks, and it became clear to her that this was not just a eucharistic celebration, but in some wonderful way it had been transformed into a Eucharist about mourning: in particular, about things not happening or things that had failed to happen in everyone's life. It became very cathartic. At the end, people told her that only a woman would have been intuitive enough to have done this. She stated that she thinks there are men who could have done it also—"it's the feminine in everybody," in her view, that can do it.

A second illustration of maternal transferences in the Eucharist is found in "hostess" imagery. A male priest related that some women wish to set a different kind of environment, one that gives them a chance to be hostess, and that this model offers a more of a "family" model of church. These women, he stated, are attempting to be more intimate, and they are concerned about setting a "good-looking table." This priest also discussed an occasion on which he had a very strong sense of a feminine presence—"the woman was really in touch with who she was and with her own identity." He said that people came away from the Eucharist feeling upbeat but were unable to articulate why.

One woman priest, who at the time of the interview was employed at a parish with a large space, elaborate liturgy, and a huge altar, told me that at first she felt overwhelmed by the space. In time, however, she came to feel like a "hostess at a banquet." Her role was to make people feel at home at the dinner party. She explained that she did not have to cook the food or even serve it in some ways. Instead, she had to present it and give people permission to eat. This imagery, in this priest's view, gets away from the notion of "mother feeding children," because adults come to the dinner party.

As a third illustration, an Episcopal laywoman offered an analogy that helps us understand the role of maternal transferences in the Eucharist. She disclosed that with male celebrants, there is a sense of "preciousness, exclusivity." With women, alternatively, she gets a "dining room" sense, the sense of preparation for a feast. She said that a woman presiding is like the food in some ways, because a woman's body is always food and women's bodies are broken. A woman's body is broken, she stated, in childbirth and in numerous other ways (i.e., women suffer bodily in many ways in Western culture). While it does not seem natural for a man's body to be broken, it does seem natural for a woman's body to be broken.

For this laywoman, a woman celebrant puts one in touch with the eating experience. To be fed by a woman, in her view, is a whole different kind of experience than to be fed by a man. There is a certain intimacy to the Eucharist, alongside issues of power. For her, it is easier to confront the sexual and intimacy issues with women—to look them in the eye—than it is with men. "It is all about mirroring," she stated, "and one mirrors the mother."

As an example, a woman priest stated that the first women clergy often encouraged physical contact at the altar rail, making eye contact and holding parishioners' hands when they put the bread in them. The laywoman I interviewed explained that the first thought she had when she took the Eucharist from a woman was, "Do I look her in the eyes?" She had never thought about looking a male priest in the eyes, although now she says she does. The power issues, she notes, were different with a woman celebrant. She felt more on an equal par with her and wanted to connect. Her experiences with women celebrants have enabled her to connect with male priests. Another woman priest I spoke with, who makes a point of looking parishioners in the eye when giving communion, said that most people really like this practice. They tell her, "It's the first time I feel like I personally have been given the bread."

A woman priest told me that the first time she heard a woman say the words of institution, she felt included in a way she had not felt previously, and that it had something to do with hearing a woman's voice say the words. The laywoman quoted earlier made the following additional remark: "To hear a man say 'the body of Christ, broken for you,' a woman thinks 'poor Jesus.' To hear a woman say it, she thinks 'oh, yes!'" The interview material suggests that maternal transferences are indeed stronger when women celebrate the Eucharist and that part of what is happening is externalization of internalized impressions of the early mother. It is because of this that the experiences are labeled "female" and that women celebrants are associated with food and perhaps even viewed as food. In sum, it has been suggested in this discussion that at a deep psychological level the female celebrant represents the figure of the early mother and that sacrifice reflects pre-Oedipal issues concerning infant-mother union and separation. On a second, patriarchal level, women at the altar symbolize the myriad ways in which women have been crucified. As Edwina Hunter wrote of the statue of Christa created by Edwina Sandys, "When many of us see the Christa we see all the women we have known and loved, and the women we have not known and yet love, shamed and cursed, tortured, raped, made the object of lust, and in sadomasochistic pornography hung on crosses."[60] On yet a third, sociocultural level, women at the altar express a gender reversal of male and female roles. Male priests have for centuries turned bread and wine into body and blood, while women do this every time they give birth.

CONTRIBUTIONS OF CATHOLIC THEOLOGY

Contemporary Catholic theology supports an emphasis on sacrifice as communion as well as expiation. While historical development of sacrifice illustrates the presence of both themes, communion is more prominent among theologians today. As stated, in recent Catholic theology sacrifice as offering is the preferred understanding: as Emminghaus puts it, sacrifice is to be taken in its proper sense of "self-giving."[61] Historically, communion is most closely associated with offering and expiation with cultic service. Both offering and immolation are found in the biblical tradition from which Christianity emerged.[62]

Power's research highlights historical shifts in the way eucharistic sacrifice has been understood in the Catholic Church. He posits that in New Testament churches, sacrifice was understood metaphorically rather than in the cultic sense attributed to Old Testament sacrifices. 1 Corinthians, for example, illustrates an indirect connection between the Eucharist and the Jewish prayer called the *todah*, a type of praise associated with the peace offering. At that time, observes Power, the Eucharist was probably understood in the metaphorical sense as "sacrifice of praise."[63] Power explains that eucharistic sacrifice in the pre-Nicene church brought together a number of themes, including "the redemptive work of the Word made flesh, prefigured in the paschal lamb and located in the humility, obedience, and suffering of his voluntary death; the recapitulation of humanity into communion with this mystery through the spiritual sacrifice of holy lives, obedient to the gospel; the offering of bread and wine as signs of gratitude for creation and acknowledgment of the one God in all things" (p. 117).

He notes that Cyprian, an early theologian, developed a more cultic view of sacrifice. The ritual of episcopal ordination in the pre-Nicene church underscored the high-priestly role of the bishop in making offerings at the altar (p. 118). After Nicea, prayers became even more tuned to cultic service and away from gift and offering (p. 140). At the Council of Trent in the mid-1500s, the sacrifice of the mass was explained entirely in terms of its reference to the cross, and the sufficiency of thanksgiving and self-offering were excluded. A key point was the nature of the mass as a sacrifice of propitiation, whereby the action of the priest in offering was viewed as distinct from the action of taking communion by the faithful (pp. 257–260).

Power explains that today the language of priesthood and sacrifice needs to be demythologized. A renewed appreciation of the term *sacrifice* as metaphor is needed. What should be emphasized, in his view, is the notion of sacrifice as "reversal":

> It reverses the quest to restore order by preparing victims and appeasing a threatening anger, whether that of God or that of the spirits that abide in the universe. Instead it points to a communion of solidarity in love in God's spirit that withstands human judgment and prevails in the midst of suffering. . . . Anxieties and fears are still to be named, but in a context wherein eschatological hope promises a divine expiation and liberation. (p. 323)

The demythologization of sacrifice, according to Power, in turn presents a new model for justice: it is not by self-oblation of desire but by giving of self for others that God's reign is promoted. Power explains that if the Eucharist is celebrated in the manner of the early eucharistic tradition, "freedom is bestowed, sins forgiven, and immortality already conferred" (p. 323).

Power's detailed overview of sacrificial theology suggests that its cultic aspect—or sacrifice as expiation—developed over time in response to particular historical circumstances. While remnants of a cultic understanding of sacrifice continue to be promoted by traditionalists, Vatican sources and Catholic theologians concur that communion is as theologically important to the Eucharist as is expiation. The Eucharist is both a ritual re-enactment of Jesus' expiatory death and a rite of mystical incorporation into the body of Christ. Communion with Christ in the Eucharist presupposes his true presence, effectively signified by the bread and wine, which become Christ's body and blood. The *Documents of Vatican II* clearly articulate that in the sharing of the Eucharist, worshipers are joined to the body of Christ. By partaking of Christ in incorporating the bread and wine, worshipers become one body with him through the power of the Holy Spirit.[64] As Catholic theologian Karl Rahner states, partaking of the "one bread" is an efficacious sign of the "renewed, deeper, and personally ratified participation and incorporation in that Body of Christ in which one can share in his Holy Spirit, that is to say, the Church."[65] The other predominant element in eucharistic sacrifice, self-offering, is visibly exemplified in the eucharistic meal, during which Christ's sacrifice to God by the church and the self-offering of individual worshipers takes place. Expiation and communion are thus linked through the consecration of bread and wine and their transformation into the body and blood of Christ.

CONTRIBUTIONS OF FEMINIST THEOLOGY

A pre-Oedipal understanding of sacrifice also finds support in some recent work by contemporary feminist theologians on sacrificial and atonement theologies. For example, feminist theologian Mary Grey states that if the word *atonement* is to be retained, it must be viewed in terms of "at-one-ment," as a "fundamental drive to unity and wholeness, which itself sparks off the creative-redemptive process."[66] Grey searches for models of at-one-ment in the dynamic of "right relation" and queries whether, by embracing this dynamic, persons can become co-agents and co-creators of their own redemption. She asks whether women can respond to the Christ event in a way "that is both self-affirming, yet self-transcending, a way that enables the voluntary assumption of suffering for the sake of a higher ideal."[67] Grey proposes the "birthing of God" as a symbol for at-one-ment. If creation is about giving birth, so must redemption, transformation, and atonement be. The birthing of God, in her view, is an expression of God's fundamental being as interrelatedness. In the birthing experience, she states, "we are given a 'letting go' of self—in pain and struggle—for the creation of new being. . . . We are held by that nurturing center: from this being-torn-apart, this sense of loss, together You and I wordlessly create new life."[68] Similarly, Elizabeth Johnson argues that the cross is part of the larger mystery of pain-to-life, of the struggle for new creation evocative of the rhythm of pregnancy, delivery, and birth.[69]

Grey's model of right relation for at-one-ment closely parallels my argument that sacrifice be re-imaged in terms of birthing and that communion be emphasized in addition to expiation. Communion is the base upon which notions of mutuality and right relation are built. Feminist theologian Carter Heyward in turn suggests that the experience of right relation is fundamental and constitutive of the human being: God "is our power in relation to each other, all humanity, and creation itself."[70] Heyward does not accept the doctrine of Jesus' sacrificial death, yet, as Brown and Parker point out, in her reconstruction Jesus redeems by showing that salvation consists of being in right relation with God.[71]

The positive dimensions of sacrificial theology for feminists are also addressed by feminist theologian Sally Purvis, who argues that the cross must be reclaimed from being used to legitimate and glorify suffering, abuse, and violence. For Purvis, the cross symbolizes the "power of God as life and love."[72] While the cross does not deny suffering, it does not justify it. Suffering is a by-product of love. The ability to reclaim the cross as a symbol of life-giving power, according to Purvis, is a function of the ability to live in communities that enact that power. "Cruciform community" operates with unity, not separation, as its fundamental state.[73] There is general agreement among theologians that the Eucharist, as a sacrament of unity and communion, should be a paradigm for just relations. How ironic it is that in restricting women's access to the altar, the sacrament is made into one of division and alienation.[74]

Procter-Smith offers a critique of attempts such as Grey's and Purvis's to find positive meaning in the cross and sacrificial theology. The attempt to redeem death by aligning it with birth, she argues, fails to recognize that birth is about "bringing life from life" rather than "bringing life from death." Also, in her view, pregnancy and birth symbolism are misplaced when they are used to refer to a brutal execution, for pregnancy and birth then become rendered in terms of sacrifice, suffering, and death.[75] To respond to these criticisms, the psychological perspective I have presented indicates that birth is not solely about bringing life from life, but that there is inevitable loss as well. To be more specific, I do not understand birth to be only the physical process of a fetus passing through the birth canal. It also includes early nurturing of new life, in Mahler's terms, separation-individuation—or one could say the birth of an individual. A pre-Oedipal view of sacrifice focuses primarily on the infant, not the mother. There is inevitable loss experienced by the *baby* in becoming separate from the mother—both physically and later psychologically. Bringing a child into the world also radically changes the lives of both parents, especially if they give it the care it requires. Parents must grieve what they can no longer do or have because of their decision to have a child. It is only because sacrifice has carried such negative connotations that some feminists do not want to see it associated with birthing. My project here has been to recast ritual sacrifice in a way that is more balanced, without, however, overlooking the expression of female appropriation and victimage in much of male sacrifice.

In addition to re-imaging sacrifice as communion, the Eucharist, when celebrated by women priests, offers a resource for feminist community-building. Whereas Elizabeth Schüssler Fiorenza argues that the Eucharist has become the ritual symbolization of the structural evil of sexism,[76] the Eucharist, with women *and* men at the altar, has much to contribute toward fostering a feminist ethic, or a "metaphysic of connection."[77] Women priests tend to promote a sense of community in the congregation. To illustrate, one woman Episcopal priest related that for thirty-eight years, the church she began serving had placed the altar up against the wall. She changed the setup after she began working there. As she explained, "We lift up together. When I come before you and my back is to you, that means that you're too stupid to offer this yourself. . . . I believe priest and people together offer the sacrifice. . . . women bring that sense of community."

Feminist ethics have at their base the restoration of right relations between women and men. One way to facilitate right relations is through recognizing that, as human selves, we are interconnected with other human selves. While the theme of pre-Oedipal communion is a model for the interconnected self (right relation on a psychological level) women at the altar also represent the restoration of right relation on a political level—the admittance of women to the priesthood. As one woman priest expressed, if parishioners are presented with an inclusive model during the eucharistic celebration, inclusiveness is going to carry over into activities apart from the Eucharist. Women sacrificing thus affirms women's bonds of connectedness and mutuality with other women and with men as well as attests to a feminist ethic of equality between men and women.

In sum, the use of feminist psychology to analyze Jay's theory of sacrifice reveals the existence of deep-seated psychological reasons to support her sociological findings. Fear and envy of maternal abilities result in male appropriation of those abilities in rituals of blood sacrifice, which in turn serve as a means of maintaining male control. Yet it is a dangerous distortion to conclude that only men *can* sacrifice, for the result would be continued justification of women's ecclesial exclusion and their sociopolitical suppression. Blood sacrifice has expressed men's appropriation of female capacities in patriarchal societies because this constellation has best symbolized the male infant-mother separative process during the pre-Oedipal period. Women sacrificing would convey the same process but no doubt in different symbolic modes characteristic of female infant-mother concerns—for example, the need to separate from the maternal body and still love the mother.[78] Thus, while Jay uncovers gender dynamics in patriarchal rituals of blood sacrifice and makes clear the roots of male sacrifice in a gender reversal, feminist psychology situates sacrifice within its more universal context of expressing the need for separateness and community, a tension that continues to inform human existence.

Thus, Jonte-Pace's criticism of my theory is unjustified on two grounds. First, there are now more than a "few women" performing sacrifice in the Episcopal Church, so that the "minor variation" I describe is becoming more prevalent and will continue to do so. Second, while there are indeed "phallic" women (those who value hierarchy and an expiatory tradition) who enter the Episcopal priesthood, they are nevertheless altering understandings of sacrifice because they are *perceived* differently by parishioners. "Mother Joanna" carries different connotations than "Father Joe." In addition, as I have shown, the nature of the transference is different when a woman instead of a man blesses the bread. Consequently, I believe that as more and more women become Episcopal priests, there will be fewer "gory crucifixes" adorning church walls. Women sacrificers do not tend to evoke images of violence.

In conclusion, a more positive reading of sacrifice is found by focusing on communion rather than on expiation, and on the pre-Oedipal instead of the Oedipal period. This more balanced interpretation also takes into account the possibility of women sacrificers. Women priests at the altar would expose the gendered roots of sacrifice in the early infant-mother relationship and in female reproductive cycles. While the nature of women sacrificing needs further exploration (see chapter 6), at a deep psychological level the phenomenon reflects the primitive relation with the mother's body, and among its manifestations are expression of the infant-mother relationship and female reproductive cycles. These images alter sacrifice beyond what the Catholic tradition is willing to acknowledge, thus explaining why, in part, the ordination of women remains so problematic. The real threat of women performing sacrifice is that it would reestablish female genealogical structures through the mother and give back to women their reproductive powers. As a result, a male-dominated social order could no longer be maintained, nor could sacrifice continue to function as a remedy for "having-been-born-of-woman."

5

CHRIST AS A WOMAN

In that celebration of women, of women asking for physical healing, for health, for wholeness, presided over by a woman, the body of Christ was suddenly a woman's body. Women's suffering and denigration was Christ's suffering and death. In a way not available to me before, I knew that God knows what it is like to have a woman's body, what it is that women suffer. Jesus died for women.
—*From Alison Peberdy,* Women Priests

The priest in the Eucharist is traditionally seen as standing in the place of Christ—as *alter Christus*. If you change the symbol, you're going to change the theological reflections on that symbol.
—*Male Episcopal priest*

My reading of sacrifice raises the issue of female imagery for Christ. Could Christ have been a woman? When I ask undergraduate students in my theology courses this question, often I receive a reply along the following lines: certainly, Christ could have been female, but she would not have been able to accomplish as much as the male Jesus did. When I point out that most people did not listen to Jesus as a man, they are temporarily quieted. But, someone answers after a pause, she would not have been able to study Torah, function as a ritual leader, and so on in the Jewish climate of the first century. And this is true. But this response has yet to get at the heart of the question, which has to do with whether a woman can symbolize Christ—and in consequence act *in persona Christi* in the mass. Asking whether Christ could have been a woman is tantamount to questioning whether God can be imaged as female. It is also to query the role of gender in salvation. As such, the question addresses core issues in feminist theology.

We now turn to the issue of women acting *in persona Christi* at the altar. Women priests would evoke a female Christ image and in so doing would give form to much recent feminist Christology. Such imagery would affect parishioners' experience in various ways. A female Christ image would be welcomed by certain individuals but be strongly rejected by others. Hostility toward female Christ symbols, and by extension continued opposition to women at the altar, can be explained in psychological terms of internalization and "psychic boundaries."

First, the category "woman" needs to be examined. Is there a common "women's experience" that can be drawn upon to explore female images of Christ? I suggest that there is, albeit contextualized. Next, the question of symbolization is raised. How do women's experiences translate into symbol? A basic understanding of the psychological significance of religious symbols is fundamental to developing a theory of how women act *in persona Christi*. Such an understanding can be gained through analyzing the psychological formation of God representations. Third, I explore the relationship of symbol to metaphor. Feminist, womanist, *mujerista*, and Asian American women's Christologies provide metaphors that describe the richness and diversity of female Christ symbols. Finally, the benefits of imaging Christ and God as female are considered, as well as how the presence of women priests causes these benefits to be either realized or resisted psychologically.

SEXUAL DIFFERENCE AND FEMINIST THEOLOGY

Vatican officials would have us believe that "woman" and "man" are biologically determined categories, the existence of which will forever prevent women from becoming priests. As we have seen, the 1976 Vatican "Declaration on the Question of the Admission of Women to the Ministerial Priesthood" put forth the position that women cannot represent Christ in the Eucharist because of their gender. The continued prohibition of women clergy on the grounds of nuptial symbolism, or bridegroom imagery, continues to be based in biological concepts of "maleness" and "femaleness." Because of the weight given by Vatican supporters to biological determinism, it is necessary to provide another perspective on sexual difference.

Feminist theorists and theologians offer a much-needed alternative viewpoint to Catholic doctrine on this topic. It is also important to discuss sexual difference before addressing the significance of female symbols for Christ. This is because the power of female Christ symbols cannot be talked about until we acknowledge that these symbols are distinct from male Christ symbols in some discernible way. Acknowledging the latter implies that women's experience can be talked about as a category. As feminist theologian Sheila Greeve Davaney points out, if there is no common women's experience, the appeal to such commonality loses its authoritative force. If feminist notions of the divine are not grounded in a universal experience or a uniquely authoritative consciousness or tradition, then there is no source of validation for these notions.[1]

In proposing that women priests will make a positive difference to the church, I am suggesting that gender matters—I believe there *are* differences between men and women. I believe one *can* talk about "women's experience," although it must be historically and culturally contextualized. This claim opens the door to questions such as the following: Will women priests make a difference because of biology or socialization? In other words, is there something inherent about being female that results in a different experience for parishioners when the priest is a woman, or is the difference the product of women's historical role as more nurturing and relational? An understanding of the debates surrounding sexual difference is therefore called for at this juncture.

First, it should be noted that many Catholic feminists shy away from notions of gender difference. This is not surprising, especially since the Vatican has used this idea to defend complementarity— the notion that men and women have different but equal ecclesial roles originating from innate, predetermined functions. Anne Carr, for example, points out that while arguments against the ordination of women imply a two-nature or dual anthropology, arguments in favor of the ordination of women generally presuppose a one-nature or single anthropology, in which there are no "preordained" roles or functions.[2] Women within the larger feminist movement have had mixed reactions to women's perceived differences from men. Some have feared that acknowledgment of sexual difference would contribute to women's subordination, by stereotyping women into certain roles and not others. Other feminist thinkers applaud gender differences, finding them a source of empowerment. It is my contention that gender differences are to be viewed as a resource but that care should be taken to avoid either "burdening" women—making them responsible for world salvation—or "essentializing" them—claiming that women's difference resides in biology. The range of views held by prominent feminist theorists helps to situate my position.

In the early 1970s, feminist thinkers such as Kate Millett and Shulamith Firestone were opposed to the idea of emphasizing differences between the sexes, asserting that historically, sexual oppression has been based on socially constructed differences between men and women. They argued for the delineation between biological "sex" and sociological "gender": while anatomy determines sex, gender is a learned or acquired feature of social life, subject to early conditioning and reinforcement. These theorists observed the pressure throughout life to exhibit gender-appropriate behavior. The time and energy devoted to teaching boys and girls to act like a "man" or a "lady" contradicted the notion that these qualities were innate.[3] Feminist focus during this period was on the idea that women were no different from men and could do anything men could do. Where differences did exist, there was an attempt to minimize them as much as possible. Firestone, for example, called for the "abolition of pregnancy," advocating that reproductive technologies be developed enabling the genesis of test tube babies.[4] Sexual difference was labeled politically dangerous, and feminists instead advocated some form of androgyny.

By the mid-1970s, this trend in feminist thinking had gradually changed. A shift occurred: from trying to reduce or deny sexual difference, feminists began to explore the resources of female difference for women's own struggle for liberation. Theorists began to find positive value in qualities that women historically carried. To illustrate, Adrienne Rich focused on the nurturing aspects of motherhood and on its potential to heal ancient Western dualisms.[5] During this period, psychology, and especially psychoanalysis, became important tools for the study of sexual difference. Jean Baker Miller, for example, argued that the very psychological qualities that allowed women to be oppressed could be a means of increasing women's strength. Because women have been taught to be nurturing, affiliative, and cooperative, Miller maintained, they possessed more truly human qualities than men as currently socialized.[6] Other psychological treatments of gender placed the blame for women's oppression on the social institution of motherhood. Both Dinnerstein and Chodorow argued that male domination of women is perpetuated by women's serving as sole caretakers of children. Rather than women giving up mothering, as Firestone would have it, Chodorow and Dinnerstein pushed for dual parenting—for men to act "maternally." Their analyses implied that men could learn maternal traits, and women, similarly, could learn paternal traits.

Feminist discussion of sexual difference in the 1980s continued the trend of acknowledging that differences between women and men exist and that some historically female qualities have societal value. This trend persisted into the 1990s, although in recent years greater emphasis has been placed on diversity among women—particularly on differences originating from age, class, race and ethnicity, and geography and culture.[7] Exploration of historically "female" qualities, and whether they are innate or culturally derived, continues to offer a context for contemporary dialogue. Feminist social theorists generally concur, for example, that women raised in Western cultures value personal relationships more than men do, and that women put more emphasis on personal nurturance. Men raised in Western cultures, on the other hand, tend to stress individuality and securing a separate identity—usually based on a career or some other external source. As Martha Long Ice explains, faced from birth with distinct entitlements and social expectations, men and women develop different "perceptual grids." Females are disposed to develop skills of personal nurturance, integrative thinking, peer negotiation, and intuitive judgment. They tend to focus on complex systems and to see the parts in terms of the whole. Males, according to Ice, are more likely to develop skills of abstract analysis, logic, and visual/spatial judgment, "aggressively imposing rational control on dynamic processes toward some desired goal or accomplishment."[8] They are likely to concentrate with high intensity on limited aspects of phenomena.

Interestingly, an emerging arena for the nature-versus-nurture controversy is the field of morality. Carol Gilligan's famous study of women's moral development provides an illustration of the flavor of the contemporary debate. Arguing that different dynamics of early childhood result in girls' focusing more on connection and boys on experiences of inequality, Gilligan asserts that social context determines the basis for the two moral visions of care and justice, respectively.[9] Gilligan holds that there is a uniquely "feminine" mode of reasoning about self and morality, which constitutes a "different voice." As Lesley Stevens puts it: "It values personal relationships over abstract principles, responsibility and care for others over universal rights, and is centered on women's knowledge of 'the importance of intimacy, relationships, and care.'"[10] Gilligan contrasts her ethic of care with an ethic of justice, associated with male morality and described by moral development theorists such as Lawrence Kohlberg. Motivated by a logic of fairness rather than the "psychological love of relationships," an ethic of justice applies universal principles of rights and justice equally to all persons.[11] While Gilligan does not claim that the "different voice" or the ethic of care is exclusive to women, she indicates that its association with women is an empirical observation.

A number of critiques of her work have emerged, among them that her study infers at times that gendered behavior is biologically determined—thus leading to separate spheres for women and men, that she attacks a straw man (it is education or social class, not gender, that accounts for women's seemingly lesser moral maturity), and that her sample is inadequate. In a rejoinder, Gilligan answers that the care perspective is neither biologically determined nor unique to women. It is, she claims, a moral perspective different from those embedded in current psychological theories and measures, and one confirmed by other studies (although her study, she states, was meant to be interpretive rather than statistical). It thus seems that Gilligan adequately answers her critics.[12]

The flourishing of "care literature" illustrates one way in which certain traditionally feminine qualities have been heralded as resources for a feminist morality. An ethic of care is generally thought to include qualities of nurturance, compassion, and networks of communication—gender traits that have traditionally been assigned to women. Various theories exist about the ultimate source of those traits: in women's reproductive role and responsibilities, women's psychosocial development, or women's cultural and economic experience.[13]

Caroline Whitbeck, for example, uses the mother-child duo as the paradigm for her "relational ontology," claiming that this relationship is so symbiotic that nothing belongs to the mother that does not belong to the child, especially during pregnancy and infancy. Whitbeck holds that women's "maternal instinct" enables them to understand the infant's experience, hence reducing difference to biology. As others have pointed out, a mother-child model of morality encounters additional dangers. For example, it suppresses and/or condemns ambivalences also found in mother-child relationships.[14] To assume that the mother is "naturally" caring of her children, as Whitbeck does, falls into the category of biological determinism. Moreover, taken to its logical conclusion, the model implies that the infant does not feel responsible for the mother, only the mother for the infant. On the other hand, the early infant-mother relationship as described by Mahler illuminates a pattern in which the well-being of two individuals is intertwined, underscoring self-other intersubjectivity.

Several examples of biological determinism in the field of theology provide additional illustrations. Mary Daly, for example, has been indicted for claiming that women have innate powers of discernment, enabling them to understand such concepts as "Be-ing" and "Eternal Essences" in a superior way to men. This criticism was made primarily of her later work.[15] Davaney pays close attention to this tendency in Daly's thought and suggests that Daly proposes that women possess a "distinctive nature and form of consciousness" that has the capacity to know "Be-ing" or "Reality." Daly, Davaney argues, believes that there is a natural correspondence, lacking in men, between the "minds of musing women" and the structures of "Reality": women's consciousness is value-laden and biophilic, which in turn responds to the biophilic dimensions of "Be-ing."[16] Davaney also finds traces in the work of Schüssler Fiorenza and Rosemary Radford Ruether of the notion that women's experience and consciousness are more adequate than men's for discerning divine purposes. The difference, in her view, is that Schüssler Fiorenza and Ruether credit female privilege with women's location in historical struggles for liberation rather than in a unique female nature per se.[17] I do not believe that women's location in struggles for liberation needs to be viewed as "inappropriately privileging" women's experience, as Davaney argues. Instead, it can be said that Ruether and Schüssler Fiorenza use sexual difference as a *valuable resource* for understanding Jesus' message of liberation. Specifically, by lifting up women's common experiences of oppression, Schüssler Fiorenza and Ruether highlight the centrality of the theme of liberation in Jesus' teachings.

Recent research in feminist theology suggests that biological determinism remains a concern for scholars but that its focus has shifted. As a field, feminist theology has changed immensely since its inception in the 1970s and early 1980s under the auspices of such scholars as Carol Christ,[18] Mary Daly,[19] Naomi Goldenberg,[20] Judith Plaskow,[21] and Rosemary Radford Ruether.[22] During these formative years, feminist scholars in religion were united by the common effort both to uproot sexism in the Jewish and Christian traditions and to discover avenues for transformative expressions of women's spirituality. Some of the issues explored were the importance of female symbols, women's religious experiences, and women's political and psychological empowerment.[23]

In its nascence, the fundamental claim of feminist theology was that women's experience is a primary context for doing theology. Feminist theologians asserted that because of the different experiences of males and females, men and women theologize in different ways. Models traditionally used to describe an individual's relationship with God, self, and nature were found in many cases to be inappropriate when the individual is a woman, hence requiring women to find their own models to describe spirituality. Before the mid-1980s—when concerns of biological determinism were first voiced—feminist theology largely spoke to the concerns of white, Western, middle-class women. As correctives to this monolithic approach, African American women, Hispanic women, and Asian American women have in turn developed theologies from their own historical and cultural contexts.

Davaney explains that while feminist theology in its early years shared basic central assumptions, themes, and commitments, today it is less a "singular identifiable site" on the theological spectrum and more appropriately characterized by varying methodological and substantive theological agendas.[24] This shift, according to Davaney, can be attributed to recent developments within feminist theology, in particular, questioning of notions of subjectivity and the normativity of feminist positions. It is worth noting that a number of methodological frameworks have emerged in recent years. Serene Jones maps the trajectories of the various types of methodologies utilized in the 1990s in her article "Women's Experience Between a Rock and a Hard Place: Feminist, Womanist, and *Mujerista* Theologies in North America."[25] These theologians now share an affirmation of the "nonessential nature of woman," yet, as Jones points out, the notion of "experience" remains essentialized by some (such as process/psychoanalytic) and radically historicized by others (such as poststructuralist).[26]

While Jones is wary of any kind of biological determinism, she admits that methodologies that tend to universalize experience are able to put forth bolder and more substantive theological visions. Davaney in turn suggests that feminist theologians need to return to women's experience, although in historicist terms. Just as there is no one, universal female nature, Davaney articulates that neither is there a singular feminist vision. From their varied positions, however, women must renew their commitment to redressing inequalities of power and to seeking coalitions across lines of difference.[27]

To this end, a psychoanalytic methodology permits development of an alternative theological vision based on a majority of women in North America. As Chodorow states, it *is* possible to make a uni-

versal claim about human subjectivity and its constituent psychody-
namic processes, and it *is* possible to generalize usefully about
aspects of many women's and men's subjective senses of gender.[28] It
remains the case that most women become mothers and are the primary caretakers and nurturers in North American society.[29] The
necessity of developing an alternative theology to Catholic system-
atics cannot be overemphasized: it is critical that the women's ordination debate utilize the "rock" that psychoanalysis provides. A
psychoanalytic approach enables development of a theology that
furthers Davaney's agenda—expunging inequalities within
Catholicism and building community among women from different
backgrounds. Through its focus on the relationship between gender, symbol, and power, a psychoanalytic methodology can function
to unite feminists, womanists, *mujeristas*, and Asian American
women in their joint struggle to overcome sexism in the Catholic
Church.

To reiterate, it is my conviction that gender differences should be
viewed as a resource rather than a liability in the quest to achieve
feminist goals. I do not believe that women priests will make a difference because of something inherent in "femininity." Gender differences exist because women have been socialized and are perceived differently than men are, particularly in the realm of symbolic analysis. In time, some of the changes to be brought by women
priests will be reflected in the pastoral style of male priests. Men
may come to symbolize nurturing and even birthgiving. These
changes cannot occur in the Catholic Church, however, until the
advent of women clergy.

To return to my earlier question, what symbolic difference would
it make if Christ were symbolized as female? I have suggested that
women priests, when they act *in persona Christi*, "flesh out" much of
feminist Christology. We now consider how this would happen.
First, a psychology of symbol is offered, using object relations theory. Then the relationship between symbol and metaphor is examined. Analyzing the relationship between psychological symbols
and theological metaphors offers a basis for responding to the above
question in a deeper way.

PSYCHOLOGY OF SYMBOL

Symbols are an integral part of Christian liturgical worship. Catholicism in particular is replete with images of the faith: icons of Mary and Christ adorn the altar, and in many parishes iconography depicting apostles and saints heralds the adjoining walls and ceiling. This iconography highlights persons and events that the Catholic Church considers important to its religious life and heritage.

Historian of religions Mircea Eliade argues that symbols reveal the deepest aspects of reality—those that defy any other means of knowledge.[30] Paul Tillich in turn maintains that symbols open up dimensions of reality that are otherwise closed and unlock similar dimensions of the soul.[31] Anthropologist Clifford Geertz interprets religion in terms of its utilization of symbols. "Religion" for Geertz is:

(1) a system of symbols which acts to (2) establish powerful, pervasive, and long-lasting moods and motivations in men [*sic*] by (3) formulating conceptions of a general order of existence and (4) clothing these conceptions with such a aura of factuality that (5) the moods and motivations seem uniquely realistic.[32]

Geertz defines *symbol* in turn as "any object, act, event, quality, or relation which serves as a vehicle for a conception."[33] Religious symbols define the deepest values of society and the persons in it, and hence shape a cultural ethos. Like genes, symbols provide a template, or blueprint, from which external processes are given definite form. Unlike genes, however, which are only models *for*, symbols are models *of*—they give meaning to social and psychological reality by shaping themselves to it and shaping it to themselves.[34] Symbols shape reality, according to Geertz, by inducing in worshipers a certain set of "dispositions"—tendencies, capacities, propensities, skills, and so on—that in turn lead to formulation of general ideas of societal order.

Feminist study on the significance of symbols suggests that male religious symbols closely correlate with men's having positions of political and economic authority over women. Carol Christ, for example, in her article "Why Women Need the Goddess: Phenomenological, Psychological, and Political Reflections," points out that religions that are centered on the worship of a male god create "moods" and "motivations" that both legitimate male political authority and keep women in a state of psychological dependence on men.[35] Similarly, Daly writes, "if God is male, then the male is God."[36] It would seem that we can predict from patriarchal social structures certain patterns in thinking about God. Ross Kraemer explains, for example, that "high grid" and "high group" cosmologies exhibit little interest in women and in the feminine divine. "High grid" societies are marked by concern for hierarchical structure and for discrimination according to race, class, and gender. "High group," in turn, indicates a strong sense of social incorporation.[37] Both characteristics are found in androcentric-patriarchal cultures.

Interestingly, the two most prevalent female images in Christian heritage—Mary and Eve—dichotomize femaleness into purity or whoredom. It is inferred from both symbols that women should be subordinate to men and should deny their sexuality. Although in certain Catholic cultures Mary has even been described to function as a "goddess,"[38] her humble submission to God is mirrored in societal pressure for women to submit to men in those cultures.

A psychological interpretation of symbol offers an understanding of the way in which the internal psychological world gives form to external events. Psychologically, symbols mediate between internal psychic perception and external reality. As Meissner states, in a loose sense symbols can be regarded as the *unio oppositorum*, where an extrinsic object or form is adopted as a vehicle for expressing something from a subjective realm.[39] Symbolic functions are exercised by encounters between interior desires and their actualization in external expressions. Symbolic acts thus unite several levels of human reality—conscious and unconscious, individual and social.[40]

The classic Freudian interpretation of "God as Father" provides a starting point for a psychological exploration of religious symbols. Ultimately, however, it proves inadequate. For Freud, the "Father God" symbol is a result of a primordial longing in the human psyche for the protection of the father. As an atheist, Freud believed that God was no more than a projection of desirable human qualities that persons longed for in fathers. Ernest Wallwork puts it aptly: "Like the infant who reacts to helplessness by picturing an omnipotent father whose love and protection can be obtained by obeying his commandments, the anxious adult projects the image of a heavenly being who possesses the attributes the father once seemed to possess—omniscience, omnipotence, the power to love, protect, and punish."[41] While Freud provides an explanation for the prominence of male symbols in a patriarchal society, he does not offer a general theory of symbol formation. For example, Freudian theory does not explain symbols like a flag, a crucifix, or the bread and wine in the Eucharist. Nor does he account sufficiently for the existence of female symbols. Goddesses are passé for Freud—a product of an earlier, less "civilized" stage of societal development.[42]

I believe that an object relations perspective better encompasses the depth and complexity of symbols, and of religious symbols in particular. According to Winnicott, for example, symbol formation occurs in the "intermediate" area of experiencing, or in transitional space—that is, in that gray area between self and other. As explained, transitional objects gradually come to replace infants' illusions and lay the groundwork for the emerging capacity for symbolism. For adults, real external objects and experiences can become vehicles for the expression of similar subjective dimensions of life, and thereby take on a symbolic dimension. As Meissner observes, their symbolic quality participates in the intermediate realm of illusion and is constituted by elements from external reality intermingled with subjective components.[43] For example, a teddy bear is often used as a mother substitute by children, and it represents comfort and security. As adults, we continue to seek comfort and security (the subjective components referred to by Meissner), but we utilize other objects and experiences—such as certain foods, pieces of clothing, and activities—to elicit similar feelings. We saw that in the case of the Eucharist, the body and blood of Christ function transitionally, permitting a union/separation dialectic between Christ and believer.

According to object relations theorists, the first representation of

God emerges from the child's experience of the early mother. For psychiatrist Ana-Maria Rizzuto, God is a special type of transitional object. She states: "In the first period of narcissistic relation to the object, the child needs the object to see him as an appealing, wonderful, and powerful child *reflected in the maternal eye*." In Rizzuto's view, this is the first direct experience used by the child in the formation of the "God representation." The face and eyes of the mother are the child's first mirror, which in turn reflect the first "image" of God.[44] Later the God representation evolves due to paternal and other influences. It is important to note, however, that the first symbol of God is based on internalized sensations of the mother. Rizzuto's stages can be summarized as follows:

1. The child internalizes interactions with the world in terms of a variety of "object representations." The phenomena internalized may include somatic sensations, affects, concepts.

2. These memories are consolidated into increasingly complex sets of representations. For example, an internalized representation of the mother may include sensations, sounds, and feelings, in conjunction with the child's needs.

3. All children have questions about the origin of the world. The idea of God is developmentally necessary in order to ground the earliest awareness of existence.

4. The representation of God is put together from portions of object representations the child has at her or his disposal. It is the end product of a process of consolidating object representations into a coherent inner object world.[45]

Rizzuto maintains that the difference between God and other transitional objects is that the others are eventually outgrown and discarded, while God becomes more important in the psyches of most individuals. Yet belief in God, for Rizzuto, will be discarded by those unable to find coherence between their God representation and their self-representation. At the same time, Rizzuto posits that the God representation remains a part of the psyche, even for unbelievers, and that it is available for potential later integration.[46]

A good illustration of emergence of a latent God representation is the phenomenon of religious conversion. In this case, before conversion the individual generally rejects God. If we assume that the preconverted individual is of an agnostic or atheistic persuasion, then at that time the God representation is not active in the psyche. God beliefs, however, do not suddenly "materialize." They emerge from internalized God representations previously disavowed because of their failure to coincide with the individual's self-perspective. During religious conversion a shift in self-perspective occurs, which is usually provoked by an external event. The individual may come to view himself or herself, for example, as a helpless sinner. If the latent God representation is characterized as omnipotent Lord and savior, God now becomes accessible at a conscious level.

Meissner is careful to qualify that the God representation, while determined in large measure by transferential derivatives from parental figures, is articulated within a community of believers in an existential framework. Because the subject is "God-talk," questions of meaning arise, e.g., how does belief in God shape my views about my purpose in life? Meissner states that theology informs and elaborates upon psychically derived representations.[47] In other words, the God representation cannot be said to be solely the product of parental transferences. Each religious tradition passes down its own theology concerning the meaning of God's existence for human life. This theology in turn influences believers' understandings of God. Thus, one's view of God is shaped by parental figures, but also by one's understanding of life's purpose and meaning, which theology addresses.

The female priest would represent Christ as female—a new symbol for the Catholic faith. Psychologically, the representation of Christ as a woman, evoked by the woman priest acting *in persona Christi*, is based on maternal transferences. As discussed, maternal transferences are likely to be stronger when women are celebrants. While male priests reinforce paternal transferences and a "Father God" image, women clergy call forth a pre-Oedipal God representation, and hence a female depiction of deity. Existentially, the image is grounded in women's experiences of what a female Christ image means—that is, how it provides a sense of meaning for them. A female Christ symbol, unlike images of Mary and Eve, would not require women to dichotomize femaleness into purity or whoredom. Nor would the representation of a female Christ function to keep women in a state of psychological dependence on men. Advances made by feminist, womanist, *mujerista*, and Asian American women theologians in the field of Christology demonstrate ways in which the relationship between symbol and metaphor contributes to understanding the significance of women priests.

A FEMALE CHRIST

Hans Urs von Balthasar articulates that the figure of Christ both reveals and expresses the nature of God. Because Christ *is* God, he is the source and content of our knowledge of God. In Christ we see "who and what" God is.[48] Critical questions arising from earlier discussion are, What *difference* would it make to have Christ symbolized as female? How would it affect one's God representation? How would it affect one's understanding of meaning in life? Recent work in feminist Christology offers a beginning point for answering these questions.

At this point the metaphorical character of all God language must be stressed. A metaphor is a way of speaking about one thing in terms suggestive of another. Metaphors provide tools with which to talk about divine reality, which can be expressed only symbolically. Like symbols, they open up dimensions of reality that are otherwise closed. Theologian Alister McGrath lists three common features of metaphors: (1) they imply both similarity and dissimilarity between the things compared, (2) they have an open-ended character and cannot be reduced to definitive statements, and (3) they may have powerful emotional overtones.[49] For example, "God is a lion" infers that God is a wise protector, but surely not that God is a cat. It is a suggestive comparison; God as lion takes on diverse meanings for different people. Finally, "God is a lion" has emotional overtones associated with strength, honor, and power. James Earl Jones in the film *The Lion King* gives voice to some of these emotional overtones associated with the lion metaphor.

Metaphors break down when concretized, as do symbols when they are viewed as mere "signs." As we have seen, taking the metaphor *in persona Christi* too literally leads to exclusion of women from priestly representation. Historical Jesus scholar Marcus Borg points out that the multiplicity of images for speaking of Jesus' relationship to God (e.g., as *logos*, Sophia, Son) make it clear that none of them is to be taken literally. They are all metaphorical. The metaphor "Son of God," for example, in his view points to the deep and intimate relationship that Jesus had with God. If taken literally, it narrows the scope of Christology to only one image. Borg explains that a multiplicity of Christological representations carries a richness of meaning not possible with only one image.[50] An overview of female Christ symbols as offered by feminist, womanist, *mujerista*, and Asian American women theologians furnishes additional metaphors for use in discussions of Christology. These metaphors provide existential meanings that extend our view of the significance of religious symbols.

Ruether was among the first feminist theologians to advocate that Christology be saved from its patriarchal underpinnings. She begins her task by exploring the dualistic anthropology that has prevented women from attaining equal status with men in the Catholic Church. In particular, she looks at the view articulated by the early church fathers—and perpetuated through much of Christian heritage—that women are not "human" in the same way that men are. The Aristotelian biological notion that the male alone provides the seed or "form" of the offspring, while the female provides the substance, led to the belief that females were a result of a defect in gestation and were consequently defective humans. Thomas Aquinas applied Aristotle's notion to theology, arguing that for Jesus as Christ to represent humanity as a whole he must be male, "because only the male possesses the fullness of human nature."[51] The contemporary Catholic Church, as we have seen, clings to a patriarchal anthropology by elevating Jesus' human maleness to an ontologically necessary significance. Ruether argues that patriarchal anthropology must be rejected in favor of egalitarian anthropology and asserts that gender symbols must be used to affirm that God both transcends and includes the fullness of humanity of both men and women. Women must be affirmed as equally "theomorphic" with men, and God must be imaged as both female and male. One must be able to encounter Christ as black, Asian, Aboriginal, female, for, according to Ruether, only in this way is Jesus' paradigmatic message of liberation truly conveyed.[52] Ruether proposes that the Jesus of the Synoptic Gospels be the foundation for a feminist Christology. Mythology that portrays him as Messiah or divine Logos, along with the accompanying masculine imagery, must be rejected. As pointed out by Mary Hembrow Snyder, if this is done Jesus is recognized as the "iconoclastic prophet" who castigated existing social and religious hierarchies for their authoritarian practices. Jesus sought, according to Ruether, to reverse the social order, "making empowerment and the liberation of the oppressed the meaning of servanthood."[53] As a result, he broke down the justification for religious and social domination based on leadership and service roles.

Ruether asserts that Jesus is a liberator of all the oppressed, but especially of poor and lower-class women.[54] Her argument for an egalitarian anthropology establishes the groundwork for moving away from solely male metaphors of Christ. While Ruether advocates that Christ be represented as female, she does not explore in any depth female symbols for Christ. To find these we must look elsewhere.

Significantly, female images of Christ can be found in certain strands of Asian American women's theology. Hwain Chang Lee, for example, points out that "Asian women very often portray Jesus as a mother figure, because 'mother' is the one who cares for the family, who is able to communicate every aspect of family life, and who bears the burdens and suffering of their families."[55] As observed by Chung Hyun Kyung, while the most prevailing image of Jesus for Asian women is that of the suffering servant, new images of Jesus are emerging. These include Jesus as liberator, revolutionary, political martyr, mother, woman, and shaman. Chung asserts that many Asian women portray Jesus in the image of mother because they see him as a compassionate individual who feels deeply the suffering of humanity and who suffers and weeps with them. As Chung puts it: "Since Jesus' compassion is so deep, the mother image is the most appropriate one for Asian women to express their experience of Jesus' compassion."[56] The metaphor of Jesus as mother shows Asian women that human redemption comes through the one who shared the suffering of all humankind.

The emotional overtones associated with a female Christ metaphor can elicit powerful bonds of identification. Chung comments, for example, that some Asian women see Jesus Christ as a female figure in their specific historical situation. Park Soon Kyung notes that even though Jesus had a male physical form, he is a symbol of "females and the oppressed" because he identifies with those who suffer. On a symbolic level, therefore, Jesus is the "woman Messiah," who is in the suffering and struggle of Asian women.[57] For some Korean women, Jesus is identified with a Korean female shaman, because he is easily accepted as the exorcist and healer of the sick. Since women play a central role in Korean shamanism, when Korean women see Jesus as the priest who exorcises *han* (sin), they connect with a female image of Jesus more than with the male image of Jesus.[58]

Asian American women theologians are just one source for illuminating the theme of a female Christ in contemporary theology. In Western cultures, Sophia, or feminine wisdom imagery, is being used to understand the Christ symbol in ways that are more inclusive of women. Elizabeth Johnson, for example, argues that wisdom is portrayed in the Jewish tradition as sister, mother, bride, prophet, teacher, friend. Sophia is also creator and fashioner of all things. Johnson argues that Jesus was closely associated with Sophia and is even presented in certain New Testament writings as an incarnation of her.[59]

Wisdom personified offers an augmented field of female metaphors with which to speak about God symbolized as female. Johnson notes that scholarly debate illuminates at least five perspectives on the interpretation of personified wisdom: (1) Sophia is the personification of the cosmic order, (2) she is the personification of wisdom sought and learned in Israel's schools, (3) the symbol stands for a divine attribute, (4) Sophia is a "quasi-independent divine hypostasis" who mediates between the world and a transcendent God, and (5) Sophia is a female personification of God's own being in creative and saving involvement with the world.[60] Johnson favors the last option because of the "functional equivalence," in her view, between the deeds of Sophia and those of the biblical God. Johnson argues that what Judaism said of Sophia, Christian hymn-makers and epistle writers came to say of Jesus. By the end of the first century, Jesus is presented ultimately as an embodiment of Sophia herself.[61] It is thus not too big a leap, for Johnson, to confess Jesus Christ as the "incarnation of God imaged in female symbol."[62]

Schüssler Fiorenza, alternatively, presents Jesus as sage and prophet of Sophia. According to the Gospel of John, in her view, it is debated whether Jesus is wisdom incarnate or whether he replaces her. For Schüssler Fiorenza, Christ can be understood as the mediator of the first creation and as the power of a new, qualitatively different creation.[63]

Borg also finds the Sophia metaphor useful to support the notion of God personified as female. He observes that in the wisdom tradition of Israel Sophia is closely associated with God—there is a functional equivalency between Sophia and God as argued by Johnson. Thus, language about Sophia, for Borg, is personification of God in female form—"a lens through which divine reality is imaged as a woman."[64] Borg argues that Jesus speaks of himself as both emissary and child of Sophia. In John, for example, Jesus is presented as the incarnation of divine Sophia.[65] Again, the metaphorical character of God language must be emphasized, lest Christian feminists fall prey to the same rigid literalism as those who insist on the maleness of Christ because only men can be "sons." Borg explains that Jesus is both *"Sophia* of God" *and* "Son of God."[66]

Feminine wisdom imagery provides an expanded set of metaphors with which to depict Christ as universal savior. In recent years this metaphor has found greater popularity outside the seminary environment. Several Episcopal women I interviewed, for example, mentioned use of wisdom imagery. A laywoman I spoke with indicated that she was hesitant to make wisdom into a "goddess" but acknowledged that the metaphor was important as a poetic figure. She believed that Mary was a possible avenue for Anglican women to explore further, especially the Mary of the

Passion. In turn, a woman priest suggested that Wisdom incarnate in the person of Jesus the man allows an interaction, a balancing of male and female. Numerous interviewees stressed the importance of having a balance of male and female imagery at the altar. As one female priest explained, if Christ was fully human, the full range of humanity should be engaged in the ministry of the church.

A male priest suggested that women celebrants tend to make the same kind of difference as black celebrants or Asian celebrants. Significantly, the metaphor of Christ as a black woman has been advanced by womanist theologians. Jacqueline Grant, for example, posits that in the experience of black women, Christ *is* a black woman.[67] Kelly Brown Douglas expands upon this notion: "Although Christ can certainly be embodied by a black woman, it is more in keeping with black women's testimonies to Jesus and Jesus' own self-understanding if womanist theology describes Christ as being embodied wherever there is a movement to sustain and liberate the entire black community, male and female."[68] Douglas explains that womanist portrayals of the "Black Christ" endeavor to lift up those persons, especially black women, who have worked toward bringing greater wholeness to the black community. That is, Christ can be seen in the faces of Sojourner Truth, Harriet Tubman, and Fannie Lou Hamer, as well as in the faces of the poorest black women.[69]

Again, the metaphorical nature of God language must be underscored. These theologians are not suggesting that the historical Jesus was a black woman. From a sociopolitical standpoint, there are compelling reasons for not limiting ourselves to one depiction of Christ—even if we could ascertain Jesus' phenotype with historical accuracy. If the only image of the incarnation is white and male, white men become viewed as closer to God, and consequently this image contributes to the oppression of women and minorities in North America. If Christ is truly to be understood as a "representative human," as many images of Christ are needed as there are types of people in the world. In addition, as stated by Borg, a multiplicity of metaphors attests to the richness and diversity of beliefs about Christ. Christ cannot be reduced to one image, nor can a definitive statement be made about any one image. Through their physical presence, the advent of women priests would enhance and deepen Christological metaphors, bringing powerful emotional overtones to abstract concepts.

Finally, the subject of female Christ symbols has also been addressed in *mujerista* theology. Maria Pilar Aquino, for example, observes that for Latin American women, a fruitful line of reflection is the rediscovery of Jesus' relation with women and women's activities. Ana Maria Tepedino in turn points out that since an inherent part of Jesus' project is the humanization of the person, women's bodies are restored as the primary place of divine activity.[70] Latin American women's Christology stresses that both men and women constitute the new humanity and the body of Christ—they too are *alter Christus*.[71] This is shown clearly in Ada María Isasi-Díaz's description of a *mujerista* liturgy celebrated by a Hispanic women's group called Las Hermanas in 1989. As part of the liturgy, a woman spoke the following eucharistic blessing after lifting the cup at the altar: "This is the milk which comes from our bodies and nourishes life. It is mixed with honey, for milk and honey was the symbol for our ancestors of the promised land, of a better future, of liberation. We bless it by drinking of it for it will sustain us in the struggle."[72] Isasi-Díaz observes that this was the first time that some of the women who participated had experienced a woman breaking the bread. She explains that in relocating the sacred in the midst of the marginalized, poor, and oppressed, *mujeristas* saw themselves made in the image of God.[73] Isasi-Díaz explains: "We wanted to enable Hispanic women to understand that if we believe God became human in the person of Jesus, all of us, not only priests and pastors, participate in the divine. We believe we accomplished this, particularly for the Hispanic women who had a leadership role in the liturgy."[74]

In sum, some of the ways in which the notion of women as *alter Christus* is informed by Asian American women, *mujerista*, womanist, and feminist theologians are in relation to women's suffering, women's liberation, and wisdom personified. Woman-Christ is healer, fellow sufferer, compassionate mother, mediator of creation, *imago dei*. Such metaphors support the claim that actual, historical women are created in the image of God and are bearers of the image of Christ—that it is precisely in their female bodily existence that baptized women are *imago Christi*.[75] Women at the altar, acting *in persona Christi*, would evoke one or more of these metaphors in the psyches of parishioners, depending on their internalized images of Christ, on their prior experiences with women (particularly women who were influential early in their lives), and on which images are the most meaningful for them. Like Ruether and Schüssler Fiorenza, I view the effects of women's historicized sexual difference as a valuable resource for Christology. The metaphors for Christ described above allow women to identify with Christ in a way not possible with a male Christ image. Women can view themselves as equally "theomorphic" with men—they, too, are formed in the divine image. As such, the images open up levels of reality that were previously closed to them.

In addition, because female Christ symbols have an open-ended character, they will be viewed differently as women encounter changes in their own lives. In twenty years perhaps the metaphor of a woman-Christ will not be so closely identified with themes of suffering and liberation from oppression as she is now. Because metaphors convey multiple meanings, they remain useful far longer than do literal images. Moreover, the rich emotional overtones carried by female Christ symbols further fuel women's efforts to achieve personal goals. Female Christ images, symbolized by women priests at the altar, would inspire female parishioners to make advances in their own lives.

This raises the question of the emotional effects for men of a female Christ image—do they as a result feel "less" theomorphic, less like God? Next, the psychological benefits of female Christ symbols for women and men are addressed more fully. Psychoanalytic notions of transference and internalization can be used to explore the variety of reactions that parishioners would have to a woman acting *in persona Christi*. While the priest at the altar in some ways functions like the analyst in a psychoanalytic consultation, the situation becomes more complex when the priest also acts *in persona Christi*, for parishioners are faced not only with a female authority figure but with a female image of deity. When outward images of deity change, internalized God representations are also forced to shift. An analysis of how this happens in terms of "psychic boundaries" will prove helpful.

PSYCHOLOGICAL ANALYSIS OF FEMALE CHRIST SYMBOLS

Earlier it was emphasized that male religious symbols correspond with men having positions of political and economic authority over women. Naomi Goldenberg observes that until recently public officials were conceived of only as adult males and that as long as this image of the male authority was held, God was pictured solely as an old man.[76] The implication of solely male imagery is that men's domination is divinely ordered and sustained by God.[77] Do female religious symbols subvert this patriarchal ideology? Anthropologist Mary Douglas has argued that while we can predict cosmology from social structure, the reverse is fraught with difficulties.[78] In other words, we cannot look at cosmologies that display a reciprocity of gods and goddesses and prognosticate the existence of an egalitarian social structure in those societies. It is true that not all cultures that worship female deities evince egalitarian religious systems— India, for example, does not. Evidence suggests, however, that many women in North American societies find female religious symbols to be psychologically empowering. This section further outlines the benefits to women of envisioning deity in terms of female symbolism. I then explore *how* these benefits are realized psychologically, drawing upon the mechanism of internalization. In some cases, the fruits of female symbolism are *not* realized in the psyche. Resistance to and ambivalence toward female Christ symbols must therefore also be addressed.

In the article by Carol Christ discussed earlier, she argues that goddess symbolism affirms four dimensions of women's being: female power, the female body, the female will, and women's bonds and heritage. First, women can acknowledge that the divine principle is in themselves and that they need no longer look to men or male figures as saviors. Second, goddess symbolism assists the process of naming and reclaiming the female body and its cycles and processes. This reclaiming results, according to Christ, in joyful, positive affirmation of the female body, as well as acceptance of aging and death. Third, women who participate in goddess rituals refuse to be subordinate to others, and they believe that they can achieve their wills in the world. And fourth, asserts Christ, goddess symbolism encourages celebrations of women's bonds to each other, particularly the mother-daughter relationship.[79]

Referring to divinity as "God the Mother" affects women in ways that calling God "Father" cannot. Most important of these is that the metaphor God as Mother allows women to identify with the divine directly, rather than through the "glasses" of male experience. Nelle Morton writes:

> Now, call on "God the Mother" or the "Goddess." What happens? For women she appears. She says your life is the sacred gift. Pick it up. Receive it. Create it. Be responsible for it. I ask nothing in return. It is enough that you stand on your own two feet and speak your own word. Celebrate the new Creation that is you. Move in the new space—free. The response from women who have become aware is an overwhelming sense of acceptance and belonging and identity.[80]

Morton implies that envisioning God as female increases women's sense of self-esteem and independence. Jann Clanton, in *In Whose Image? God and Gender*, reaches a similar conclusion. If a woman accepts that she is not "quite as fully created in the image of God as is the male," Clanton states, "then she will have difficulty accepting her full potential to reason and to create."[81] In her research sample, Clanton found a statistically significant relationship between masculine concepts of God and feelings of shame and deference in women, which suggested to her that masculine God imagery negatively affects women's self-esteem. Alternatively, the women in the sample who spoke of God as "more than masculine" scored higher in self-confidence than those who held a solely masculine view of deity. From this material, Clanton concludes that women who can conceive of God as androgynous or "beyond gender" experience greater internal freedom to develop their own creative and intellectual potential.[82]

Clanton observes that persons who can imagine and verbalize an inclusive God are more likely to be inclusive in their views of priesthood and ministry: according to her study, approximately 83 percent of Roman Catholics with an androgynous or gender-transcendent view of God also believe that women should be ordained as priests (as compared with only 25 percent of those with a masculine view of God).[83] My own research suggests that the advent (and acceptance) of women priests will in turn facilitate more openness to inclusive God imagery. To illustrate, I relate some responses from my interviews to a question concerning use of inclusive-language liturgies.

An Episcopal laywoman attested that there is a connection between acceptance of women ministers and support for inclusive language: "It's a chicken-and-egg kind of thing. I don't know how you would argue cause and effect . . . but there is very definitely a connection." Children, she said, make the connection very quickly—the minister represents God and therefore God cannot be just a boy. She observed that in seminaries now there is more interest in balancing male and female imagery and less resistance by women toward using occasional male imagery.

A male priest who was very ambivalent toward women clergy told me that a lot of negative work is being done in inclusive-language liturgies—in which masculine titles for God are being reduced in order to build up feminine images. A second male priest informed me that substituting *God, Redeemer,* and *Sanctifier* for *Father, Son,* and *Holy Ghost* is blasphemous. He explained that he would not personally refer to God as *Mother,* but that Isaiah's maternal imagery for deity demonstrates that the metaphor is not sacrilegious.

Most of the women priests I interviewed were much more supportive of inclusive language for God, or at least not adamantly opposed to it. One woman priest told me that women priests are necessary for women to be seen in the image of God. Another female priest indicated that questions regarding the appropriateness of certain inclusive metaphors arise out of parishioners' experience of having both male and female priests. She suggested that women priests are altering images of God, but at a deep level that is difficult to put into words. A third priest indicated that women priests are helping people envision the image of God as masculine and feminine. In her church, for example, the norm is to have both a man and a woman at the altar. Another clergywoman explained that in her experience, women who were abused by their fathers have difficulty praying to God the Father. Inclusive language for God, in her view, allows these women to envision God as both masculine and feminine.

An active laywoman I spoke with explained that the root of exclusive liturgical language is that "men do not want women to have the things they have, and they base that on a God who is a man. If they accept that God could be anything else, it would mean losing the privileges that they've had for centuries." She believes that as more and more women are ordained, feminist theology will become more acceptable and necessary. To illustrate, one woman priest I spoke with experienced great difficulty using exclusive language in eucharistic liturgies. She told me that it is very frustrating not to be able to delete or change words when they are exclusive: there are times when she wants so badly to say, "God of Abraham and Sarah, God of Jacob and Rachel." But adding to the printed rites, she explained, is not permitted in the Episcopal Church.

In sum, some of the benefits made possible by female God imagery are women's increased sense of self-esteem, independence, and freedom to develop their creative and intellectual potential; greater valuation of their capabilities and bodily cycles; and affirmation of connections with other women. It is now appropriate to ask how these benefits are realized psychologically. In other words, what are the means by which women come to reap these benefits? Given the nature of the benefits discussed, why are some women and men resistant to female Christ symbols?

Internalization

The above questions concern the relationship between one's self-identity and one's internalized God representation. It is important, therefore, to gain some understanding of this inner psychological relationship. In order to do so, first we must explore how religion shapes who people are. How do religious beliefs affect self-concept?

A starting point is provided by James Fowler, in his research regarding the relationship between individual psychological development and the formation of religious identity.

In his book *Stages of Faith*, Fowler utilizes Erikson's eight stages of psychosocial development as a base from which to explore religious identity, or faith development. According to Fowler, during the first stage (Intuitive-Projective Faith) children generally construct an image or images of God, pieced together from story fragments and images provided by their culture.[84] Fowler explains that during the second stage (Mythic-Literal Faith) the following occurs:

> The person begins to take on for him- or herself the stories, beliefs, and observances that symbolize belonging to his or her community. Beliefs are appropriated with literal interpretations, as are moral rules and attitudes. Symbols are taken as one-dimensional and literal in meaning. (p. 149)

Ten-year-old Millie, for example, describes God as "an old man with a white beard and white hair wearing a long robe. . . . he has a nice face, nice blue eyes. He can't be all white . . . he has blue eyes and he's forgiving" (p. 138). Chronologically, Mythic-Literal Faith corresponds to a child's school years. Stage three (Synthetic-Conventional Faith) corresponds with adolescence. In this stage, symbols and ritual representations expressive of the faith are not separable from what they symbolize. As Fowler explains, "Any strategy of demythologization . . . threatens the participation of the symbol and symbolized and is taken, consequently, as an assault on the sacred itself" (p. 163). While stage three typically emerges during adolescence, Fowler points out that for many adults it becomes a permanent place of balance. If persons are to move to the fourth stage (Individuative-Reflective Faith), they generally must encounter a clash between valued authority sources, or have experiences that lead to critical reflection, such as "leaving home" (pp. 172–173). It is only during the fourth stage that symbols can be "separated from their meanings" and translated into propositions, definitions, or conceptual foundations (p. 180).

Thus, if most children conceptualize Jesus as a white male—as given to them in cultural stories—this God representation will be understood literally until, as adults, their faith becomes mature enough to allow them to separate the depiction from its underlying meaning. It is interesting that African American children are often presented with images of a black Jesus rather than a white one.[85] Do those African Americans, in consequence, view Jesus as black when they become adults? In a survey of African American Catholics, sociologist Julia Rath found that the majority indicated that Jesus was black, or at least not white.[86] Rath observes that a typical response to her survey was the following: " 'We found out even in the King James version that if His skin is like that of bronze and his hair is like that of wool, then that sounds like that Man was a black Man.' "[87] In contrast, there is no evidence that churches led by women have attempted in any systematic way to portray Jesus as female to young girls. At this point in time, it is fairly safe to say that most male and female children in Western culture grow up with the image of Jesus as male.

"Christlike" *behavior* is also associated with a male image of Christ. In Christian theology, Christ is the central figure for development of ethical standards: one's behavior should be modeled after Christ's. Believers are admonished to be Christlike, which involves incorporating qualities believed to be part of Christ's character as identified in the Gospels. Included among these are compassion, love, and altruism. How exactly does one become more Christlike? Theologians might answer with the notion of "sanctification," a process that takes place through God's grace and the Holy Spirit's guidance. A broader query is, How does anyone become more "like" another individual? Psychoanalysts address this question through the concept of internalization.

As already noted, internalization involves the way in which external persons and objects become integrated into the internal psychic structure of an individual. The crux of internalization is encapsulated in the yen to imitate the behavior of a lost loved one. Loewald's assessment of Christ as an "ego ideal"—exemplifying the internalization and sublimation of all earthly relationships—hails the figure of Christ as a model for imitation within the psyche. As explained by Robert Nye, "ego-ideal" refers to the part of the superego that serves as the idealistic internal measure or standard of what the person should be.[88] In this case, the internalized Christ serves as a template by which to measure how "Christlike" one is and can be.

Like the son who becomes more like his father after his father's passing, the internalization of Christ is, for the most part, not a conscious process. In this regard, internalization is related to the psychological notion of "identification." Nye defines identification as "a psychological process which originates in the wish to be like another individual in some way, and eventuates in the assimilation of attributes of the other into stable and permanent elements of the personality."[89] Roy Schafer notes that the major identifications— those that contribute significantly to early systemic development and later systemic change—typically are based on models provided by parents, siblings, and others with whom the individual is in early and dependent association. The individual later may identify with other persons, fictional characters, ancestors, and significant figures in history or myth.[90] For those raised within the Christian tradition, Christ is one such likely figure for identification.

While Loewald and Schafer help to address the way in which the psychological Christ becomes internalized as a replacement for the crucified Jesus, what can be said about the particular image of Christ? Does that become internalized as well? I believe that it does. As Schafer notes, identification with abstract concepts is apprehended unconsciously in terms of concrete persons or things[91]—in other words, with certain images of those concepts. The precise nature of identification with and internalization of Christ depends upon a number of factors: the individual's own experiences with other Christians and with Christian teachings about Christ, God representations derived from parental derivatives, and pictorial depictions. In sum, Christlike qualities, such as goodness, altruism, and so on, are internalized in the context of a particular image or symbol of Christ.

It is important to reiterate that in terms of Fowler's faith stages, symbols are not seen as separate from their meanings until the fourth stage, a stage that is not generally reached until young adulthood, if at all. When Christ is internalized as an ego ideal, therefore, a specific image of Christ is internalized as well. This image provides a measure of one's own self-concept. For most individuals, unless they are presented with nonwhite or female images of Christ in childhood (or confronted by them in adulthood), that image is of a Caucasian man. It follows that when whites see the white male Christ pictorially depicted, their self-concept as potentially Christlike is affirmed. Women and nonwhites, I suggest, also internalize a white male Christ if that was the predominant image presented to them in childhood. This remains particularly true for women in highly patriarchal settings such as fundamentalist churches.

What happens psychologically if one is confronted with a nonwhite or nonmale image of Christ? In an article titled "Christology Crossing Boundaries: The Threat of Imaging Christ as Other Than a White Male,"[92] I use the concept of internalization to explore psychological origins of resistance to multiple representations of Christ—particularly those that cross gender and racial boundaries. Because acceptance of women priests requires psychological integration of a nonmale image of Christ, these insights are also applicable to women priests acting *in persona Christi*.

Resistance

Psychologically, a variety of responses would be generated by Catholic women priests at the altar—from "that was great" to "that wasn't any different" to "that made me extremely uncomfortable." I believe that one cause of discomfort and hostility to nonwhite, nonmale images of Christ—and, by extension, to women priests—lies in how the Christ image coheres with or disrupts self-concept as internalized from childhood. The remainder of the section demonstrates the following points. First, boundaries of gender and race are formed early in childhood and are significant factors in the development of self-concept. Second, the extent to which an individual identifies with a female Christ image reflects the degree of fluidity of her or his "psychic boundaries." And third, psychic boundary transgression is unconsciously expressed in such emotions as anxiety, hostility, discomfort, or offense.

While it is true, as Clanton argues, that women's self-esteem is often enhanced when they able to envision God as female—i.e., like

themselves—I suggest that the process of shifting God representations is complex and often difficult. Does one's God image become
more nurturing as that individual is more capable of being nurtured,
or does one become more capable of nurture when presented with
a more caring God? I think it can work both ways, but I lean toward
Rizzuto's notion that the God representation must find coherence
with the self-representation in order to be accepted within the psyche. In an undergraduate psychology of religion course, a student
shared with the class that she was only able to shift her God representation from an authoritarian tyrant to a more caring image with
increased self-esteem through therapy. Rizzuto implies that embracing a more caring God is unlikely unless one's self-concept has also
shifted, which usually means reworking one's relationships with
internalized parental imagos.

Several important questions arise. First, what is the psychological significance of growing up with an image of Christ that is like or
different from one's self-concept? Those individuals, for example,
with a phenotype similar to that of the traditional Christ as depicted by primarily male European painters (in some cases blond and
blue-eyed) will be more deeply affirmed in experiencing their self-
concept as potentially "Christlike" than those who do not share this
phenotype. On the other hand, if one is raised with depictions of
Christ unlike one's own image, then at some level the self is negated as Christlike, although Christ could still function as an ego ideal.
Social norms no doubt play a role in which images are internalized
as ego ideals. For the most part, to be white and male is normative,
"good," and powerful in Western society.

Second, what are the implications of trying to "switch" Christ
images? In particular, what is the response of those individuals who
already embody the "norm" when they are presented with Christ
images divergent from their self-concept? I suggest that for men,
internalizing a female Christ involves crossing a gender boundary,
while for white women and men, internalizing a black Christ
involves crossing a racial boundary. Imaging Christ as other than a
white male forces crossing of the racial and gender boundaries that
maintain self-concept as either identified with or different from
one's internalized image of Christ.

Crossing a gender boundary is generally more threatening for men than it is for women. I believe that imaging Christ as female can be troubling for women as well—not primarily because of gender boundary transgression, but because of their unconscious internalization of a white male Christ as privileged and powerful. Chodorow's work is useful in exploring boundary transgression in the context of gender.

As we have seen, Chodorow observes that girls grow up with a sense of continuity and similarity to their mother, which results in more flexible ego boundaries in girls than in boys.[93] On the other hand, boys grow up with a sense of separateness from the mother, a process that is further promoted in the course of forging a masculine identity by boys' repudiation of the mother and of their own feminine identification. Gender difference thus becomes central for males—"core gender identity and the sense of masculinity are defined more negatively, in terms of that which is not female or not-mother, than positively."[94] Chodorow explains that while the maternal identification represents what is "generically human" for children of both genders, because men have power in our society, they have come to define maleness as that which is generically human, and women as "not men." Men institutionalize their unconscious defenses against repressed feminine identification and attachment in the form of sexist attitudes and behaviors.[95]

Using Chodorow, we can see how the neat package of "white maleness is next to godliness" is undone when Christ is symbolized as other than a white male. Internalizing a female Christ causes repressed feminine identifications to surface in men, threatening core masculine identity. Since men unconsciously define maleness as both a human and a divine norm, in order to internalize a female Christ men's self-concept can no longer be defined as "not female," and female can no longer be defined as "not God." In identifying with a female Christ, men are forced to acknowledge their own repressed feminine attachment and identification, which is tantamount to being engulfed by what might be called the "nebulously overwhelming archaic mother." In other words, they must cross a psychological boundary that is unconsciously defended against. Women, on the other hand, have less difficulty in identifying with a male Christ, because gender difference is less threatening to women—that is, the boundary is more fluid. Some women, as I have mentioned, may find a female Christ problematic because it severs their internalized connection with patriarchal power.

Similarly, while many white individuals experience dissonance in identifying with a black Jesus, a minority of nonwhites in Western culture may be uncomfortable with a black or Asian Jesus, for the same reasons that some women may be uncomfortable with a female Christ. Because whiteness is considered normative in Western culture, crossing a racial boundary causes uneasiness as well. Racial identity is more difficult to discuss than gender identity, because there is less agreement around precisely how race is determined. It would seem that racial identity is both an external and an internal category: children perceive themselves as African American when others view them as such, and adults can choose to self-identify as African American. In this vein, it is significant that children as young as three years old seem to be aware of racial differences and their associated meanings or values.[96] The Clarks' famous doll test, for example, was designed to demonstrate race consciousness and preferences in preschool children. *Race consciousness* here refers to "consciousness of self as belonging to a specific group which is differentiated from other groups by obvious physical characteristics."[97] The Clarks' doll test demonstrated that a majority of African American children between ages three and seven rejected a brown doll in favor of a white doll. While the study is dated, there seems to have been little change in the racial attitudes of African American preschool children over the past forty years. Even today, the African American child will want to identify with what represents good and will form a way of thinking that essentially favors white.[98]

"White" racial identity, I believe, is defended against on a basis similar to that of masculine gender identity. In order to internalize a black or Asian Christ, a white individual such as myself must cross a racial boundary in terms of self-concept. In identifying with a dark Jesus when my self-concept is formed around whiteness, I am forced to question my own racial identification. I am also forced to confront the notion that race, like gender, is a social construct. In doing so I must acknowledge that I too am "raced," just as men are "gen-

dered," and must encounter the complexities of this issue. This is
more difficult for whites than for nonwhites, because of the Western
cultural construction of whiteness as normative and "good" and
because of its very real association with political power. Just as
African American children want to identify with what represents
good, adult Western Christians desire that their image of Jesus
reflect Western values. Whites seldom are able to see *themselves* in a
black Christ, nor does the image of a black Christ reflect the accepted values of their culture. Some African Americans have no difficulty internalizing a black Christ—those children, for example, who
are raised with images of a black rather than a white Jesus. Others,
like whites, may find a black Jesus problematic because this symbol,
like the male Christ for some women, breaks their internalized connection with cultural privilege and power.

In my view, the root cause of discomfort and hostility to nonwhite, nonmale images of Christ lies in how the Christ image
coheres with or disrupts self-concept as internalized from childhood. Identifying with an image that is different from one's self-concept is a primary source of psychic boundary transgression, which
is one origin of discomfort toward plural images of Christ and, by
extension, toward women priests. I will now illustrate all of these
themes, drawing from the image of a black female Christ and other
ethnographic material.

CHRISTA: AN EXAMPLE OF
BOUNDARY TRANSGRESSION

Perhaps the most graphic Western symbolic depiction of a black
female Christ was Edwina Sandys's sculpture of the naked body of
a woman hanging on a cross, titled *Christa*.[99] *Christa* provoked a
great deal of outrage and was described by opponents as "reprehen-
sible and desecrating . . . totally changing the symbol."[100] Bishop
Walter Dennis, for example, charged that the display was "theologically and historically indefensible."[101] When the Center for Women
and Religion at the Graduate Theological Union attempted to do
publicity in the Bay Area for an event featuring the sculpture, a

mock newsletter was planted with a picture of *Christa* with a tail, titled *Animalia*.[102] These examples of resistance illustrate negative types of reactions when gender and racial boundaries are transgressed. Yet many women and men expressed equally strong positive reactions to *Christa*. Some women made a strong association between this sculpture and women's suffering at the hands of patriarchy. Edwina Hunter, for example, argues that this statue of a crucified woman "makes real" the symbol of the cross: "It puts us back in touch with the reality that the Cross is a scandal and the one who hangs on it is cursed."[103] As Hunter points out, the true scandal is not *Christa*, but that she is a clear representation of what has happened historically to women. The Right Reverend Paul Moore, then bishop of New York, asserted: "The Word became Flesh and dwelt among us. . . . This means that the Incarnation of the second person of the Trinity involved the taking on of humanity, of all 'flesh,' male and female."[104] After seeing *Christa* in the context of a seminar called "Issues of Sexuality in Ministry," a feminist minister from Korea wrote: "Christa, she is a symbol of suffering woman. Christa, she is a symbol of new humanity of woman. From the suffering, life comes out again."[105] Psychologically, one might say that because the Korean minister's self-concept was consistent with a God representation of suffering deity, the metaphor "suffering woman" took on redemptive value for her.

Viewing *Christa* had a liberating effect on another feminist minister, Rev. Dr. Smallwood, suggesting to her that there is more to God and Christ than maleness. She relates her experience as follows:

> I had heard that Christa was a crucified woman, but the first time I saw her, it was impossible to ignore that she was a Black woman. I had had no idea that this woman would come out to grab me and make me feel as though we were old friends. . . . But I knew also that Christa was all women, all people of color. She was the reminder of injustice and oppression. As I looked on her I could feel the suffering that comes when one is poor or different.[106]

This quotation indicates the ability of metaphors—made concrete through symbols—to evoke powerful emotional overtones. Dr. Smallwood's response also supports the point made earlier by Carol Christ regarding the power of female symbols to affirm women's bonds and heritage. Significantly, while the depiction of a male black Jesus, who redeems the particularity of black suffering, has provoked little outrage, the image of a female Christ in the form of *Christa*—who speaks to women in their suffering—has been labeled scandalous. Eleanor McLaughlin suggests that this response is a reminder of the power of body, and of Jesus' historically particular male body.[107] It also is a recognition of the power of visual symbols versus spoken or written metaphors.

The range of responses to *Christa* illustrates the varied degrees of fluidity of racial and gender boundaries. Of the viewers discussed, those whose self-concept is dependent upon an internalized white male Christ (i.e., the "opponents") had trouble crossing the racial and gender boundaries necessary to accept this image. Reverend Moore, however, was able to find coherence between this female God representation and his self-concept, even though it involved "switching" God symbols. Thus, it seems that his self-concept was "fluid" enough to permit crossing to occur without enormous psychic resistance. The feminist minister's internalized God representation allowed her to identify with the metaphor of God as a suffering woman. We do not know whether she had to "switch" God representations in order to do so or whether a suffering female deity was a component of her religious background.

Diverse responses to Episcopal women clergy at the altar also demonstrate different degrees of psychic boundary fluidity. A male priest told me, for example, that sometimes people walk out when a woman is presiding. Sometimes they don't show. Another male priest offered this reasoning for choosing to be absent when women are celebrating: "Is it better to be absent from the Eucharist or to be present and angry? I think Matthew tells us it is better to be absent." A woman priest related that a few parishioners have crossed their arms at the communion rail as a message of defiance. Another woman priest told me that pockets of hostility toward female clergy still exist. At meetings, for example, some male priests treat her as if she were invisible: "There are priests that will do just about anything to not be in conversation with you."

A third clergywoman told me about an event that took place in January 1974, before Episcopal women's ordination to the priesthood had been approved. At a major conference, a woman deacon was assisting at the Eucharist by passing the chalice. While she was doing so, a priest grabbed her hands and tried to make her drop it. She explained:

> Now in the Episcopal Church, we believe the same thing Catholics do—it is the real thing. It is the blood of Christ. You cannot spill it. So he's trying to get her to drop the chalice. And she wouldn't. She held on—she wouldn't drop it. At which point he let go, told her to go to hell, and scratched the back of her hand.

Another priest told me that a woman had scratched her palm when she was holding the chalice, in "absolute fury" that a woman could be behind the altar rail. This same priest has also had people tell her, "I've never felt so close to God as I have when you're celebrating the Eucharist. When you are delivering the chalice, when you're delivering the bread, I've never felt so close to God." She served in a church where she co-celebrated with a man, and she found that inevitably some people crossed the aisle to get to his side and, less frequently, parishioners crossed to get to her side.

Sometimes opponents to women clergy change their minds when they experience a woman at the altar. In these cases it is likely that on a psychological level, "switching," or perhaps expanding, one's internalized God representations is occurring. To illustrate, a woman priest related that a man approached her after a service and said, "You know, I knew it was going to be different having a woman priest at the altar, and it was—you sang an octave higher!" She explained that most people who have experienced her ministry for the first time tell her that "it's different," but "it's not bad," and they actually like it.

I have suggested here that a white male Christ is "internalized," or identified with, in the psyche of individual Christian believers from an early age. For men or Caucasians, imaging Christ as other than male or white, respectively, forces crossing of gender or racial boundaries that serve to maintain important dimensions of self-structure. This phenomenon in turn threatens self-identity, causing discomfort and hostility. For women or nonwhites in Western culture, the situation is more complex. For some, the internalized image of a white male Jesus affirms their self-concept in terms of existing structures of power. Others, however, can more easily imagine Christ as Asian, black, female, and so on (i.e., like themselves).

The principles used to account for resistance to plural images of Christ also apply to the controversy around women priests. In the above examples, Episcopal women priests evoke a variety of reactions from parishioners because, psychologically, people have different levels of tolerance for plural images of Christ. Those with little tolerance for gender boundary transgression may choose not to be present when a woman is celebrating. Alternatively, they may react with defiance, for their internalized God representation is being challenged. They may react with a counterchallenge, as did the priest who tried to force the Episcopal woman deacon to drop the chalice. Other parishioners experience in female Christ symbols an affirmation of their self-identity in a way they have never felt before. Psychologically, they are able to cross the boundary from God as male to God as female; or perhaps they have internalized a latent image of God as female. Theologically, they find a female Christ symbol empowering on emotional, bodily, and intellectual levels.

It should be said that while not all Episcopalians view the priest as a representative of Christ, many do, and it is the official Catholic view. I find it interesting that most of the women priests I interviewed did not consider their presence to be affecting images of Christ, even though a number of them acknowledged that they are altering images of God. I think that shifting Christ symbols is even more threatening than changing God representations, because doing so challenges people to think symbolically rather than literally. Jesus was indeed a man, but Christ represents liberation and universal salvation—qualities that are symbolized in different ways for different people. Again, one of the benefits of multiple metaphors is their ability to express the richness and diversity of meanings attached to a single symbol.

Because women at the altar are acting *in persona Christi*, they function as visual representations of Christ and, as such, evoke similar psychological identifications and resistances as would a picture or statue of a female Jesus in the church sanctuary. It is worth noting that not long ago, African Americans were refused priesthood/ministerial ordination in some denominations on the grounds that *they* did not adequately resemble Christ. In addition to enfleshing a female image of deity, women priests would alter the nature of christological debates in other ways, by raising issues of body, maternal functions, and sexuality. If God is female as well as male, is God immanent as well as transcendent, as argued by many feminist theologians? What is the place of sexuality in the schema of creation, sin, and salvation? What role does sexual difference play in *this* context? Drawing upon a psychoanalytic approach known as French feminist theory, it is to these questions that we shall now turn.

6

GENDER, SEX, AND GOD

Symbolically, I believe the woman at the altar enlarges people's understandings and imaginings about God. In prayers
and in celebration, the ordained person is representative of
the people to God and God to the people. If the image is
always male, God is represented only as male. As women are
included symbolically as representative people, the image of
God is larger.

—*Episcopal laywoman*

If sexuality is not part of the human nature which Christ has
taken with him into heaven, then it calls into question
whether sexuality is redeemed.

—*Male Episcopal priest*

Thus far female symbolism for Christ has been explored largely in
the context of feeding and nurturing, but do women call forth other
modes of divine representation? Can the maternal image be viewed
in other ways? Do women priests always evoke a maternal image? If,
as a woman priest informed me, women clergy mirror God a little
differently than men do—and "that happens whether we teach on it
explicitly or preach on it or just stand there"—what more can be
said about how women priests would affect contemporary theology?
What more can be said about their significance for the priesthood,
parishioners' experience, and the church at large?

Ethnographic data reveal the need for models for God other than
strictly maternal ones. A woman priest told me, for example, that
while it is important for people to have an image of God as mother
as well as of God as father, the female image carries with it the same

problems as the male metaphor. The parental image is not always a positive image, nor is it complete. Another woman priest voiced a concern with domestic imagery. A lot of feeding imagery, she stated, conveys the sense of congregation as children. When her parish experimented with inclusive-language liturgies, women in particular resisted the heavy dose of domestic symbolism, especially God as feeder, child caretaker, homemaker, and housewife. Domestic God imagery, she explained, puts women back in the kitchen. The metaphor of female Wisdom seemed less maternal to parishioners, yet they wondered if there were other useful models.

An excursion into French feminist psychoanalytic theory enables us to answer the questions entertained above. The body of work known as "French feminist theory" has become important on the North American scene since at least the mid-1980s. Influenced by Simone de Beauvoir's feminist existentialism and Jacques Lacan's linguistic psychoanalysis, the writers dubbed "the French feminists" offer insight into what difference it makes that the priest is a woman, particularly in the area of symbolic analysis—including voice, body, and mirroring the maternal. An examination of the work of Julia Kristeva and Luce Irigaray will allow us to extend arguments made earlier on what difference women priests would make in the context of the Eucharist. French feminist psychoanalytic theory provides additional tools for understanding pre-Oedipal dynamics, including expanded notions of sexual difference and differentiation, the mother-daughter relationship, and the significance of female symbols.

In particular, Kristeva and Irigaray provide as yet unexplored resources for Christology, or the study of beliefs about Christ. For example, through French feminist "glasses," women celebrating the Eucharist represent the nature of Christ as both human and divine. By facilitating dissolution of categorical distinctions between gendered humanity and divinity, and between divinity and the world at large, women celebrants enable a more immanent and inclusive Christology. Two models are offered here to further aid understanding of the symbolic significance of the woman at the altar: (1) the maternal body and (2) the erotic body. Kristevan and Irigarayan views of sacrifice serve to elucidate these two models. The models, in turn, lead to a Christology in which (1) Jesus is viewed as mother, giving birth, (2) transcendence and immanence blur as rigid dichotomies, and (3) female sexuality becomes a focus.

First, the ways in which Kristeva's and Irigaray's work strengthens that of object relations theory are addressed. Then I show how their views of sacrifice illustrate a means of expanding upon object relations theory. Kristevan and Irigarayan perspectives also suggest how the woman priest at the altar symbolizes both maternal body and erotic body. The significance of these priestly representations for Christology is the focus of subsequent discussion.

THE KRISTEVAN "SEMIOTIC" AND
THE IRIGARAYAN "IMAGINARY"

Some preliminary background in French psychoanalytic feminism will assist in comprehending terminology that at times is arcane. French feminist psychoanalytic theory developed in reaction to the work of French psychoanalyst Jacques Lacan. Lacan is especially known for his reinterpretation of the early Freud in terms of symbolism and language. The Oedipus complex, for example, in marking the period of the boy's repression of love for his mother and identification with his father, linguistically expresses the child's entry into the world of language and culture—which Lacan calls the "Symbolic." He dubbed the internalized moral values of the superego the "Law of the Father" and hypothesized two additional levels of experience—the "Imaginary" and the "Real." The Imaginary has been equated with the pre-Oedipal period of object relations theory, that time when the relationship between the mother and the infant is central and the infant does not have a clear sense of identity. The Real is beyond comprehension and signification. Key issues for Lacan are the development of sexual difference and the "phallus" as the prime signifier of that difference. Lacan uses the term *phallus* instead of *penis* and interprets phallus in terms of what the penis *symbolizes*—namely, cultural power rather than anatomical privilege.[1] So, for example, Freud's famous dictum "penis envy" meant, for Lacan, not that little girls envied the fact that little boys had penises but that they coveted the power and authority that those with the organ had in society. In Lacan's view, because girls lack phalluses, women themselves represent loss and lack.

French feminist psychoanalytic thinkers such as Luce Irigaray and Julia Kristeva in general follow Lacan in acknowledging the importance of symbolism and language to personality formation. Like Lacan, they focus on the development of sexual difference, but they do so from the standpoint of the pre-Oedipal period instead of the Oedipal. Whereas Lacan is similar to Freud in attaching primary importance to the Oedipal period, Irigaray and Kristeva are akin to the object relations theorists in placing primary importance on the pre-Oedipal period or the Imaginary. Both Kristeva and Irigaray stress the necessity of changing the representational or symbolic system in order to alter social and economic structures. In addition, both believe that while representation has to do with the Imaginary, in changing the Imaginary the patriarchal Symbolic order is also transformed. As philosopher Kelly Oliver notes, the French feminist thinkers emphasize the necessity of allowing more of the prelinguistic Imaginary to erupt into the Symbolic.[2]

In much the same way that certain object relations theorists expose Freud's misogynism, French feminist theorists provide critiques of Lacan's. As stated, in their view the Symbolic order— ruled by the "Law of the Father"—can be changed by allowing more of the prelinguistic Imaginary (or, for Kristeva, the "semiotic") to erupt into the Symbolic. *Semiotic* is Kristeva's corollary term for those sounds and rhythms discharged within language that are associated with the maternal body, or, as Oliver puts it, the "subterranean element of signification that does not signify."[3] As a linguist, Kristeva indicates that by *Symbolic* she is referring to the "discursive practice that adheres to the logical and grammatical rules of speaking" and by *semiotic* she means "drive-related and affective *meaning* organized according to primary processes whose sensory aspects are often nonverbal (sound and melody, rhythm, color, odors, and so forth)."[4] Kristeva's semiotic has been correlated with Irigaray's Imaginary and with the pre-Oedipal period.[5] The semiotic emerges from the relationship between mother and infant, is prior to culture and language acquisition, and is dependent upon the body's drives.[6] Both Irigaray and Kristeva link emergence of the Imaginary and semiotic, respectively, with expression of the repressed feminine. Irigaray focuses in particular on language, and Kristeva, on "maternal" forms of signification.

Concerning sexual difference, Kristeva takes the position that because there is no opposition between masculine and feminine in pre-Oedipality, the mother cannot be reduced to an example of "femininity." Males and females are not innately different but become viewed differently because of their "positions" in society. Thus, any strengthening of the semiotic, in her view, would lead to a weakening of traditional gender divisions. As Toril Moi observes: "Kristeva's emphasis on marginality allows us to view this repression of the feminine in terms of *positionality* rather than essences. What is perceived as marginal at any given time depends on the position one occupies."[7] For Kristeva there is no such thing as an "essential" womanhood, not even a repressed one.[8]

Kristeva's assertion that the pre-Oedipal period is lacking in gender distinctions could easily be seen as contradicting Chodorow's research. This need not be the case, however. As discussed, Chodorow argues that there is a greater degree of infant-mother merging for girls than for boys. Boys, because of their experience of early-developed, conflictual core identity problems, must repudiate their feminine identification in order to forge a masculine identity. Chodorow indicates that in order for this scenario to develop, boys and girls are *treated* differently from infancy. Kristeva suggests, however, that boys and girls do not cognitively *perceive* themselves as different until entering the Symbolic or Oedipal phase of development. Kristeva's work expands object relations thought to take into account women's marginalized status in contemporary society. Her emphasis on femininity as patriarchal construct—to be viewed in terms of a marginalized position—offers an additional dimension to theories of sexual difference. As Jonte-Pace points out, Kristeva's work, in its project of encountering the internal otherness of the self, unfolds new possibilities for recognition of the "otherness" of both the self and the other.[9]

While Kristeva's position on sexual difference has largely escaped feminist criticism, this is not true of Irigaray's. Irigaray's work has been read by some to perpetuate a radical, even ontological, rather than socially constructed, disjunction between sign/mind/male and body/nature/female.[10] In other words, she has been accused of being an essentialist. As we have seen, essentialism is controversial in that it designates some aspect of human nature as pre-given, innate, biological, and hence incapable of change. Irigaray has been charged with grounding women's qualities in their reproductive biology. In "This Sex Which Is Not One," for example, women's speaking is made analogous to vaginal lips coming together and separating again.[11] Philosopher Rosemarie Tong attempts to refute essentialist accusations leveled against Irigaray. Tong explains that because Irigaray is a deconstructionist thinker— and deconstructionism is about breaking down dualisms, categories, and statuses—to call her an essentialist is a contradiction in terms. Most postmodern feminist texts, according to Tong, maintain a distinction between (1) women as biological and social entities and (2) the "female," "feminine," or "other," where "female" stands metaphorically for the genuinely other in a relation of *difference* rather than opposition.[12] Thus, Tong would suggest that Irigaray's reading of feminine language be taken in a symbolic sense, and references to female reproductive processes viewed as ways to describe pre-Symbolic, pre-Oedipal sensations, without claiming that only women are capable of participating in or experiencing them.

Whether sexual difference is socialized or innate, women priests would bring changes in some of the directions suggested by Irigaray's work. Like Kristeva, Irigaray expands upon the contributions made through object relations theory. In particular, her emphasis on language allows for further discussion of the significance of symbol and metaphor for women priests. In addition, Irigaray's position that sexual difference is a resource for women— and her focus on desire, sexuality, and bonds between women— enables development of modes of female symbolization that are nonmaternal.

Interestingly, the scholarship of Kristeva and Irigaray has increasingly overlapped the field of religious studies. In recent years, these two thinkers have expressed not only interest in but appreciation for the power of religious themes. At the same time, they offer critiques of certain aspects of the Christian tradition. For example, Kristeva believes the intent of biblical food taboos was exclusion of the mother. She reads the Old Testament book of Leviticus, for example, in terms of a pre-Oedipal dynamic of maternal separation. Separating from the mother, rejecting her, resuming contact with her, defining oneself according to her, and rebuilding her constitute, in Kristeva's view, a narrative expression of the Hebrew struggle against pagan maternal cults.[13]

Yet both Kristeva and Irigaray view religion as a possible vehicle for greater interaction between the Symbolic and the semiotic/Imaginary, which they argue is sorely needed by women and men in modern society. While Kristeva has not explicitly addressed the Catholic women's ordination movement, Irigaray makes reference to it in her critique of Schüssler Fiorenza's book *In Memory of Her: A Feminist Theological Reconstruction of Christian Origins*. Irigaray states: "What interest can women have in being disciples or priests at all? The important thing is for them to find their own genealogy, the necessary condition for their own identity."[14] Irigaray asserts that if contemporary Catholicism involves only men and their "mother-wives," those women who cannot find their identity in this scenario would be best advised to go elsewhere.[15] Yet, as has been shown, women priests would bring to religion needed feminine representation so passionately argued for by Irigaray. Because Irigaray posits that the divinization of femininity takes place apart from women's regaining a sense of autonomy and identity within the church, she constructs a false dichotomy between "equality" and "divinity."[16]

Both Irigaray and Kristeva view maternal themes as hidden under paternal ones in the Eucharist. The sacraments, for Kristeva, involve both Symbolic and semiotic modes of language and seek to negotiate the line between them. The semiotic and Symbolic are separated by what Kristeva calls the "thetic cut," which can be seen as the passage from an infantile, largely semiotic state of connection with the mother to a rational, largely Symbolic one with the father. Negotiating this line involves both the establishment and the transgression of taboo.[17]

The role of the Eucharist, for Kristeva, is to remove guilt for archaic maternal relations. Partaking of the body and blood of

Christ is psychologically equivalent to satiation at the mother's breast.[18] In the Eucharist, an osmosis takes place between spiritual and substantial, the corporeal and the signifying, the result of which is that a speaking subject is reconciled both to the body of the mother and the law of the father.[19] Kristeva explains that the Eucharist is the "ritual par excellence of identification with God's body" and a basis for all other identifications.[20] For Kristeva, the psychological concept of identification can be correlated with transubstantiation, since, in her view, the psychic issues are the same. She understands identification in terms of the various aspects involved in the process of becoming a subject: "The 'I' transferred to the Other becomes One with the Other through the entire range of the Symbolic, the imaginary, and the real."[21] Kristeva admonishes that the loving incorporation of the father must not hide its underlying aggressiveness, for the father's body carries the memory of the mother's (i.e., the pre-Oedipal underlies the Oedipal).

Irigaray, on the other hand, attributes the pre-Christian meaning of the Eucharist to be giving of the fruits of the earth, which became sacrificial when put in the hands of men. In her discussion of the resurrection of the normatively male body, she refers to the Eucharist in terms of repressing dependence on the mother and eliminating women from creation/redemption:

> So when this minister of the so-called one God, of the
> Father-God, pronounces the eucharistic words, "This is my
> body, this is my blood," in accordance with the rite of shar-
> ing food, which is our age-old rite, perhaps we might remind
> him that he would not be there if our body and our blood
> had not given him life, love, and spirit. And that it is us,
> women-mothers, that he is giving to be eaten too. But no
> one must know that. That is why women cannot celebrate
> the eucharist . . . Something of the truth which is hidden
> therein might be brutally unmasked."[22]

Thus, that which is offered to be eaten is always a maternal body.[23] In sum, we can see that both Irigaray and Kristeva underscore maternal themes in the Eucharist, offering further support for Ross and Ross's contention that the mass is as much about pre-Oedipal dynamics as it is about Oedipal ones. In addition, their views on sexual difference support a reconfiguration of the meaning of "otherness" and sexuality in eucharistic theology and experience.

SACRIFICE: WOMAN PRIEST AS MATERNAL BODY AND EROTIC BODY

We can begin to envision what this reconfiguration might mean through exploring the theme of religious sacrifice as understood by Kristeva and Irigaray. Their views on sacrifice also illustrate how French feminist theory expands upon object relations thought when applied to theology. As is Freud's view of sacrifice, the perspectives offered by Kristeva and Irigaray are incomplete. Their notions of sacrifice, however, do underscore that (1) "death-work" is as much a part of sacrifice as is communion and (2) when women celebrate the Eucharist, a gender "re-reversal" is taking place, in which women are reclaiming their reproductive and nurturing roles. As well, when Kristevan and Irigarayan theories are applied to sacrifice, models of woman as "maternal body" and woman as "erotic body" are rendered by the presence of female priests. These models offer resources for exploring the significance of women clergy for Christology.

Both Kristeva and Irigaray view sacrifice in terms of repression of the maternal. According to Kristeva, rituals of sacrifice largely express fear of the mother's generative power. In particular, blood stands at the crossroads of the mother's abjection, and menstrual pollution points to maternal conflict.[24] As psychologist of religion Martha Reineke explains:

> Without the ladder to the symbolic offered to the child by
> the imaginary father, the mother is the primary site of abjec-
> tion. Fluids from her body evoke for the child its violent
> expulsion from the maternal interior in all of its risk. Her
> blood and milk—source of life and death, nourishment and
> threat—are first witnesses to the drama of archaic differentia-
> tion.[25]

In this way Kristeva accounts for the concealment of the mother behind sacrificial substitutes in rituals. Purification rites, food taboos, and pollution fears are governed by the threat to survival experienced in the state of primary narcissism, when the first boundaries of identity are drawn.[26] Sacrifice and maternal conflict seem inextricably connected for Kristeva, so much so that Kristevan scholar David Crownfield is prompted to ask: "If the archaic root of that [founding] violence [in Christianity] is maternal, evoking the scapegoating of women, can this substitution of the Son be maintained, and how? If not, what alternative understanding of the sacrificial motif in Christology might derive from the Kristevan analysis?"[27] This question can be extended to the issue of women priests: if sacrifice, for Kristeva, is based on maternal abjection, what does a Kristevan analysis yield for the issue of women celebrants?

It is significant that both Irigaray and Kristeva, like the other sacrifice theorists discussed earlier, developed their theories in reaction to Freud. Moreover, both retained his notion that violence is central to sacrifice. In Irigaray's accusations that Freud forgets the more archaic murder of the mother, for example, she draws from the same Greek mythos as did Freud.[28] Sacrifice thus is now "matricide" rather than "patricide." Jonte-Pace points out that Kristeva's project in *Powers of Horror* is almost identical to Freud's in *Totem and Taboo*. She explains that while for Kristeva, sacrifice "reenacts the violent separation of abjection," taboo " 'forestalls sacrifice,' making it unnecessary by maintaining clear boundaries between pure and impure."[29] While Irigarayan and Kristevan notions of sacrifice have some applicability, such as the murder of the goddess by patriarchal gods, it is difficult to develop a general theory of sacrifice using matricide. The mother clearly is absent in the examples of father-son sacrifice discussed earlier, but has she been murdered or merely hidden from view?

A possible reading of Kristeva is that sacrifice is the attempt to ward off the feared repressed maternal resulting from a "necessary matricide,"[30] which is metaphorical of the infant separation-individuation process. Kristeva, like Nancy Jay, emphasizes the patriarchal expression of sacrifice in terms of repression of the abject feminine. Yet she pays little attention to the push-pull dynamic inherent in both male and female individuation, which is also played out in sacrificial rituals. Kristeva focuses on expiation to the neglect of communion.

In her book *Sacrificed Lives: Kristeva on Women and Violence*, Reineke offers a helpful interpretation of the contemporary culture of violence against women using Kristeva's notion of sacrifice as matricide. Positing a distinction between "death-work" and sacrifice, Reineke suggests that in patriarchy women become victims of sacrifice when they "are made hostage to others' dramatic efforts to repeat individuation from the maternal matrix."[31] Death-work is an inevitable result of the mother-infant differentiation process: "failure to be" (negativity) emerges from a "desire torn between a longing to be oneself and a longing for a return to origins."[32] While this negativity, for Kristeva, is inherent in human identity, sacrifice (not inevitable) requires that it be translated onto the body of a victim.[33]

According to Reineke's interpretation, sacrifice necessarily involves violence against women. She argues that it is only through distinguishing sacrifice from death-work that violence against women can be stopped. Her efforts to discern death-work that is not sacrificial parallel my investigations into expressions of sacrifice that are not matricidal. In both cases we are attempting to disrupt the conflation of infant-mother separation-individuation with violence against women. I do not share her view, however, that sacrifice is always matricide. I believe that death-work can take place within the context of sacrifice without necessarily victimizing women.

In fact, Reineke's focus upon "necessary death-work" in Kristevan thought expands our object relations view of sacrifice. As discussed earlier, according to an object relations perspective, sacrifice expresses the separation-individuation process for both men and women. Separation-individuation constitutes the child's effort to form a distinct identity from the "other." While object relations thought emphasizes communion as an aspect of this process, Kristevan thought admonishes that the theme of separation, or death-work, cannot be dismissed altogether from sacrifice theories. One cannot remain forever enmeshed in the mother. As well, the work of Kristeva, like object relations thought, emphasizes that the maternal body is at the heart of rituals of blood sacrifice.

Irigaray also rejects the term *sacrifice* completely, equating it solely with matricide and repression of the feminine. She argues that the
primordial sacrifice is of natural fertility; beneath animal or human
sacrifice are hidden vegetable sacrifice and disappearance of goddesses.[34] As Reineke has pointed out, Irigaray finds two substitu-
tions to be characteristic of sacrificial traditions in which gender
considerations are paramount.[35] In Christianity the (male) Word
takes the place of the (female) flesh. The visible victim is Christ, yet
the body and blood ritually consumed are female—the hidden murdered mother.

Irigaray's efforts to reclaim a pre-patriarchal, anti-sacrificial tradition are useful for further exploring the implications of women
celebrants. In its focus on sacrifice as "fertility," her work expands
our object relations view of sacrifice as birthing. Irigaray asserts: "A
woman celebrating the Eucharist with her mother, sharing with her
the fruits of the earth she/they have blessed, could be delivered of
all hatred or ingratitude towards her maternal genealogy, could be
consecrated in her identity and her female genealogy."[36] The
metaphor of fertility, for Irigaray, acknowledges the need for words
or symbolization of women's rites.[37] Since women's rites have
always been bound up with cosmic rhythms, what is needed, in her
view, is a new style of collective relations to include "relationships
which reject the body-mind split and contrive constant growth without any sacrificial break."[38] A possible source for women's rites is
the natural cycles of fertility, including symbolization of women's
bodies and blood.[39]

A weakness in Irigaray's theorizing is her failure to see sacrifice
as a manifestation of the separation-individuation process inherent
to both male and female development; instead, she views it as only
an expression of matricide. In rejecting the term *sacrifice*, she is
neglecting to account for the necessary loss that accompanies separation from the mother and the push-pull dynamic that both boys
and girls go through in the process of differentiation. In fact, fertility cycles illustrate the tension between separation and connection
that I described in rituals of sacrifice.

At the same time, Irigaray's view of sacrifice makes important
contributions to the women's ordination debate. Whereas object

relations theory proposes that a gender reversal is occurring in the Eucharist, Irigaray's work suggests that a female-celebrated Eucharist can be classified as a gender "re-reversal"—a reclaiming of female reproductive abilities and maternal genealogies. It points to the Eucharist, with women priests, as a celebration of women's relationships with their bodies and with one another. Irigaray's focus on fertility also lifts up the theme of the woman priest as erotic body. The metaphor of fertility, in addition to birthing, includes relationships between men and women, and between women and women. As such, it raises the issue of sexuality and its significance for eucharistic theology and experience.

The two models suggested by Kristevan and Irigarayan theories—woman priest as maternal body and erotic body—have wide-reaching implications for the future of Christology. Both models enable a more immanent and inclusive Christology. For example, Kristevan theory supports the notion that the maternal body is a site for dissolution of Western dualisms, such as nature/culture and human/divine. Irigaray's work, in turn, allows for a reenvisioning of Christology in terms of eros and relationality. The paradigms of woman priest as maternal body and erotic body lead to a Christology in which the three points made earlier are elucidated: (1) Jesus is viewed as mother, giving birth, (2) transcendence and immanence break down as rigid dichotomies, and (3) female sexuality becomes a focal point.

KRISTEVA: WOMAN PRIEST AS MATERNAL BODY

We have already examined how women priests at the altar, giving of body and blood, symbolize the early relationship to the maternal body. In addition to birth, a Kristevan understanding of the maternal body grounds maternal generativity in the context of suffering and death. A Kristevan paradigm of the maternal body points to a Christology in which, in the context of women celebrants, the body of Christ represents the maternal body, broken in childbirth.

Thus far, we have explored several ways in which women acting *in persona Christi* represent Christ as the maternal body. For

Kristeva, the maternal body is the site of the "abject." Abjection is the expression of a division between the subject and its body, and a merging of self and other.[40] The abject is both a necessary condition of the subject and what must be expelled or repressed by the subject in order to attain identity and a place within the Symbolic. As Elizabeth Gross observes, abjection is a reaction to the recognition of the "impossible but necessary transcendence of the subject's corporeality."[41] The abject is similar to the object relations notion of pre-Oedipal space. Kristeva, in fact, suggests that "potential space," elaborated by transitional objects, perfects the necessary conditions for semiotic functioning and the transition to language acquisition.[42] Thus the abject is a site of intermediacy, in which the boundaries between other and self are not distinct. The abject should be seen in the context of the semiotic and, as such, is repressed upon entry into the Symbolic order. It is associated with the repressed feminine.

The abject maternal body, for Kristeva, is a split subject. She illustrates this idea through describing the mother's experiences of pregnancy and birthing. Kristeva argues that pregnancy, like abjection, is a borderline phenomenon, blurring yet producing one identity and another.[43] Pregnancy is a sort of "institutionalized, socialized, and natural psychosis"—a dramatic splitting of the body, the division and coexistence of self and other.[44] Like the abject, maternity expresses the splitting and fusing of a series of bodily processes beyond the control of the subject, affirming the woman-mother's position as a hinge between nature and culture.[45] As Kristevan scholar David Fisher observes:

> The subject that emerges from this unnameable division [the "chora"] is a split subject, identifying its previous, fragmentary experience with the source of life, imagined as the mother's body. Because the maternal body is experienced as *both* the originating, nurturing source of subjectivity (hence desired) *and* rejected as abject or horrifying in light of the "perfect" image that the subject now wishes to become, the maternal image is at once a source of fascination and rejection.[46]

Significantly, for Kristeva, the semiotic maternal body has been repressed in Catholic discourse on motherhood. Marian theology, for example, illuminates a dramatic splitting of the woman in which maternal generativity is cut off from sin, sex, and death. Instead, Mary is "alone of all her sex," the mother who does not die. In contrast to the Marian text, mothers are presented by Kristeva as split subjects. Mothers "live on the border, crossroads beings, crucified beings,"[47] as do all split subjects. Life and suffering, love and death, are linked to one another and to the maternal body, as exemplified in the chora—or, as Crownfield puts it, the "retrospectively imagined container that precedes the distinction of mother, self and object, and of the real and symbolic."[48]

In an article published in *Hypatia*, a feminist philosophical journal, Ewa Ziarek queries whether Kristeva's use of the maternal body as a source of resistance to the Symbolic leads to any significant transformation of cultural paradigms. Or does it merely repeat a traditional cultural gesture relegating women to a "precultural, prediscursive position"?[49] In other words, does Kristeva's use of the maternal metaphor "put women back in the kitchen"? Ziarek notes that for many feminist critics, Kristeva's association of the maternal with prelinguistic experience replicates the patriarchal hierarchy of culture/nature, paternal law/maternal body. Yet she argues that in Kristeva's theory, the semiotic process of the maternal body has the potential to disrupt language as a social code (p. 96). Ziarek believes that Kristeva encourages reconceptualization of the maternal function as an instance of "infolding of the semiotic and the symbolic," as a " 'radical form of split symbolizations'" (p. 97).

The semiotic chora, for Ziarek, should be read in terms of traces of alterity and heterogeneity operating within the linguistic and psychic economy. The event of pregnancy and motherhood, in her view, allows a discussion of otherness prior to the constitution of a separate ego and to formation of subject/object dichotomy (pp. 98–99). Because pregnancy splits the subject and shatters the symbolic notion of the body as "mine" and separate from all others, the maternal body, the "site of splitting," becomes a space of "othering."

The maternal body is, for Ziarek, both a site of "radical othering"—which must be articulated beyond the symbolic/natural opposition—and a site of symbolic inscription. *Othering* is the term for that which cannot be named according to customary taxonomies. Thus Kristeva's work initiates a different discourse on maternity, one that transgresses the "limits of the symbolic logic of separation . . . and the mystifications of unity and resemblance" (p. 99). Ziarek's argument is therefore useful because it suggests that Kristeva's maternal body cannot be categorized in traditional ways.

If self cannot be disentangled from other in the context of the maternal body, then can death and life, God and humanity, be so rigidly dichotomized in the Eucharist? I suggest that when women act *in persona Christi*, Christ becomes the site of juxtaposing death and life, nature and culture. Kristevan theory underscores my conviction that the cross is simultaneously a place of death and of birth, of abjection and of the emergence of new life.[50] A Kristevan reading of the symbol of the woman at the altar renders Jesus' body as the maternal body, the site of interconnection of death and life, nature and culture, semiotic and Symbolic. While Kristeva posits a violent split between semiotic and Symbolic, I suggest that they should be seen in terms of a continuum rather than as rigid opposites, just as separation from the mother is a continuing dialectic and not a once-and-for-all event.

Using a Kristevan paradigm, the woman at the altar becomes a locus for suffering, death, and birth in the context of maternal—instead of paternal—generativity. Christ is the mother, giving birth and feeding. When men act *in persona Christi*, they are placing themselves in the marginalized position of the "feminine," or the abject maternal. According to a postmodern interpretation, men desire the abject maternal because it represents archaic maternal connectedness. Because Kristeva is less idealistic than some of the object relations theorists, she posits this site as a place of conflict as well as merging. The abject is feared and repressed because of its position of great power and of great ambivalence, as the site of primary division and connection between self and other. While the position of the abject is not exclusive to women, women tend to occupy it, as illustrated in Kristeva's notion of the maternal body giving birth.

In sum, when a woman acts *in persona Christi*, Christ becomes the abject maternal—the taboo in a holy place. When women are celebrants, Jesus' giving of body and blood is seen in terms of the abject maternal body, which simultaneously affirms and transcends corporeality. Jesus is the mother whose body is broken in childbirth, but he is also the one whose body is positioned in a kind of corporeal contiguity with all Christians.[51] In this fashion, believers maintain a mystical connection with Jesus despite his earthly death.

A primary claim of this book is that the primordial drama of identification with and differentiation from the mother is reenacted when women priests celebrate the Eucharist. Kristeva's work suggests that because of the mother's status as a split subject, the woman celebrant allows a bridge between semiotic and Symbolic, pre-Oedipal and Oedipal, nature and culture. This bridge ruptures violently only if the subject commits "matricide"—expressed in cutting oneself off permanently from the abject maternal. Matricide is not necessary, however. Here I agree in part with Oliver, who argues that the child must reject the "maternal container" but not the mother herself as a person. "Maternal container" refers to the psychic representations of being held or enveloped by the mother, the earliest example of which is mirroring. To push Oliver a bit further, it seems detrimental to reject the maternal container entirely, because early maternal mirroring is never entirely rejected or repressed.

In terms of a Kristevan analysis, Christ is not only the maternal body giving birth, but he also represents, in the context of women celebrants, the conjunction of human and divine. If the Symbolic is the realm of the father/spirit, and the semiotic the realm of the maternal/corporeality, then women celebrants juxtapose these binary oppositions. To juxtapose is to force confrontation. To suggest that a woman at the altar represents mothers as "crucified beings," as split subjects who bridge both the body's drives and the Symbolic, nature and culture, is also to propose that when women celebrate the Eucharist, the abject maternal body becomes a locus for divine communion. The repressed maternal emerges out from under purification rites and taboos, breaking those taboos by its very presence. A female Christ forces coming to terms with the opposition between male/spirit and woman/matter—and between gendered humanity and divinity. When women bless the bread and wine in the Eucharist, transcendent, traditionally male God and corporeal woman appear in the same space: both are in the "form" of Christ. It is difficult to maintain the dichotomy between transcendence and immanence when women are imaged as equally theomorphic as men. As Episcopal priest Denise Haines puts it, women's biology inextricably binds them to the earth, making it difficult to maintain the dichotomy between sacred and profane when women preside at the altar.[52]

It is unfortunate that some feminist and womanist theologians have rejected conversation about the relation of Christ's humanity to his divinity. In doing so, they have discarded the doctrine of "hypostatic union"—or the union of divine and human natures in Christ—which was formulated during the Council of Chalcedon in 451 C.E.[53] Delores Williams, for example, in *Sisters in the Wilderness: The Challenge of Womanist God-Talk*, states that the black woman's question about Jesus Christ is not about the relation of his humanity to his divinity, or about the relation of the historical Jesus to the Christ of faith.[54] Elizabeth Schüssler Fiorenza in turn argues that the Christological doctrine of Chalcedon associated fatherhood/masculinity with divinity and eternity, placing motherhood/femininity in the temporal realm of humanity. The doctrine, in her view, introduced not only gender dualisms but dualisms between church and world, religion and nature, heaven and earth.[55]

According to Kristevan analysis, however, a female Christ symbol finds compatibility with Karl Rahner's understanding of hypostatic union, or God's becoming material. As Rahner states: "Whenever God—by his [*sic*] absolute self-communication—brings about man's [*sic*] self-transcendence into God . . . there we have a hypostatic union."[56] When women act *in persona Christi*, God becomes material, and the material (i.e., woman) becomes divine. A female Christ symbol makes it impossible to retain the dualisms warned against by Schüssler Fiorenza. The Reverend Eleanor McLaughlin has suggested that Jesus is a "Third One, who dismantles the dualisms, male/female, law/gospel, insider/outsider, friend/enemy, God/world."[57] This role becomes even more clear when women represent him.

It also becomes impossible, using Kristeva, to retain a gender dichotomy when women celebrate the Eucharist. As stated, for Kristeva the maternal body is not an essentialist function of *woman per se* but a position taken by women in the context of culture. Kristeva wants to move away from a discussion of sexed bodies, to the position that there is no body in itself, no *natural* sexual difference. Rather, in her view sexed bodies are always matters of representation.[58] As Oliver observes, Kristeva chooses maternity as a prototype because it breaks down borders between nature and culture, subject and other.[59] Interestingly, for Kristeva the concepts "man" and "woman" are the products not of nature but of signifying practices.[60]

In sum, Kristevan theory, through supporting acknowledgment of "otherness" as an important aspect of religious practice, adds to earlier work on the woman priest as maternal body. A clergywoman is quoted in John Morgan's book *Woman Priests*, for example, as stating:

> When I give communion to people I feel a deep sense of union with them and of communicating Christ to them—and I know that when we look at each other across the communion rail we are mirrors for one another: girls and women know that they too are instruments of God; boys and men are face-to-face with an "other" which must surely help them to see God more fully and to come to know the "other" in themselves.[61]

In addition, a Kristevan reading of the woman priest at the altar indicates that the abject maternal body is a contested presence, yet a necessary one if Western dualisms are to be overcome. The model of woman priest as maternal body, giving birth and feeding, discloses that death and life are intertwined processes, just as the taboo and the holy are integrally related. An ethnographic account from *Women Priests?*, edited by Alyson Peberdy, highlights the notion that a celebrant with disease—also abject in Western culture—can break down the dichotomy between transcendence/immanence, or spirit/matter:

We asked her [Yvonne, an Anglican accepted for ordination who at the time this article was written had been diagnosed with cancer] to preside at the informal liturgy which always concluded our meeting. She took bread and broke it and said the words we say in memory of Jesus: "This is my body broken for you." As we ate that bread and passed the cup of wine, I was aware of a shift in consciousness, in my sense of self and sense of God. In that celebration of women, of women asking for physical healing, for health, for wholeness, presided over by a woman, the body of Christ was suddenly a woman's body. Women's suffering and denigration was Christ's suffering and death. In a way not available to me before, I knew that God knows what it is like to have a woman's body, what it is that women suffer. Jesus died for women. By seeing Christ as a woman, by saying God is a woman who suffers in her body, I could find new wealth of meaning in the knowledge that I am made in the image of God.[62]

Finally, Kristevan thought has the potential to rejuvenate feminist discussion on the nature of Christ's humanity to his divinity. The above quotation suggests that women priests, because historically forbidden, have the power to shift parishioners' understandings of Christ in ways such that suffering and wholeness, and humanity and divinity, truly converge.

IRIGARAY: WOMAN PRIEST AS EROTIC BODY

Like Kristevan theory, Luce Irigaray's work also offers powerful insights in the area of Christology. It does so primarily through investigating the model of woman priest as erotic body. The issue of sexuality, moreover, is not adequately addressed by Kristeva.[63] Through a discussion of female sexuality—and male sexuality in relation to it—Irigaray offers much in the way of providing non-parental and non-domestic imagery for God and Christ. This imagery broadens the context in which we think about priestly representations of Christ.

Irigaray argues that the "natural," i.e., biological, division into two sexes cannot be ignored, because it has provided the Imaginary basis for the patriarchal division of roles.[64] In the effort to downplay Jesus' maleness, for example, little attention has been paid to the notion that Jesus, as a "representative human," was also a sexed individual. While Jesus' anatomical maleness is certainly not essential to the Christian notion of salvation, the fact that he was human is an integral part of his identity. As a male priest asked me, if sexuality is not part of Jesus' human nature, is sexuality in fact redeemed? When women priests represent Christ, their sexuality as an aspect of "representative humanity" must be addressed.

In sorting out this complex configuration of women, Christ, Eucharist, and sexuality, it is useful to explore two theological approaches to the relationship between sex and the sacred: the Roman Catholic viewpoint on reproductive sexuality and a feminist theological perspective on eros. Material from Episcopal women clergy is included to further analyze the feminist outlook. The ethnographic data establish that women priests indeed raise issues of sexuality in the context of the Eucharist. Irigaray's work, in turn, offers positive meaning to women's sexual presence through exploring the significance of Jesus' own corporeal nature. In the context of women priests celebrating the Eucharist, her research presents several ways in which "cultivation of the sexual" would be beneficial to the future of Catholic faith.

Roman Catholic Viewpoint on Reproductive Sexuality

According to Catholic doctrine, only sex within heterosexual marriage is acceptable, and women's sexuality is generally negated. Maria-Teresa Porcile-Santiso observes, for example, that contemporary Roman Catholic teaching on sexual morality finds its basis in three fundamental points: (1) the Bible regards sexuality favorably, (2) love is the standard for sexual behavior, and (3) a "fully human" sexual relationship entails equality between men and women, complementarity of the sexes, and the sexual drive to union (except in cases of sublimation).[65] Sexual sin, on the other hand, is defined according to Catholic doctrine as follows: "Any activity which is individual and solitary (masturbation), or with persons of the same sex (homosexuality), or without love (prostitution), or extra-institutional (pre-marital relationships), or which is an evasion of procreation (contraception), or a denial of marital fidelity (adultery), is always considered sinful."[66] Within the heterosexual marriage relationship, Catholic teaching stresses the transmission of life. Porcile-Santiso notes that in the papal encyclical *Humanae Vitae* (1986), the church's most recent view on sexuality, the fundamental admonition is thus: "Every conjugal act must be open to the transmission of life." Similarly excluded is "every action which, either in anticipation of the conjugal act, or in its accomplishment, or in the development of its natural consequences, proposes, whether as an end or as a means, to render procreation impossible."[67] Reasons for such exclusion are (1) respect for the natural biological order (i.e., the natural rhythms in women) and (2) the fear that men, "growing used to the employment of anti-conceptive practices, may finally lose respect for the woman and . . . may come to the point of considering her as a mere instrument of selfish enjoyment."[68]

It is common knowledge that women's sexuality has generally not been regarded positively in the Catholic tradition. As examples, fourth-century theologian Jerome wrote extensively on virginity and praised women who followed the path of celibacy. During the same period Augustine admonished that sex was tainted because of the sin of Eve, the stain of which was passed down through all subsequent generations. Essentially, this is the doctrine of "original sin," that all persons are born with sin because of Adam and Eve. During the Middle Ages, Thomas Aquinas argued that sex was a "venial sin"—not as serious as a "mortal sin" (such as intentional murder), but a sin nonetheless. Moreover, Eve's eating of the apple in the Garden of Eden illustrated, for medieval theologians, that woman has an inherently more carnal nature than man does.

Ruether has suggested that in Catholic dogma there is a connection between the teachings of the magisterium (an organ of the church that deals with matters of faith, dogma, morals, and "natural law") and the negation of women and sexuality.[69] She argues that theologians such as Augustine and Aquinas, because they denied women's equal human status with men, have been responsible for the present teaching that women cannot be ordained because they cannot "image" Christ. Morever, she insists that the continuing refusal of the Vatican to accept female altar servers reflects a tradition in which the female body is by definition excluded from the holy.[70]

Ownership of woman's body, particularly her fertility, for Ruether is foundational to male control over women. She explains that the theological reasoning behind *Humanae Vitae*'s claim that love cannot be viewed as a valid "end" of sexuality is because women and men, in the pope's view, are not equal. According to Ruether, the roots of this perceived inequality lie in a lower regard for the female role in procreation, stemming from Aquinas's belief that the male provides the "form" whereas the woman provides only "matter."[71]

Feminist Theological Perspective on Eros

It is important to be aware that alternative perspectives to the official Catholic view on reproductive sexuality exist within the Christian tradition. Feminist theologians, in particular, have increasingly addressed the erotic in an attempt to explore sexuality as a resource for liberation rather than as a source of sin. For example, Rita Nakashima Brock's notion of "feminist eros" is as an "incarnation of divine love," emerging from "heart" and the fundamental power of life—healing, empowering, liberating.[72] Using Audre Lorde, Carol Christ calls for a celebration of eros, suggesting that the erotic has the power to transform our lives and our world.[73] For Carter Heyward, the erotic is the most fully embodied experience of the love of God and, as such, is the source of transcendence as well as immanence. Heyward finds Christa a transitional symbol of sacred power, stating that our "most fully christic [liberating] experiences are our most fully embodied (sensual and erotic) connections in relation to one another, other creatures, and the earth."[74]

These theorists have not escaped criticism. Kathleen Sands, for example, points out a tendency to idealize eros, to ignore sin or fault, or to expect sex to encompass the entire content of the moral good.[75] While Sands is right to stress that feminist theologians must cultivate a "practical sexual wisdom,"[76] I believe the erotic offers important resources for understanding love, healing, and liberation. Sexuality can be sacred in the proper context. Along with Brock, Christ, Heyward, and others, I would like to overturn the age-old Augustinian dictum that sex is sinful and instead see sexuality embraced as a potentially positive spiritual force in people's lives.

Ethnographic material attests to the fact that sexuality matters in the context of the Eucharist, especially when women are celebrants. The following accounts beg for further analysis. A parishioner told a priest I interviewed, for example, that he was sexually aroused when a woman celebrated the Eucharist and felt he could not partake of the sacrament in that state. In contrast to his perspective, Episcopal priest Alla Bozarth-Campbell writes: "Seeing a female priest at the altar assures me that I don't have to leave my sexuality at the church door when I come to worship, but that I can worship with my body as well as my heart and soul and mind, wholly joining the Great Dance."[77] A third woman priest told me that there is a lot of erotic power involved with women priests. She acknowledged that male sexual arousal was an argument used against ordaining women as clergy. After women were ordained, she noted, discussion came to revolve around whether women clergy were "priestesses": the term stirred up connotations that women priests were involved in pagan fertility rites. Since the approval of women priests, she observed, attractive women have at times been barred from ordination on the grounds of "promiscuity."

There are several ways to approach the issue of sexual arousal. One is to explore its causes more fully. Do some men feel aroused because they have never considered the idea that the priest is a sexual being? Or is their arousal rooted in seeing a woman in a historically taboo setting? Either way, it is likely that the issue of sexual arousal will become less threatening for those men who regularly participate in Eucharists celebrated by women. Interestingly, many of the early questions about female Episcopal priests concerned women's sexual nature in the context of a sacred ritual. While the Catholic male priest, a celibate, has traditionally been viewed as asexual, the woman priest is automatically seen as a sexual being, forcing the issue of sexuality into the theological arena. This would be true even if celibacy were required of women priests.

With the advent of women clergy, it will be necessary to rethink theological meanings of sexuality, particularly in some of the directions suggested by feminist theology. The presence of women celebrants will force parishioners to confront their own views of sexuality. As has been shown, this notion is supported by ethnographic data. A woman priest explained to me, for example, that when only men could be clergy, one never thought about the priest's gender. Now that both sexes are represented, it has dawned on parishioners that most clergy are male, as opposed to neuter. Another woman priest I interviewed commented that having a female colleague gives a male priest's own maleness "back to him."

The realization that priests are gendered has spawned debates in the Episcopal Church on the issue of homosexuality. It is significant that the subject of ordaining gay men and lesbians was never openly discussed until the ordination of women was authorized.[78] The advent of Catholic women priests would also raise questions regarding homosexuality. Many priests and parishioners would feel threatened, but many others would experience a lifting of the veil and would welcome the opportunity to talk about an issue that previously had been kept underground. Again, the Episcopal tradition provides apt examples of issues that might be raised. An Episcopal laywoman I interviewed, for example, articulated one way in which homosexuality was used as an argument against women priests. She explained: "I was told by one priest . . . that a woman presiding at the Eucharist was incestuous. It's homosexual, it's perverted, like the Eucharist is some kind of sex act. And that's exactly how he saw it . . . a male priest and a female church." Many in the hierarchy expressed outrage when one of the first ordained Episcopal women priests was an out lesbian. At the 1998 Episcopalian Lambeth Conference, an international meeting held once a decade, a coalition of conservative African, South Asian, and U.S. bishops passed a resolution declaring homosexuality incompatible with Scripture and advising against the "legitimizing or blessing of same-sex unions" and the "ordination of those involved in those same-gender unions."[79]

The interview material with Episcopal priests leads one to conclude that Pandora's box would indeed be opened if Catholic women were ordained to the priesthood. Many conflicting and controversial views on sexuality would surface, and additional discussions on the issue would be critical. I believe Irigaray's perspective would be extremely beneficial to these discussions. Through establishing that Jesus himself—a representative human—had a sexual nature, Irigaray's research suggests avenues by which women's sexuality can be given positive meaning when women are celebrants.

Implications of Jesus' Sexuality for the Eucharist

The work of Irigaray enables us to explore further the significance of sexuality for the Eucharist. Her theories also allow us to address subjects such as women as other than mothers, desire, the relationship between nature and culture, and female divinity. Fundamentally, Irigaray acknowledges that every individual is "sexed," even Christ. Jesus' sexuality offers clues for interpreting the co-presence of sexuality with spirituality in the context of the woman priest as erotic body.

Irigaray asks: Do you know of any asexual life? Nature and sexuality, for Irigaray, are a locus of creation of ourselves as body and flesh.[80] Our relationship to sexuality, and to nature, is the last irreducible reality of our lives as human beings.

Irigaray argues that the denigration of Christ's incarnation as a sexual being has blocked an understanding of his sexual nature.[81] Indeed, the more that Jesus "the Christ" became Hellenized and spiritualized in Christian heritage, the more Jesus "the human being" became neutered. As Robert Goss indicates, ecclesial portrayals of an asexual Jesus came to promote misogyny, homophobia, and denigration of sexual pleasure.[82] For Irigaray, Jesus' life illustrates that "spiritual becoming" and "corporeal becoming" are inseparable. She observes that every stage in the life of Christ is an event of the body: "conception, birth, growth, fasting in the desert, immersion in the River Jordan, treks to the mountain or walks along the water's edge, meals, festivals, the laying-on of hands, the draining of physical strength after a healing, transfiguration, trials, suffering, death, resurrection, ascension."[83] Because Christ was flesh and blood, living in the confines of a body, Irigaray concludes that he must therefore have been sexual.[84]

If Christ was sexual, then those who represent him are obviously sexual beings as well. While celibate men are not asexual any more than are women priests, we have seen that the latter force the issue of sexuality out into the open. In particular, women priests raise the question of the significance of Christ's incarnation for human sexuality. An Irigarayan perspective, I propose, suggests that Christ's redemption of the world makes the incarnation of all bodies potentially divine. As Irigaray puts it, each man and woman is virtually a god.[85] She argues that if Christianity were to make explicit the fact that "spiritual becoming" and "corporeal becoming" are one and the same thing, then Christianity could be seen as promoting cultivation, rather than renunciation, of the sexual.[86] While orthodox patristic theologians did affirm that Christ was truly human and truly divine, they did not take the next step to declare corporeal nature a "good" of creation.

What would cultivation of the sexual mean in the context of the Eucharist? Three possibilities present themselves. First, a focus on sexuality liberates women from a solely maternal function, empowering women's symbolic connectedness with their own mothers and with other women. Second, such a focus enables development of a relational Christology, through the affirmation of desire. Third, cultivation of the sexual in the context of women celebrants attests to women as "divine beings."

First, a focus on sexuality frees women from being viewed solely in terms of maternal functions. Irigaray argues that an unsymbolized mother-daughter relationship makes it nearly impossible for women to have an identity in the Symbolic order distinct from the maternal function. She discusses the function of the maternal-feminine as "container" or "envelope" for both the man and the child. Since this status has not been interpreted, the maternal-feminine remains inseparable from the work or act of man.[87] There is no place for the woman to be a container for herself. While the maternal function serves to mediate the generation of the son, it sets up no genealogy between mother and daughter. Irigaray explains that love of self among women is difficult because, traditionally, self-love is not differentiated from the mother-daughter relationship. In patriarchal society, if women are to be desired and loved by men, they must relinquish their mothers, substitute for them, or eliminate them, all of which destroy the possibility of love between mother and daughter.[88]

Irigaray indicates that women, unable to create their own words, remain in an immediacy without any transitional object. They take and give without mediation, commune without their knowing it, with and in a flesh they do not recognize.[89] She states: "We have to discover a language which does not replace the bodily encounter, as paternal language attempts to do, but which can go along with it, words which do not bar the corporeal, but which speak the corporeal." We must find words that speak the most archaic relationship with the mother, "sentences that translate the bond between her body, ours, and that of our daughters."[90] For Irigaray, it is necessary for a symbolism to be created among women for there to be love between them.[91]

Irigaray argues that in order for a woman to have access to her sexuality, she needs to be able to identify with, and at the same time differentiate and distance herself from, her own mother.[92] She needs to develop words, images, and symbols to express her intersubjective relationship with her mother as well as with other women. This is also necessary if she is to enter into a nondestructive relation with men.[93] Irigaray points out that while one can readily think of examples of the mother-son relationship, there is no maternal genealogy enshrined in Christian doctrine and iconography.[94] Woman today is orphaned, without a spiritual genealogy. In Irigaray's view, it is essential that women find themselves through female images already deposited in history, and not through man's genealogy.[95] Women must construct an identity model enabling them to situate themselves as women.[96] Irigaray offers ways in which this might happen, such as displaying images of the mother-daughter couple (Mary and her mother, Anne, for example) in non-exploitative ways.[97]

I have suggested that women priests celebrating the Eucharist would reclaim a maternal genealogy, expressive of the infant-mother relationship and female reproductive cycles. Women priests at the altar, giving the host to other women, would also help bring mother-daughter issues to the fore. This would be especially true for those priests who take on the title "Mother," corollary to the moniker of "Father" for male priests. Women priests who use "Mother" could help parishioners expand their perceptions of this term. One woman priest told me, for example, that using the title Mother allows parishioners to go beyond the domestic image. As priestly Mother, her relationships with others express an ongoing bond of intimacy, yet permit growth and change. Parishioners, she explained, can see that even the mother needs to be mothered.

In addition, women's different physical presence at the altar, especially voice, hair, and body, would alert parishioners to the symbol of woman as sexual as well as maternal being, empowering woman-woman connections. An Episcopal laywoman, for example, indicated that most of the women she has seen celebrate tend to be "very high on the expressivity scale," and their ritual gestures tend to look more genuine than the men's. She explained:

> One of the things I like about women celebrants is that women have different voices than men do. Their voices are on another register, and have more expression. The body is another difference: I knew two priests who were "big, curvy women, with big hairdos," who were into bodywork. One could not look at them and not think about questions like what does it mean for a woman to be a priest.

Irigaray further elucidates the symbol of the woman celebrant in terms of women's archaic relationships with other women. Since the first object of desire is a woman, women, for Irigaray, always stand in a primal relationship with homosexuality, while men stand in an archaic relationship with heterosexuality.[98] Thus, in addition to affirming their own bodies as givers of life, women celebrants symbolize a homosexual economy (i.e., symbol system) between priest and female worshiper and a heterosexual economy between priest and male worshiper.

The second possibility rendered by cultivation of the sexual is the affirmation of desire. Irigaray's discussion of desire is often framed in the context of *jouissance*, a term that generally refers to sexual ecstasy but that also encompasses spiritual, mental, and emotional pleasure. Irigaray asserts that woman's sexuality is *plural*: the pleasure of both the "vaginal caress" and the "clitoral caress" contribute to woman's pleasure.[99] *Jouissance*, in her view, is found in the return to the repressed female Imaginary. Female *jouissance*, expressed in the idea of lips that overlap by retouching one another, is, for Irigaray, an avenue for woman's becoming: "Female *jouissance* would be of the order of the constant and gradual creation of a dimension ranging from the most corporeal to the most spiritual, a dimension which is never complete and never reversible."[100]

Irigaray's notion of *jouissance* celebrates bodily connectivity while pointing to spiritual and emotional connection. In the context of women priests celebrating the Eucharist, desire should be acknowledged as a potent force for healing and connection. As feminist theologians have demonstrated, the erotic is a fundamental source of relationality and creativity, an important dimension of what it means to be human. Desire is healing and transformative when expressed in the context of loving and mutual relationships.[101]

In terms of Christology, to acknowledge desire is to profess the "self-in-relation." As discussed previously, eros from a feminist theological perspective is the manifestation of every individual's deep needs for connection with other human beings. To say that Jesus of Nazareth—the Christ—was sexual is to acknowledge that he had needs for connection with other human beings. But is that all there is to it? Jesus was never married, and despite contemporary movie portrayals such as *The Last Temptation of Christ*, he was not known to have had sexual relations. While some affirm the "queer Christ,"[102] the important message about Jesus' sexuality for our purposes is that he possessed incredible libidinal energy, which he in turn extended to others. Using Brock's notion of eros, by this I mean that Jesus drew upon healing, empowering, and liberating life forces. Borg describes this aspect of Jesus in terms of "spirit person" and "mediator of the sacred." "Mediators of the sacred," according to Borg, become funnels for the power or wisdom of God to enter this world. Historically, Borg states, Jesus was perceived both as an exorcist who cast out demons and as a healer of diseases.[103]

The woman priest, as a "representative human," expresses Christ as the self-in-relation, the human being who, through his teachings and life, wielded transformative libidinal power. Receiving the Eucharist is a very intimate experience between priest and worshiper, especially if the priest makes eye contact, as many women do. To experience the divine in the sacrament of the Eucharist, or Christ embodied for the forgiveness of sins, entails deep connection. Interestingly, while the woman priest decentralizes Jesus' maleness, she reemphasizes Christ's corporeality and the corporeal nature of the sacraments. As Catholic theologian Edward Schillebeeckx writes, "The incarnation of the divine life therefore involves bodily aspects. Together with this we must remember that every human exchange, or the intercourse of men [*sic*] with one another, proceeds through man's [*sic*] bodiliness."[104]

Several examples from ethnographic material illustrate how women priests would affirm a relational Christology, through fostering bonds of intimacy and connection between priest and parishioners. A woman priest told me, for example, that she was "blown away" the first time she saw a woman celebrant kneel down to give communion to the children—she put herself on their level. Since then this priest has also knelt when giving children communion, but she has never seen a man do this in all of the years she has been in the church. Another clergywoman I spoke with indicated that both men and women have told her the Eucharist has become more meaningful to them when she is celebrating. People feel more connected, and they say that her saying the words is an emotional experience for them. She related:

> In the early days, a lot of my anxiety came from how it was going to be for me and for others. Concern for the mechanics made it difficult to approach the Eucharist prayerfully. Now the important moments tend to be at the recitation over the cup, and over the bread, or at the anamnesis or epiclesis. The sacrament is an incredibly personal thing, and it is not to be made impersonal, rote, but an incarnation. I don't agree that the celebrant needs to be like a blank slate.

Similarly, a third woman priest I interviewed stated her belief that women clergy are more emotionally invested in the people than are male clergy during a eucharistic celebration. She noted, for example, that she looks at the congregation when she consecrates the elements, and she also uses the first names of parishioners when administering the bread. She knows priests who are too eager to move on to the next person, and she comments: "To me it needs to be a couple at that moment . . . it just needs to be the two of you. It needs to be finished before you go on to the next person. You just don't stuff a wafer in his face and keep mumbling words." Women priests, in her view, capture the eucharistic "holy moment" better than men do, because they allow themselves to feel in ways that men do not.

There are theologians who argue that a reformulation of Christology must be conceptualized in solely sociopolitical categories, to the exclusion of relationality. Schüssler Fiorenza, for example, offers critiques of Heyward's and Brock's relational Christologies, arguing that an epistemology of relationality reinforces the middle-class, white stereotype of feminity.[105] My own opinion is that the debate should not be either/or. Liberation and healing can take place on many levels, only one of which is political. Moreover, a commitment to social justice emerges *out of* relationality: that is, the recognition that one's self is part of the larger human community and that when anyone suffers, on some level we all do. Nor do I believe that relationality is equivalent to stereotypical femininity. A male priest I interviewed suggested that his model for women priests was a "mother with character," a mother who can say "my child is wrong" but still love her child. In the context of feminist theology, a variety of Christological reconceptualizations are necessary, among them political, psychological, emotional, and spiritual. As discussed, the advent of women priests would affirm right relation on many levels.

Third, a cultivation of the sexual in the context of women celebrants opens the door to acknowledgment of women as divine beings. Irigaray conceptualizes the divine as (1) corporeal, (2) sexuate, either male or female, (3) subject to becoming, (4) multiple, and (5) incarnated in us here and now.[106] God, for Irigaray, is a "sensible transcendental": a term designating "a material process of completion and integration, a movement always tending toward and becoming its own ideal."[107] Irigaray's understanding of God makes possible the view that nature and culture are a continuum rather than dichotomous. Why must God always remain "inaccessible transcendence," she asks, rather than a "here and now" realization through the body?[108] In her view, there should be a continuous passage of the natural into the cultural, and of the spiritual into the natural. She states: "God is beyond this world, but supposedly he [*sic*] already ensures its coherence here and now. Fluid, an interstitial flux, that cements everything and allows us to believe that the love of sameness has been overcome, whereas in fact that love has been raised to an incalculable power and swallows up the love of the other—the maternal feminine other—which has been assimilated to sameness."[109] God, for Irigaray, is the "principle of the ideal, a projection of the (sexed) subject onto a figure of perfection, an ego-ideal specific to that subject, a mode of self-completion without finality."[110] Irigaray's view of God shares much in common with process theology, which I will say more about shortly. God, for Irigaray, acts in the world like a fluid or glue, yet is beyond anything in this world. As she explains, "Transcendence is thus no longer ecstasy. . . . It is respect for the other whom I will never be, who is transcendent to me and to whom I am transcendent."[111] In other words, God is in us, and we are in God.

Irigaray states that the loss of divine representation has brought women to a "state of dereliction": it has left them without a means of symbolizing themselves, deprived mothers and daughters of mutually respectful mediums of exchange, and subjected them to a reproductive order governed symbolically by men.[112] Irigaray envisions an alternative Symbolic, which, by making a place for the woman, would enable a relation between the two parents. It would not replace the paternal metaphor with a maternal one but would allow the woman as lover, and mother as co-parent, to enter into the Symbolic.[113] Irigaray asks how a time and place can be established whereby the two sexes can touch each other without loss or residue, where one does not occupy the negative and the other the positive—where there is mutual recognition. Such a relation cannot exist if either sex has no positive identity, no relation of autoeroticism, no positive relation to members and ideals of its own sex.

While men have had to relinquish autoeroticism, women, as discussed earlier, have had to give up homosexual, particularly maternal, connections.[114]

If women alone continue to represent the body, or the sensible, then they are excluded from the ideal or transcendent. Irigaray suggests that the body should be recognized and symbolized in such a manner that women are no longer the sole guardians of the corporeal.[115] Obviously, this means that ways must be found for men to symbolize the corporeal as well. Irigaray is arguing for a "symbolic redistribution," so that men can accept the part of themselves that is "nature" and women can take on transcendental functions previously relegated to men.[116] The advent of women priests would help in this regard. For as we have seen, the Catholic priesthood would no longer be viewed as an asexual vocation but would be fraught with bodily significance. Several Episcopal women priests told me that the advent of women clergy has enabled issues of the body, such as rape, abortion, and domestic abuse, to surface in a way that they had not previously done.

God, language, and woman are linked, for Irigaray, in the idea of "becoming." God or language is defined in terms of becoming, as are woman and man.[117] Women's identity, for Irigaray, consists in the systematic non-split of nature and spirit, in the "touching together of these two universals."[118] Woman's "birth" into transcendence is both carnal and spiritual.[119] For Irigaray, it is only insofar as woman can become divine in and of herself, and not simply as mother, wife, or lover, that a notion of divinity appropriate to women becomes possible.[120] As woman becomes God, God is incarnated in woman.

In addition, in Irigaray's view a divine exchange between the sexes can occur only if women have their own concepts of God. Spiritual progress should be understood, for Irigaray, as the development of individual and collective dialogue between the sexes,[121] which can take place only insofar as each can "sample" the other's spiritual and sensible dimensions. A woman priest told me, for example, that she was uncomfortable with an all-female celebration and admonished that we need a "whole imagery" of priesthood.

Irigaray's notions of God as corporeal, in the process of becoming, and incarnated are not far from certain contemporary feminist theological views. Mary Daly's notion of God as "Be-ing"—intransitive and dynamic—for example, approximates Irigaray's understanding of God as becoming.[122] Nor, as stated earlier, are Irigaray's views foreign to a "process" understanding of God. Process theology emerged in the late 1970s and early 1980s and was strongly influenced by the philosophies of Alfred North Whitehead and Charles Hartshorne. According to Hartshorne, process theism is "dipolar": there is both an "abstract essence of God" (which is eternal, absolute, independent, and unchangeable) and a divine "concrete actuality" (temporal, relative, dependent, and constantly changing).[123] In contrast to the view of God in contemporary fundamentalism, God in process theology is not omnipotent, nor does God rule the world like a monarch. A divine being is not in absolute control of everything that happens. Instead, God is a "creative participant in the cosmos":[124] God influences us in the best possible direction but is not coercive.

Feminist theologian Sally McFague's concept of the "cosmic Christ" also embraces the process concept of the coming together of nature, culture, and spirit. In her view, the entire cosmos is the habitat of God, who is known through the physical world. Because God's body is coextensive with the natural world, for McFague creation is the place of salvation.[125] Jesus' paradigmatic ministry, in particular, is available through nature and is mediated through bodies. For both Irigaray and McFague, all bodies can be open to divine presence. I believe that both would find women at the altar, giving of body and blood, to be a powerful symbol of the natural world that provides bread and wine as physical sustenance. Women acting *in persona Christi* thus represent not only Christ as female but McFague's notion of the world as God's body: birthing, dying, renewing itself. This symbolism connects women with nature's capacities for renewal and regeneration, conjoining nature, humanity, and divinity. Interestingly, Paula Cooey offers a reconstruction of the doctrine of the incarnation (God's enfleshment in the person of Jesus) along these lines, making clear the full implications of "sentience." Cooey suggests that the doctrine "provides the foundation for a sacramental theology that transfigures pain and death without circumventing them, even while celebrating life."[126]

It is thus not surprising that a male priest I interviewed who objected to "downplaying the maleness of Jesus" also opposed liturgies that carry a tone of "naturalistic pantheism," an "overemphasis on God's revelation of God's self in creation." Birthing images also bothered him, for he saw them as breaking down the distinction between creator and created. In contrast, a woman priest I spoke with stated that women clergy help all people to see themselves as *in persona Christi*. One way she visually conveys this message is in the spatial arrangement at the front of the church. There is no typical communion rail, she explained, and the step on which the altar is situated is round and reaches out into the congregation. Another woman priest asked during our interview, "Do women, and also men, begin to understand themselves in a much more present, tangible way, as being made in the image of God, because of having male and female ministers at the altar?" Irigaray's work yields an affirmative answer.

Irigarayan theory suggests that whereas the anticipation of a woman celebrant may cause anxiety, her physical presence can affirm the co-presence of sexuality and the sacred. To illustrate, one woman priest I interviewed stated that she felt uneasy before she experienced her first woman celebrant, thinking, What's this going to be like? Is this wrong? Will God be upset? But as the woman began to celebrate, she told me, "she had the most melodious voice. It was loud enough to be heard and yet it was so feminine and strong and Godly all at the same time. And I experienced receiving Christ at the altar." She explained that in the course of that hour-long service, the "final brick from the wall" that had been keeping her from moving forward was removed. "That's how I changed my attitude about a woman celebrant at the Eucharist. . . . I had to be there. I had to see it. I had to see her own sanctity in it all. And I saw it." For this woman priest, "femaleness" was a contested presence at the altar until she actually witnessed a woman celebrant. The woman's actions at the altar enabled her to experience positive meaning in the juxtaposing of female sensuality—expressed here through voice—and a sacred rite.

In sum, Irigarayan theory suggests that when women celebrate the Eucharist, Christ represents not only woman as mother but also woman as daughter and lover. As such, women priests acting *in persona Christi* affirm desire or *jouissance*. A female celebrant also points to the fundamental *relational* nature of Jesus as "representative human," affirming the self-in-relation. Finally, a woman at the altar renders nature, culture, and God as a continuum rather than as the rigid dichotomies declared at Chalcedon, thus blurring the distinction between immanence and transcendence.

Before leaving Irigaray, I would like to return for a moment to sexuality. I have suggested that if women celebrated the Eucharist alongside men, the issue of sexuality would force its way into conscious awareness. Women clergy would open the Pandora's box of repressed sexual desire, desire that the Vatican has attempted to keep closed through perpetuation of a solely male priesthood. In a postmodern understanding, women priests would make a place for a female homoerotic economy—i.e., women symbolizing relationships with other women, including female divinity—as well as for a heterosexual one. Women clergy would force into awareness women's primary and archaic homosexual economy and men's primary and archaic heterosexual one. Taken to its conclusion, the presence of women celebrants would force men to acknowledge desire for the "other" of their earliest relationship, namely the mother. Notwithstanding the diversity of adult forms of erotic expression, I have postulated that all men have a residual desire for the mother. This desire often cannot be acknowledged because of the threat to masculinity of maternal engulfment—the fear of sinking back into feminine identification, of losing a carefully constructed male identity to the chaos of the pre-Oedipal or Imaginary. Similarly, so also do all women possess a deeply rooted desire for the object of their earliest relationship. The admittance of women to the priesthood would expose maternal desire on the part of both sexes, and, in the context of both men *and* women priests, would make possible a maternal as well as a paternal genealogy.

In sum, the work of Irigaray and Kristeva allows us to envision priestly representations of Christ that both enlarge on and take us beyond the maternal image. The pregnant woman-Christ lifts up themes of maternal generativity and "othering," as well as illuminates the cross as site of abjection and emergence of new life. Through symbolizing woman as divine being and relationships among women, the woman priest as erotic body offers important resources for finding positive meaning in sexuality and the sacred. The erotic woman-Christ also opens up possibilities for envisioning a more relational and inclusive Christology. Both models, woman priest as maternal body and woman priest as erotic body, juxtapose dualisms of transcendence and immanence, nature and culture, human and divine. Because they situate the taboo in a holy place, these priestly representations would be controversial. At the same time, they would offer enormous possibilities for the future enhancement of the Catholic faith.

7

WHEN WOMEN BECOME PRIESTS

I see women in a prophetic role, questioning the patriarchal foundation of institutional Christianity. To do that, you have to be in relation to the institution. That's why I'm here.
—*Female Episcopal priest*

Day-in-and-day-out relationships are really what begin to change how we act in the world. Here [at the parish] women are more and more not the "odd" thing. As it becomes true of women priests, it becomes more and more true of each woman.
—*Female Episcopal priest*

The shortage of priests in the Catholic Church has been a matter of concern for some time now. Between 1966 and 1984, the church witnessed a 20 percent drop in the number of active diocesan priests, and some predict that there will be an additional 20 percent decline in the number of such priests between 1985 and 2005. As noted by sociologist Ruth Wallace, the most significant factor is recruitment: by the late 1990s the ordination rate was 69 percent lower than it was in the mid-1960s. In addition, 46 percent of active diocesan clergy will be fifty-five years of age or older by 2005, and only 12 percent will be thirty-five or younger.[1] Despite these unsettling figures, Vatican officials remain vehemently opposed to ordaining women. To further discourage theologians from discussing the issue, in 1998 Pope John Paul II issued a statement declaring that deviations from Catholicism's "definitive truths"—among which were cited female priests, euthanasia, and sex outside marriage—constitute a violation of church law.[2]

Yet the title of this book implies that at some point in the future women will be ordained as priests in the Catholic Church. In the course of this project many people have asked my opinion on which will take place first: women becoming priests or priests getting married. If Catholic married men were ordained, the changes to the church would not be as radical as if women were allowed to become priests. Married male priests would raise the issue of sexuality but not that of women's "bodiliness." Gender reversal and maternal envy would remain primary dynamics of the Eucharist even with a married male priesthood, and Christ and God would continue to be viewed in terms of male symbolism. Perhaps this is why the Vatican has spoken more frequently and forcefully against ordaining women than against ordaining married men—and has in fact ordained certain Episcopal married priests who have converted to Catholicism.[3]

It is my conviction that women priests will not be officially permitted in the Catholic Church until there *are* women priests. In other words, Catholic women must be seen in a priestly role, in particular celebrating the Eucharist, in order to be approved and ordained as priests. I have spent much time here discussing the power of symbols, arguing that women priests celebrating mass would transform individuals and the social institution in powerful ways. Female symbols at the altar would underscore the "feminine" role of priest as feeder and nurturer. The symbol of a woman at the altar would bring pre-Oedipal components of the Eucharist to the fore and would provide a template for maternal transferences to parishioners. Women clergy would foster a less violent, less misogynistic notion of sacrifice, shifting the theological emphasis toward communion and birthing. The symbol of a woman at the altar would encourage an immanent, female image of divinity and would also raise issues of sexuality for the church.

In short, the ordination of women would empower women in the pews. It would also subvert the status quo by resisting and undermining androcentric-patriarchal power structures. The advent of women priests would attest to the ritual power of the Eucharist to bring about transformation in the Catholic Church. I begin by turning my attention to the subject of how women's ordination might take place. In this regard, it is helpful to explore the struggles experienced by Episopal women in attaining ordination to the priest-hood. I review the process by which Episcopal women achieved ordination in the 1970s in the United States and discuss battles that Episcopal women priests still have to face. It is also instructive to take a look at the steps that some Catholic women and men are taking in order for women to achieve greater visibility in priestly roles. I then reflect on how a psychological approach has addressed what difference women priests would make: for the priesthood, for parishioners' experience, for theology, and for the church. In conclusion, I answer lingering questions and offer a possible direction for the future.

HOW WILL WOMEN BECOME PRIESTS?

Episcopal Battles: Historic and Present-day

The lessons of history are often useful. I began by discussing changes that women Episcopal priests have brought to the church since the approval of women clergy in the United States in 1976. A review of the events leading to this landmark event brings perspective to movements of change ensuing in the Catholic Church today. An evaluation of these events also attests to the power of symbol and ritual to effect institutional change, for in the Episcopal Church, women did not officially become priests until they were already functioning as priests. I believe this will also be the case in the Catholic Church.

Most scholars would agree that the movement for women's ordination emerged as part of the larger struggle for gender equality within the Episcopal Church. Before the 1950s, in most dioceses women were prohibited from serving on parish vestries or representing the parish at diocesan functions.[5] Historian Pamela Darling observes that a 1969 action rendering women fully eligible to serve as lay readers, together with a 1970 ratification of the constitutional change admitting women to the House of Deputies (a national voting body within the Episcopal Church) were important legal adaptations improving women's status.[6] Two important changes in church law in the 1960s on the status of deaconesses laid the groundwork for the women's ordination movement: (1) mandatory celibacy was no longer enforced, and (2) the language of the installation of deaconesses was changed from "set apart" to "ordered."[7] The use of the term *ordered* meant that deaconesses were ordained to the diaconate the same way that men were, and it gave deaconesses the same ecclesial status as male deacons. Becoming a deacon is a necessary requirement for eligibility to the priesthood. Being "ordered" to the diaconate signified that women, similar to their male colleagues, were only one step away from becoming priests. These changes prompted a study committee to raise the question of admitting women to *all* orders of the church's ministry. The committee's report concluded that there were no dogmatic or biblical reasons against ordaining women and that there were psychological and sociological factors favoring it.[8]

The 1970 General Convention—the central governing body, composed of bishops, priests, and laypersons, which meets every three years—eliminated all distinctions between women and men as deacons. In 1971, Suzanne Hiatt became the first woman in the United States to be ordained to the diaconate under the new canon. According to one priest I interviewed, it was largely under her leadership that the movement for women's ordination surfaced and grew to such large proportions. An important aspect of Hiatt's work was *networking* among women around the country who were interested in being ordained. Hiatt was a trained, experienced community organizer,[9] and by 1973 several groups in support of women's ordination had been formed, among them the Episcopal Women's Caucus, Women's Ordination Now (WON), and the National Coalition for Women's Ordination to the Priesthood and Episcopacy.[10] The wider women's movement was advantageous and timely—the Episcopal women's groups gained some of their strength and momentum from consciousness-raising and other feminist groups who were strongly advocating women's rights.

As Darling explains, beginning in 1965 and extending to the first authorized ordinations in 1977, the campaign for women's ordination included about eight years of "conventional" politics, three years of "escalating confrontation and disobedience," and a follow-up period of reaction and adjustment. While women's inclusion in the diaconate was a long, slow process—in which deaconesses were willing to operate submissively within the bounds of acceptable feminine behavior—that was not to be the case for women's ordination.[11] When the movement for women clergy was defeated at the 1973 General Convention and a conservative presiding bishop was elected, many supporters felt a sense of futility about the political process. Some decided to seek ordination outside official channels, choosing to reinterpret authority and power in the church by claiming them for themselves.

   In 1974 an "irregular" ordination occurred. On July 29, eleven women were ordained to the priesthood in Philadelphia by three retired or resigned bishops, without prior diocesan approval. Four more women were ordained as priests in Washington, D.C., on September 7, 1975. Hiatt believes that the irregular ordinations were the only way for women to have achieved ordination.[12] The embedded message in these ordinations was that restoring equality between men and women as symbolized in priesthood was a greater good than following church discipline.[13] The ordinations were declared illegal and invalid by the reigning council of bishops—in fact, the bishops declared that no ordinations had occurred.[14] Interestingly, official reaction focused on punishing the ordaining bishops and male priests who invited women to celebrate the Eucharist, primarily on the grounds of violation of "collegiality." Moreover, censure statements revolved around a legalistic concern for order rather than theology or women's role. While Darling states that no disciplinary action was taken against the ordinands, Hiatt indicates that several of the women were admonished or suspended for exercising their ministry as priests.[15]

   Despite legal actions taken against male clergy supporters, women priests continued to celebrate the Eucharist in both private and public places. This action was significant in that it gave them *symbolic* and *political* power. People could see women functioning as priests, even though the bishops had declared that they were not. Hiatt explains that in the rite of ordination, the bishop does not "confer" priestly ordination but simply tells the ordinand to assume it. This is what happened in the case of women's ordination.[16] As one woman priest put it, "They simply took the authority, and they [the Episcopal Church] simply had to come 'round." It seems that not ordaining women had become more trouble than ordaining them.[17] On September 16, 1976, the sixty-fifth General Convention of the Episcopal Church in the U.S. voted to affirm the right of "fit and qualified" women to be admitted to the priesthood.[18] The first "regular" ordination of women clergy took place on January 1, 1977.

On February 11, 1989, the Episcopal Church in the U.S. appointed its first woman, Barbara Harris, to the episcopacy—i.e., to the office of bishop. It is interesting to note the controversy stirred up by this action. One reason given was that a priest is generally required to have been ordained for ten years before being eligible for the episcopacy, and Harris had been a priest for only eight years. Other reasons for the controversy were that she was divorced and was without a college degree. A more significant reason for opposition was that bishops have the power to confer ordination on deacons seeking the priesthood. At issue here was a woman's political power. Some opponents argued that when women gained power to ordain other women, the number of priests would mushroom and would get out of (men's) control.[19] Traditionalists objected on the grounds that as long as women were ordained only to the diaconate and priesthood, they could either avoid or exclude them. But a woman bishop would have a place in the authority structure that would make these options impossible. How would one know, for example, whether a male priest celebrating the Eucharist had been ordained by a woman bishop?[20]

Significantly, Bishop Harris at her consecration co-celebrated the Eucharist with a Chinese woman ordained to the priesthood in 1944 in Hong Kong. Research shows that the Reverend Li Tim Oi had never renounced her orders, despite requests that she do so.[21] Though this discussion has focused solely on the American situation, Episcopal women continue to struggle for ordination worldwide. The Anglican Church of England voted to admit women to the priesthood in 1992. Hiatt reports that in that same year, half of the provinces in the Anglican communion (fourteen out of thirty-four) ordained women to the priesthood.[22] Eleven women bishops were present at the 1998 Lambeth Conference.

Now that "the priest *is* a woman," issues of gender equality are far from resolved in the Episcopal Church. While statistics show a steady increase in Episcopal women priests over the past twenty years, ambivalent and even hostile attitudes toward their presence remain. The Reverend Alla Bozarth-Campbell expressed in 1984: "I'm worried because the question of ten years ago, 'Are we doing the right thing, or are we just opening up the male priesthood to create female patriarchs?' has not yet been fully answered. It's very lonely for women priests with no female role models. We have to create our own role models."[23]

The same year, the Reverend Nancy Hatch Wittig noted that "women are not taken seriously in terms of jobs, ministry, or even presence."[24] One important manifestation of ambivalence toward women is in terms of jobs and pay.[25] According to a study in *Clergy Women: An Uphill Calling*, published in 1998, the mean salary for full-time Episcopal clergywomen was $40,489, compared to $47,173 for full-time Episcopal clergymen.[26] Louie Crew of Rutgers University indicates that in 1998 women priests constituted only 9.7 percent of 3,902 rectors (sole pastors of parishes that can pay their salaries) in the United States, and 17.7 percent of 1,062 vicars (pastors serving congregations that cannot pay their salaries).[27] As mentioned earlier, approximately 13.8 percent of Episcopal priests in the United States in 1998 were women.

My interviews confirm that women priests do not get the same types of jobs or compensation as male priests. A male priest I spoke with indicated that very few churches that are large enough to employ an assistant have a woman as senior pastor. A woman priest told me that one of the differences between men and women priests in her diocese is that women have to settle for less. Another clergywoman explained that women are still not accepted as rectors of parishes. An Episcopal laywoman related that several of the first women priests indicated to her that if they had had any idea of the kind of emotional abuse they were going to be subjected to, they would have chosen not to be ordained.

Related to this issue of women's full equality in the church, Paula Nesbitt discusses the recent phenomenon of "dual ordination tracks" and their impact on men and women Episcopal clergy.

Beginning in the mid-1970s, substantial denominational attention focused on redefining and professionalizing the role of the permanent deacon, including development of training programs specifically geared for that ordination track. The primary difference between the permanent deacon and the priest is that the permanent deacon does not have the authority to celebrate the Eucharist or to give blessings or absolution. Nesbitt observes that by 1985, the sex composition of those entering the permanent diaconate had changed from predominantly male to female and that the trend has remained steady since. She concludes that while the newer ordination track may serve legitimate organizational needs—and is a response to increasing pressures of "occupational feminization"—it may have a negative influence on the careers of women clergy. In particular, it leaves open the possibility for marginalization, segregation, or discrimination in opportunities for women priests.[28]

As well, the fear is increasing that the Episcopal priesthood is becoming structurally identified with femininity rather than masculinity. An Episcopal laywoman I interviewed suggested that fear of loss of status fueled objections by male priests to women clergy in the 1960s and 1970s. Studies indicate that candidates entering diocesan ordination processes are increasingly female, predominantly middle-aged, and openly homosexual. While figures indicate that young men began choosing other professional fields well before women started entering graduate programs in religion, women's entrance into the priesthood has been blamed for the decline in numbers of male clergy.[29] A priest I interviewed echoed this concern, stating that one of her personal fears is that ordained ministry will become viewed as "women's work" and hence devalued.

As of 1999, women clergy are still not entirely accepted in the Episcopal Church. One issue that surfaced at the 1998 Lambeth Conference was that of "compulsion": that is, must bishops make ordination accessible to all, regardless of gender, in countries where the ordination of women is permitted? The resolution that passed advises Anglican provinces to "uphold the principle of 'open reception' as it relates to the ordination of women to the priesthood," while "recognizing that there is and should be no compulsion on any bishop in matters concerning ordination or licensing."[30] In other words, bishops opposed to women as priests do not have to ordain them. This resolution calls into question a canon passed at the U.S. General Convention in 1997, mandating that all bishops allow women priests to minister in their dioceses. Shortly after the resolution passed, Bishop Chilton Knudsen of the diocese of Maine reported that it was internally inconsistent, "because reception requires exposure and [the action] limits exposure of people to the ministry of women."[31] The Lambeth resolution has the potential to affect several dioceses in the United States that, as of 1999, still do not ordain women or allow women priests to function.

Harbingers of Change in Catholicism

If acceptance of women priests requires exposure to women priests, how can women claim symbolic and political power in the Catholic Church—especially when separate, autonomous, legislative bodies do not exist nor is there lay involvement in decision-making processes? For at this point, there are no Catholic women deacons, nor is there a Catholic equivalent to the Episcopal House of Deputies. Interestingly, in recent years some have discussed establishing a separate order of Catholic female deaconesses. In support of this, the 1994 apostolic letter addresses only whether women can be priests, not whether they can be deacons.[32] The recovery and re-creation of the distinct ministry exercised by women in the New Testament has been argued.[33] In my view, female deaconesses are not likely to be approved very quickly, particularly since religious orders are an option for Catholic women called to religious life.

Like the "Philadelphia Eleven" and their supporters, a growing number of Catholics committed to women's equality have become impatient with formal channels and are choosing to disobey church law. As with the Philadelphia ordinations, this activism is likely both to engender greater support for women priests and to heighten tensions within the church. I see three ways in which women are gaining greater symbolic power within the Catholic Church: as women "pastors," through the actions of courageous priests, and by celebrating the Eucharist "unofficially."

First, one legal means by which women are becoming more visible in priestly roles is as administrators of priestless parishes. In

1983 revised canon law included a provision for persons other than priests to exercise pastoral care. This opened the door for recruitment of women as pastoral administrators.[34] Ruth Wallace focuses much of her attention in *They Call Her Pastor: A New Role for Catholic Women* on exploring the differences that women pastors make in the lives of their congregations.

Wallace reports that under the guidance of supportive priests, women pastors read Scripture, preach the sermon, and sometimes distribute communion alongside the priests in the sanctuary. Several women pastors indicated that they share the baptismal rite with the priest. In cases of priestly "no show," the woman pastor presides at a "word and communion service" instead of mass (pp. 114, 144, 137). Wallace observes that sometimes this role causes conflict: "Older and more conservative Catholics are especially bothered by the sight of a woman leading the services at the altar" (p. 141).

Yet there is strong indication in Wallace's book that the presence of women in a ministerial capacity can change people's attitudes concerning women clergy. As one woman pastor stated regarding her role: "It's a problem for the hierarchy; it isn't a problem for the average people. . . . It was taught to them, and they can learn to get past that, just as they can learn to get past judging a person because they are black or Mexican or Oriental" (p. 157). Wallace observes that even parishioners who described themselves as traditional Catholics told her that they had changed their attitudes regarding women in the church as a result of their woman pastor. The overwhelming majority of parishioners interviewed, she reports, are opposed to patriarchy and gender discrimination (p. 165).

Several of the women Episcopal priests I spoke with indicated that, of the parishioners who initially objected to their ministry, many came to accept them as priests after witnessing the fruits of their work in the church. One priest stated: "I have had men and women come to my office, usually shaken and in tears, saying, 'When you first came, I did not think it was right that you were a priest. But because I've seen God work through you, and I see the Holy Spirit in your ministry here, I have no doubt now that you're doing what God called you to do.'" Another woman priest told me that when she was standing in line to go in for her ordination, half of the congregation came up to her and said that they had changed their minds and that now they were extremely happy she was being "priested." During the announcements portion of the service, a priest who had been opposed to her ordination stood up and declared, "They say a leopard can't change its spots, but I'm here to tell you that a leopard can." She reported that the congregation gave him a standing ovation. A third priest indicated that when parishioners get to know her as a person, often prejudices fall away. A number of men have told her that before her ministry in the church they never would have accepted a woman priest, but because of their experience with her, they have changed their minds.

Wallace foresees that as the shortage of priests becomes more critical, the laity will be asking in increasing numbers—"Why *not* women pastors?" and "Why *not* married priests?" (p. 177). Not surprisingly, the point of greatest tension for women pastors is that because only an ordained priest can celebrate the Eucharist, they cannot totally minister to their parishioners. One must raise the question of whether an individual can be a good sacramental minister without also exercising pastoral leadership in the community. In a book banned by the Vatican, Lavinia Byrne argues that by refusing to ordain women, the church risks separating its teaching from its sacramental authority, a division that is both artificial and false to the deepest instincts of Catholicism.[35] If some kind of ministerial link is not maintained, does not the Eucharist risk being cut off from the rest of the life of the community?[36] This is often what happens in priestless parishes.

A second way women are becoming more visible in priestly roles is through male priests' risking their careers to put them there. This is illustrated by a controversy stirred up by a priest in Rochester, New York. In 1998 Father James Callan was "fired" from Corpus Christi Church by the CDF (Congregation for the Doctrine of the Faith). Under his twenty years of leadership, the membership of Corpus Christi had grown from 200 in 1976, the year before Father Callan arrived, to approximately 3,400 in 1998.[37] As reported by Callan, reasons given for the reassignment were the church's ministry to gays, active leadership roles for women—including "priest-like participation"—and distribution of communion to persons of all Christian denominations.[38] At the time, Callan commented: "I am being reassigned to another church so that this church can be brought more in line with what the Vatican would like" (p. A1). Catholic Citizens for a Decent Community, a group sharply critical of Callan, had sent copies to the Vatican of a photo of a woman holding an uplifted communion chalice at the church. The Vatican responded by criticizing Callan for allowing a female pastoral associate to wear a stole, the symbol of the diaconate and priesthood. Callan refused to back down, stating: "To me this is an embarrassment. . . . when we have a world filled with such big problems and they are worried about Mary [Ramerman] wearing the stole and holding the bread and wine" (p. A1). Callan remained undaunted in the face of his future reassignment, explaining, "I plan to take the same values and work towards the same goals. I hope wherever I go I will be joined by women and men in leadership positions. I hope to have a complete gay ministry and an openness to everyone at the Communion table" (p. A1). The news of Callan's reassignment sparked an uproar in the church, and many members vowed to carry on his principles even after his departure. After his firing, between four hundred and five hundred members of Corpus Christi Church began regularly assembling at a downtown Presbyterian church, where Ramerman, who lost her job as pastoral associate, was leading services.[39] This example further illustrates parishioners' support for women in priestly roles. As of December 1998, Callan had been suspended by the bishop, an action that strips him of his ability to perform priestly functions.[40]

A third way in which women are claiming symbolic power in the Catholic Church is through celebrating the Eucharist "unofficially," i.e., without consecration by a priest. Sheila Durkins Dierks investigates a number of such informal groups, identifying more than one hundred eucharistic gatherings that meet at least once a month.[41] In addition, a group called Critical Mass celebrates the Eucharist publicly in major cities. I find it interesting that a critique of Critical Mass offered by Bishop John Cummins focuses on the "misuse" of the Eucharist, but not on the issue of whether the women are indeed celebrating a Eucharist.[42] Dierks indicates that of 102 responses to a question concerning eucharistic theology on her questionnaire, 56 percent answered that at "WomenEucharists" (WE) it is believed that the bread and wine become the body and blood of Christ. Most responses, states Dierks, reveal a belief that Jesus is really present in the elements of bread and wine during WE.[43] The women who answered in this way believe that women and laypersons have the same ability to consecrate the elements that a priest has. Similarly, a position paper issued by Critical Mass organizers declares: "We believe that when the Christian community celebrates Eucharist, Jesus is truly present, as He is truly present whenever we gather for prayer, feed the hungry and clothe the naked, mourn with those who suffer, work for justice and peace, and celebrate, heal and reconcile in His name."[44] To illustrate, journalist Jane Redmont reports of a Critical Mass celebration held in Oakland, California, on October 5, 1997:

> We hold the loaves of bread and the cups of red wine close to our hearts: This is my body, this is my blood. First in a circle, facing the altar, then facing the assembly, the rest of the wide circle in which we stand. After placing the gifts back on the table, we touch each other's arms. We repeat: This is my body; this is my blood; and move into the congregation to share and spread this gesture and these words. . . . I understand the body of Christ in a way I had not before, not at any rate as deeply, with a knowledge inside the flesh.[45]

Critical Mass loosely follows the structure of the Catholic mass but uses drama and music to reinvent the ritual from a feminist point of view. One of the group's functions is to transform the Eucharist into an empowering ritual for women. While in general WE groups do not seem to share an explicitly feminist agenda, a frequent result of shared celebration is women's greater sense of affirmation and agency. Dierks writes that women need to see women handling the bread and wine, not just as eucharistic ministers but as consecrators, "with the deed recognized and affirmed as sacred."[46]

The examples cited illustrate ways in which women are beginning to assume greater sacramental roles in the Catholic Church. These women, over time, will cause parishioners to view them symbolically as priests. We can see that Episcopal women clergy attest to the power of symbols to affect people's psyches in deep and enduring ways. Episcopal women achieved ordination by taking advantage of the transformative power of ritual. Through celebrating the Eucharist, they convinced others that women's ordination was just and also beneficial to the church. In time, Catholic women will do so as well.

WHAT DIFFERENCE WILL WOMEN PRIESTS MAKE?

Psychological Findings

It is helpful to reflect here on what difference women priests would make for the priesthood, for the parishioner, for theology, and for the church at large. How has a psychological approach furthered our discussion of the questions asked in the introduction? Which questions remain to be answered? I believe that a theological methodology is insightful but insufficient to account for resistance to women clergy and how they would make a difference. The psychologies of Freud, object relations theorists, and French feminist psychoanalytic thinkers allow a deeper reading of the issues at stake in women's ordination to the priesthood and also enable readers to more fully appreciate the extent of difference that women priests would bring to the Catholic Church.

First, what difference would women clergy make for the priesthood? We have seen that the priesthood is integrally tied to the sacrament of the Eucharist. Psychology discloses the existence of maternal themes in both the Eucharist and the priesthood. The primary issues of union, separation, and reparation—concerns pertinent to the early relationship between mother and infant—are expressed in eucharistic theology. When only men are allowed to be ordained as priests, a gender reversal of male and female reproductive and nurturing roles occurs. Through using a psychological method, I showed that if women were allowed to co-celebrate with men, the priesthood would embody inclusiveness on both divine and human levels.

A psychological perspective advances the idea that maternal transferences are stronger when women celebrate than when men celebrate, and that this difference has implications for theology. As for priesthood, transference has an effect on leadership styles. Models of the priest as a "hostess" who is concerned about setting a "good-looking table" and a "family model" with "mother presiding at dinner" emerge when a woman presides at the altar. These models indicate that women priests bring a less authoritative style to eucharistic celebration.

We have seen that, psychologically, opposition to women priests resides in gender identity issues. Internalized images of a white male Christ, along with rigid psychic boundaries, can fuel additional ambivalence toward women as priests. The fact that women clergy have been historically forbidden can also make problematic the way women celebrants are received by parishioners. Since women have not generally represented the holy in Christian heritage, women priests illustrate the tension inherent in juxtaposing the taboo and the sacred. We have also seen that the dichotomy between the taboo and the sacred breaks down when women celebrate mass. The woman priest comes to represent *both* divinity and humanity, because God, humanity, and nature are viewed on a continuum when women are at the altar.

Second, what difference would women priests make for the parishioner? Clearly, women priests would bring a very different physical presence to the Eucharist. Object relations theory provides an explanation of how and why the benefits of women's presence at the altar are realized psychologically. Women's blood, for example, can be given positive meaning for parishioners in terms of birthing. Maternal transference furnishes an explanation for increased accounts of nurturing and feeding imagery reported by parishioners when women celebrate. Through transference, women can also identify their own suffering with the suffering of Christ. While women's menstrual blood remains a contested presence, it is a necessary one if women and men are to overcome the notion that the female body is impure. As well, the juxtaposition of sexuality with spirituality at the altar can be viewed affirmatively when women are celebrants.

A psychological approach elucidates underlying resistances by some parishioners to women priests, especially maternal fear and envy and consequent male desire for feminine identification. Interestingly, while I was completing the final draft of this manuscript, a man (who happened to be a conservative Catholic) came to my apartment to repair my printer. When he learned the subject of my book, his immediate response was, "Well, men cannot become pregnant. There are some things women cannot do." I have not yet addressed to what degree male gender identity issues are found in parishioners versus priests—this could be an area for future exploration.

Third, what difference would women clergy make for theology? I believe women priests would have far-reaching effects on the field. The ordination of women to the Catholic priesthood would cause both Catholic and Protestant theologians to think deeply about the nature of God and Christ. Through its symbolic analysis of the woman at the altar, a psychological approach expands contemporary feminist thought on sacrifice, Christology, and how we contemplate God. My use of psychology illuminates that the figure of the early mother becomes present to the believer through the eucharistic elements of bread and wine. Thus, women celebrants would make more explicit the underlying pre-Oedipal themes in the Eucharist. In demonstrating that the Eucharist expresses maternal as well as paternal themes, I established the need for both female and male symbolism at the altar.

Among the most profound theological effects of women priests would be shifts in understandings of sacrifice and Christology. A psychological method also brings to the fore the effects of sexuality on theology. Women's presence at the altar cannot help but be a sexual presence, and sexuality is an inevitable component of a theology of immanence. Psychology also illuminates how the presence of women priests functions to break down Western dualisms. Moreover, a psychological approach emphasizes the importance of a relational Christology, with Christ as the "self-in-relation." Women priests are altering symbols of God at a very deep level, causing images and experiences of divinity to expand in ways that both affirm women's functions and roles and present new possibilities for them.

Lastly, what difference would women priests make for the church? Clearly, women clergy would alter the androcentric-patriarchal foundation of the institutional church. While women's ordination to the Catholic priesthood would certainly not eliminate all resistance to women as priests, their advent would make possible enormous positive change for the church at large. I have addressed the latent "feminine" nature of priesthood and church in numerous ways in this study. Since the priest acts *in persona ecclesiae* as well as *in persona Christi*, changes in the priesthood would also manifest themselves on an institutional level, thus creating a vision of a "feminine church." What might this mean?

If women were ordained, the church as the "body of Christ" would be more inclusive than it currently is. Parishioners would see both men and women at the altar, and as a result they would have a more complete picture of the church. Women priests would enable the church to address a wider realm of human experience. Because of their history of oppression, women priests would heighten the cause of overturning injustice worldwide. Issues that particularly affect women—such as rape, poverty, and domestic violence—would also receive greater attention.

Since women celebrants would bring unique resources to their ministries, their presence would result in a different notion of "church." Leadership style is one dimension of this difference. Women bring a less authoritative style to eucharistic celebration, and this would lead to a less authoritative church. We have learned that women priests raise the human element to greater awareness, including sexuality. They also present a model in which everyone represents Christ. These two aspects of women's ministries—the priest as human and the layperson as *alter Christus*—would foster a more holistic notion of church. Women priests would affirm that the heart of the church is not the Vatican, but the body of the faithful worldwide. I believe the ordination of women to the priesthood would generate greater global membership. More women would join Catholic churches in order to gain the benefits women priests have to offer. While conservative men would leave Catholic churches, liberal men would convert or return to Catholicism because of the image of wholeness and inclusivity fostered by women priests. Catholic men who feel a call to be part of this inclusive model would enter the priesthood. Catholic women would likely enter the priesthood in large numbers, especially those women who have experienced a call for years.

The ordination of women to the priesthood would be of enormous symbolic significance for the Catholic Church at large. A more egalitarian church would further the notion of the "catholic" (or universal) church as a community in which all are equal before God and all have equal access to salvation. The advent of women priests would improve ecumenical dialogue. The Catholic Church could function as a beacon of equality in those cultures that still do not grant women the same legal rights as men. The advent of women priests would also cause a shift in the way the church understands itself in relation to the "ideal" or "saved" church. While there will never be a utopian church on earth, the earthly church with women priests would come closer to representing a future eschatological, or saved, community.

Many questions remain to be explored about what difference women priests would make. I have not discussed *which* women will become the first Catholic women priests—pastoral associates who are already assuming the priestly role, members of female religious orders, or perhaps Anglican clergywomen who convert to Catholicism. Nor have I addressed how women priests might affect the church's stand on other controversial issues, such as married priests, abortion, or contraception. I have not looked at cross-cultural issues that the advent of women priests could raise, or the possible schisms in the church as a result. The timing of the Vatican's approval of women's ordination is also out of range of a psychological purview. In discussing these four subtopics, I have tried to demonstrate how a psychological approach is best equipped to answer questions regarding the "how" and "why" of ordaining women priests, particularly as these questions pertain to religious symbolism.

Lingering Questions

This section is structured as an informal "Q and A." Some of the following questions were posed to me by others, and some reflect my own musings.

Q: Your argument suggests that women will make *better* priests than men. Are there any redeeming qualities for males in the priesthood?

A: I have argued that women will make *different* priests than men. Does that make them better? Women bring different resources and histories to priesthood than men do. They present different models, especially for women, models that are currently unavailable within Catholicism. The interviews suggest that women clergy tend to be more relationally oriented and more self-consciously interested in fostering bonds of intimacy and connection than male priests have been. But that certainly doesn't mean that male priests aren't interested in these things also. In fact, my experience in seminary was that male seminarians were more comfortable in nurturing and caretaking roles than those who fit the average profile of an American man and that women seminarians were more "phallic," to use psychoanalytic parlance, than the average American female. What I think happened was that the early female Episcopal priests had to be more traditionally "masculine" in order to make it through the process and survive in parishes. With time, women clergy have become more accepted, and they have brought with them resources and concerns such as those that I have discussed. Women are feeling more comfortable with who they are, and they are modeling this to parishioners. For example, a friend of mine who is an ordained United Church of Christ minister has changed her hairstyle over the years. She has naturally curly, thick black hair, which she wore up in a bun when she began her career because she felt it was too wild and feminine. Now she wears it down, loose around her shoulders. Today she feels she can be seen as both a woman and a religious authority, whereas a decade ago she wasn't sure that she could. This doesn't necessarily make her a better minister than a man, but she does present a model for women that they didn't have before.

Presenting alternative models of masculinity is where I think the redeeming qualities of male priesthood can be found. Over the centuries, a solely male priesthood has contributed to some extremely patriarchal theology and a sense of male exclusivity. What male priests can do today is offer examples of masculinity that are less androcentric-patriarchal and more tolerant and inclusive. It would be wonderful if we reached a point where male priests symbolized birthing, connection, and communion to people to the same degree that women priests can. But we are not at that point yet. Given the rigid image of masculinity presented by many contemporary fundamentalists, we need male priests who are willing to take on the caretaking role—the "nurturing father" image. Nurturing fathers are sorely needed if boys are to grow up to be well-integrated men, and male priests can help foster that image. In addition, women will not get very far in their struggle for ordination without supportive male priests and bishops. While this book primarily concerns the significance of women priests, it does not negate the need for good male priests.

Q: Is it always better to be relationally oriented? Doesn't this book stereotype women and men? Aren't men as capable of understanding themselves as "selves-in-relation" as women are?

A: Over the years I have come to believe that, yes, it is always better to be relationally oriented. This is because spirituality is *about* relation—with God, other, cosmos. This notion is found not only in monotheistic traditions but even in nontheistic Buddhism, where the goal of practice is to realize selflessness—to embrace that there really is no difference between self and other. Relationality is indeed a goal of religious practice.

From a feminist perspective, it is a somewhat different story. Women have been accused of being too relational, of not having enough sense of self. Yet at the same time, feminists would not want to return to the Cartesian "I think, therefore I am" notion of the autonomous self (i.e., a self cut off from body and other selves). That's why the term *self-in-relation* has become important. A feminist perspective acknowledges that yes, we are individual selves, but we also live in community. The struggle then becomes how to develop a strong identity while at the same time recognizing our interdependence with others. We cause others and ourselves pain when we do not realize our connections. I think relationality in balance with self-fulfillment is a desirable goal.

Yes, I do believe that men are as capable of understanding themselves as selves-in-relation as women are, but most have not been socialized that way. This is still true. Of course, there are some male theologians who have written theologies of relation. James Jones, for example, in *Religion and Psychology in Transition: Psychoanalysis, Feminism, and Theology* points out that Schleiermacher and Buber produced very relational theologies.[47] The feminist theology that has emerged in recent years, however, has *overwhelmingly* been concerned with issues of relationality. It does not seem to be as pressing an issue for male theologians, even today.

As for stereotyping, I was a bit surprised that most of the priests

I interviewed both in 1988 and in 1998 believed that women priests brought "softer," more traditionally "feminine" elements to the Eucharist and the Episcopal tradition at large. I thought I would find that in 1998 the styles of the women were not so different from the styles of the men anymore. Perhaps in another decade this will be true, but it isn't yet. Women are still pulled in directions suggested by Chodorow and Gilligan, and their theories will probably hold true as long as women are the primary caretakers of children.

Q: Where is God in a pre-Oedipal reading of the Eucharist?

A: A pre-Oedipal analysis of the Eucharist does not remove God from the ritual. God is still there. God is most commonly experienced, however, through relationships with others. When we experience connection with mother (or father) in the Eucharist, we also encounter the divine. A psychological approach offers a means of bridging the gap between theology and psychology. Psychological theorizing deepens understandings of the Eucharist, and these understandings in turn inform the psychological methodology that I utilize. At no point do I argue that the Eucharist is *only* a pre-Oedipal ritual commemorating the relationship of mothers and infants or that the female priest symbolizes the archaic mother figure alone.

I think theologians have a great deal to learn from psychologists of religion. A basic assumption in my research is that psychological development shapes not only who we are as individuals but also how we understand the nature of God, Christ, and church. Most psychologists acknowledge that our relationships and values are initially shaped by our parents. Why not also beliefs about God and the Eucharist? I have tried to show here that there are many levels of meaning conveyed by religious symbols. Our psyches largely shape our understanding of reality, and yet psychological meaning is not usually addressed. The importance of early parental relationships to psychological development cannot be overemphasized. They are also important to religious development.[48] A pre-Oedipal reading of the Eucharist takes these insights into account.

Q: If men harbor such intense envy and fear of feminine identification, is there any hope for the future of Catholic women's ordination? Why don't we see gender reversal in other spheres of life?

A: First of all, I believe that male-dominated religions originated to deal with fear and envy of female power. This is not my own idea—

scholars such as Mary Daly and Naomi Goldenberg have put it much more eloquently. Daly, for example, discusses gender reversal in the Hebrew creation myth—the birth of Eve from Adam's rib.[49] Baptism by a solely male priesthood also expresses a gender reversal. Goldenberg gave a lecture at Nebraska Wesleyan University a few years ago titled "A Feminist, Psychoanalytic Reflection on 'The Cat in the Hat Comes Back': Exploring the Male Claim to the Ownership of Sacred Texts," in which she examined ways that the sacred texts of Judaism, Christianity, and Islam appropriate and denigrate female functions while reifying maleness.[50] Envy and fear of feminine identification are found in other spheres of life, but they are particularly prominent in those religious systems that originated in a setting of male dominance.

Where Goldenberg and I differ is in our view of the future. She argues that feminists should flee from male-dominated religions because the central beliefs of such religions are predicated on female suppression.[51] I have more hope for the future of these traditions, because I think it is possible to remain within an established tradition and bring about change. As stated, however, women's ordination in the Catholic Church will not happen without the support of men. In particular, men are needed who are comfortable with who they are and who are able to deal with their mother issues. Male priests especially must closely examine their reasons for opposing women clergy. I would not go so far as to advocate psychoanalysis, but male priests do need to come to terms with the traditionally feminine nature of their profession and with the nature of the Eucharist as a ritual of feeding and nurture. In Jungian terms, male priests need to integrate their "feminine side," which will probably mean facing their "animus" or "shadow." The future of Catholic women's ordination lies in a continual struggle for it on the part of both men and women and in a conversion of the male hierarchy.

The Future

What will the future of women's ordination in the Catholic Church be? I have suggested here that women priests will not be approved until women become more visible in sacramental roles. It is my hope that more women who are called to the priesthood will "present themselves" to their bishops for ordination, as a woman did in Kentucky in January 1998. Her story offers inspiration to all those women and men who would like to see women ordained within their lifetimes.

Before Janice Sevre-Duszynska made national news in mid-January by asking to be ordained during a ceremony at the cathedral in Lexington, Ky., she had tried the usual forms of protest to dramatize her distress over the church's ban on women priests.

In a recent telephone interview, she recited a litany of her previous efforts: wearing blue arm bands to protest outside the site of ordinations, joining in for-women-only eucharistic celebrations, speaking and writing to bishops, carry placards promoting women priests.

Last spring, she even applied for a job as pastor at the University of Kentucky Newman Center in Lexington, knowing how unlikely it was that she would get it. . . .

"What is a person like me supposed to do," she wondered aloud. "There is no dialogue."

That lack, she said, prompted her resolve to present herself for ordination at the Cathedral of Christ the King on Jan. 17, her 48th birthday and the day Charles W. Howell Jr. was being ordained a priest in Lexington.

"When I decided on it, my body shook like an earthquake for three hours," she said. "Even thinking about it, I was aware of just how much strength it would take. I honestly didn't know how I was going to move my body to get up there." . . .

Sevre-Duszynska attributes her . . .[bold] action in mid-January to newfound courage after a series of personal losses. In 1990 she lost the younger of her two sons, Brian Thomas, then 18, in an automobile accident. Subsequently, her marriage of nearly a quarter-century ended in bitter divorce. . . .

In December, Sevre-Duszynska purchased an alb and a red cincture from a Protestant supply house. She then wrote cards to supporters, including three priests in Lexington, to tell them of her evolving plans.

To the priests, she wrote, "You are my fellow priests. . . . On Jan. 17 I will take my place as your fellow priestess. We know each other, and I look to you for strength." To Howell she wrote, "I welcome you as a fellow priest to serve in the dynamic movement of human liberation from selfishness and exploitation. Sometimes, as in Acts 17:6, that means turning the world upside down. . . . At your ordination I must quietly though boldly act from my experience. I pray you'll respect and understand."

Meanwhile, she was praying, tossing and turning at night, gathering courage, she said.

On the day of Howell's ordination, she arrived early at the cathedral wearing a long coat and scarf to cover her alb. She took a seat on the aisle about 12 rows from the sanctuary.

When Williams called Howell's name, Sevre-Duszynska was ready. In an action that some described as dramatic and riveting, she strode quickly toward the sanctuary carrying her mother's hand-crocheted handkerchief and a tiger lily in her hand. The lily, she said, symbolized the year of the tiger—the Chinese sign she was born under.

Sevre-Duszynska remembers herself calling out, "Bishop Williams, Bishop Williams, I am called by the Holy Spirit to present myself for ordination. My name is Janice. I ask this for myself and for all women."

She then prostrated herself at the right of the altar, where the bishop was sitting. Williams replied, "I feel your pain and I sense that you feel you are called to ordination." Sevre-Duszynska recalls that he asked her to return to her seat, quietly accusing her of being disruptive.

She stood, reciting the names of women from the Bible and women saints, recalling, she said, the historical oppression of women.

"I said, 'I am all the oppressed of the Bible who cried out to the Lord who heard their prayer. I am Sarah, I am Hannah, I am Elizabeth, I am the woman who touched the hem of Jesus' garment, I am the woman who poured oil over

Jesus' head. I am Veronica. I came here today hoping for a miracle, inspired by my patron saint, St. Joan of Arc. I hoped you would ordain me for all women.'"

Williams said, "I feel your pain and I pray to God for women like you," though later he told the congregation that he considered disrupting worship to be "a very serious act." During his homily, he addressed Howell, saying, "Charles, I would be remiss if I did not point out to you that the division in the church today will cause you pain also."

Sevre-Duszynska said her fantasy had been that some of the priests would come forward to stand beside her at the altar.

Sevre-Duszynska returned to her seat, only to leave it again to join a line of priests laying hands on Howell in blessing. She was restrained by Fr. Gregory Schuler, cathedral rector, who told her that she could give Howell a hug instead. She recalls telling Schuler, "You mean because I'm in a feminine body I can't put my hands on him."

During the kiss of peace, Williams sought out Sevre-Duszynska in her pew and gave her a hug, a gesture she said she considered "very gracious." She objected, though, to his description of her actions as disruptive. "That is a highly charged term," she said. "What other channel is open to me?" . . .

Since the ceremony, Sevre-Duszynska said she had written to Howell and to Williams, telling the bishop that it had taken "more strength to walk up to that altar than to give birth to my two sons." . . .

"I am a seasoned, experienced woman and a daughter of the church who has a lot to offer," she said. "When you come to a sense of evolving truth and you don't act, you are committing a sin of omission. To me, this century is notorious for what people have failed to do. And when we don't take action, we participate in the spiritual violence."[52]

What are we all failing to do in order for the priest to be a woman?

APPENDIX

The ethnographic data used in the book were obtained through taped interviews with fifteen Episcopal priests and three Episcopal laywomen. Of the fifteen priests, four were men. The interviews were conducted during 1988–1989, when I was completing research for my doctoral dissertation, and in the summer of 1998, when I was finishing research for the book. The interviews spanned three dioceses, two in the Midwest and one in the Southwest. The priests were employed in a variety of professional situations at the time of the interviews, including rectors, curates, assistant pastors, teachers, administrators, doctoral students, professors, and non-parochial workers. Dates of ordination to the priesthood ranged from the late 1970s to the late 1990s.

I asked the following questions during each interview:

1. Tell me about your journey to ordination (if a priest).

2. What kinds of reactions have you received from parishioners with regard to women celebrating the Eucharist?

3. What is your own reaction to women celebrating the Eucharist? Do you find there are any differences when women celebrate than when men celebrate? If so, what are they?

4. What has your experience been with inclusive-language liturgies?

5. Why do you think individuals have objected to the ordination of women?

6. What changes, if any, are women clergy bringing to the Episcopal Church?

During the summer of 1998 I contacted those priests and laypersons interviewed during 1988–1989 (for whom I could obtain address information) and asked them whether, a decade later, their responses were substantially the same or different. Two responded to my query, and both indicated that the substance of their initial interview remained the same.

In order to protect confidentiality, no names or identifying characteristics are given for the interviewees. The issues involving women priests in the Episcopal tradition remain highly sensitive and controversial. While they were extremely interested in the substance of the project, the men and women who agreed to be interviewed often did so with reluctance. Some had never talked about issues concerning gender and the Eucharist before. Others felt at risk in discussing difficulties in their diocese. My guarantee that names and identifying characteristics would not be disclosed allowed the interviewees to feel more comfortable and to respond more openly to the above questions.

NOTES

1. INTRODUCTION

1. Two recent books that begin to address issues such as these are Hilary Wakeman, ed., *Women Priests: The First Years* (London: Darton, Longman, and Todd, 1996), and Sue Walrond-Skinner, ed., *Crossing the Boundary: What Will Women Priests Mean?* (London: Mowbray, 1994).

2. James W. Fowler, *Stages of Faith: The Psychology of Human Development and the Quest for Meaning* (San Francisco: Harper and Row, 1981).

3. Ana-Maria Rizzuto, *The Birth of the Living God: A Psychoanalytic Study* (Chicago: University of Chicago Press, 1979).

4. Hilary Wakeman, "What Difference Is Women's Priesthood Making in the Pews?" in Wakeman, *Women Priests*, p. 4.

5. Pamela Fawcett, "What Difference Is Women's Priesthood Making to Women?" in Wakeman, *Women Priests*, p. 30.

6. Wakeman, "What Difference," p. 4.

7. Judith Rose, "What Difference Is Women's Priesthood Making to the Church of England?" in Wakeman, *Women Priests*, pp. 150–151.

8. Barbara Baisely, "Being Realistic About Feminism," in Wakeman, *Women Priests*, pp. 107–108.

9. Rose, "What Difference," pp. 147–148.

10. Ibid., pp. 140–141. The style of leadership is not likely to change in a marked way, however, until the proportion of women to men in the priesthood increases significantly. On the other hand, Barbara Brown Zikmund, Adair Lummis, and Patricia Chang assert that women who are senior pastors in Episcopal and Lutheran denominations are less likely to employ a democratic leadership style than are clergywomen or clergymen in any position in all the other denominations they studied. They state that these women may feel pressured to lead in ways that are historically appropriate for senior pastors in their denominations. Zikmund, Lummis, and Chang, *Clergy Women: An Uphill Calling* (Louisville: Westminster John Knox Press, 1998), p. 62.

11. Monica Furlong, "The Guardian of the Grail," in Walrond-Skinner, *Crossing the Boundary*, p. 23.

12. Jane Williams, "Lady Into Fox: Friends Into Priests," in Walrond-Skinner, *Crossing the Boundary*, p. 91.

13. Christine Farrington, "Renewing the Place," in Walrond-Skinner, *Crossing the Boundary*, p. 76.

14. Jane Sinclair, "Of Priests and Presidents," in Walrond-Skinner, *Crossing the Boundary*, p. 155.

15. Williams, "Lady Into Fox," p. 87.

16. Mary Lou Suhor, ed., "Women Clergy Double Over 5 Years," *Witness* 70, no. 10 (October 1987): 13.

17. Mary D. Donovan, *Women Priests in the Episcopal Church: The Experience of the First Decade* (Cincinnati: Forward Movement Publications, 1988), p. 15.

18. Louie Crew, "Female Priests in the Episcopal Church," http://newark.rutgers.edu/~7Elcrew/womenpr.html, January 6, 1999.

19. Kathleen J. Greider, "The Authority of Our Ambivalence: Women and Priestly Ministry," *Quarterly Review* 10, no. 4 (Winter 1990): 24–25.

20. Ibid., p. 25.

21. Lesley Stevens, "Different Voice/Different Voices: Anglican Women in Ministry," *Review of Religious Research* 30, no. 3 (March 1989): 266.

22. Ibid., p. 267.

23. Greider, "Authority," p. 34.

24. In John Morgan, *Women Priests* (Bristol, Ind.: Wyndam Hall, 1985), p. 171.

25. Ibid., p. 173.

2. GENDER REVERSAL

1. For a literature review of the arguments against women's ordination, see Women's Ordination Conference, *Women and Priesthood: A Bibliography*, parts 1 and 2 (Fairfax, Va.: Women's Ordination Conference, 1995), and James R. Roberts, *Women Priests: Reflections on Papal Teaching* (Vancouver: Langara College, 1994).

2. R. W. Connell, *Gender and Power: Society, the Person, and Sexual Politics* (Stanford: Stanford University Press, 1987), p. 140.

3. Gilbert Herdt, *Guardians of the Flutes: Idioms of Masculinity* (New York: McGraw-Hill, 1981), and *The Sambia: Ritual and Gender in New Guinea* (New York: Holt, Rinehart, and Winston, 1987).

4. This term is Susan Nowak's, in "The Girardian Theory and Feminism: Critique and Appropriation," *Contagion: Journal of Violence, Mimesis, and Culture* 1 (1994): 19–20 n. 3. For Nowak, "patriarchy" is the structural expression of an androcentric worldview, or a pattern of thinking that posits the humanity of dominant male human beings as normative for all human beings.

5. Marija Gimbutas, *The Civilization of the Goddess* (San Francisco: HarperSanFrancisco, 1991).

6. Riane Eisler, *The Chalice and the Blade: Our History, Our Future* (San Francisco: HarperSanFrancisco, 1987).

7. Susan Faludi, *Backlash: The Undeclared War Against American Women* (New York: Anchor Books, 1992).

8. Denise Carmody, *Women and World Religions*, 2d ed. (Englewood Cliffs, N.J.: Prentice-Hall, 1989), p. 41.

9. See Mary Jo Weaver, *New Catholic Women: A Contemporary Challenge to Traditional Religious Authority* (San Francisco: Harper and Row, 1986).

10. Later I will mention instances of women baptizing in an "unofficial" capacity.

11. Anne Carr addresses this issue in *Transforming Grace: Christian Tradition and Women's Experience* (San Francisco: Harper and Row, 1988), pp. 40–42.

12. Ibid., p. 40.

13. Mary Hunt, "Thinking Anew About Ordination," *New Women, New Church* 14, nos. 4–6 (July 1991–February 1992); 15, no. 1 (July 1991–February 1992): 3–5.

14. See, for example, P. Francis Murphy, "Let's Start Over: A Bishop Appraises the Pastoral on Women," *Commonweal*, September 15, 1992, 11–15; Michael H. Kenny, "Which Way the Pastoral?" *America* 167, no. 4 (August 22, 1992): 76–77; and Kenneth Untener, "Forum: The Ordination of Women: Can the Horizons Widen?" *Worship* 65 (January 1991): 50–59.

15. Antoinette Iadorola, "The American Catholic Bishops and Woman: From the Nineteenth Amendment to ERA," in Yvonne Yazbeck Haddad and Ellison Banks Findly, eds., *Women, Religion, and Social Change*, p. 466 (Albany: State University of New York Press, 1985).

16. Rosemary Radford Ruether, "The Roman Catholic Story," in Rosemary Radford Ruether and Eleanor McLaughlin, eds., *Women of Spirit: Female Leadership in the Jewish and Christian Traditions*, p. 374 (New York: Simon and Schuster, 1979).

17. Weaver, *New Catholic Women*, p. 114.

18. Congregation for the Doctrine of the Faith, "The Vatican Declaration: Women in the Ministerial Priesthood," *Origins* 6 (February 3, 1977): 517–524.

19. U.S. Bishops, "Partners in the Mystery of Redemption: A Pastoral Response to Women's Concerns for Church and Society," *Origins* 17, no. 45 (April 21, 1988): 757–788; U.S. Bishops, Second Draft of Pastoral on Women ("One in Christ Jesus: A Pastoral Response to the Concerns of Women for Church and Society"), *Origins* 19, no. 44 (April 5, 1990): 717–740; U.S. Bishops, Third Draft of Proposed Pastoral Response to the Concerns of Women for Church and Society ("Called to Be One in Christ Jesus"), *Origins* 21, no. 46 (April 23, 1992): 761–776; U.S. Bishops, Fourth Draft of Response to the Concerns of Women for Church and Society ("One in Christ Jesus"), *Origins* 22, no. 13 (September 10, 1992): 221–240.

20. Murphy, "Let's Start Over," p. 13.

21. Daniel McGuire, for example, outlines three ways in which the exclusion of women from orders is unjust: (1) it is unjust to the women who wish to offer this type of service, (2) it is unjust to the church members who are not served by these women, and (3) it does spiritual and moral harm to persons. He writes: "It insults women by treating them as a sacramental obstacle and by arbitrarily frustrating their spiritual desires for ordained ministry. Furthermore, it denies ordained ministry to increasing numbers of Christians who desire ordained ministry and do not have it, even though women and men married to women are ready and able to assume this service. . . . Finally there is the injustice of scandal. . . . In a scandalous way this comforts a society which also excludes women from top positions in government, business, the professions, and even the arts." Daniel McGuire, "The Exclusion of Women from Orders: A Moral Evaluation" (Cross Currents: 1984; reprinted by Priests for Equality and the Women's Ordination Conference).

22. Roberts, *Women Priests*, p. 1.

23. See, for example, Alan Cowell, "Pope Rules Out Debate on Making Women Priests," *New York Times*, May 31, 1994, p. A8; Peter Steinfels, "Vatican Says the Ban on Women as Priests Is 'Infallible' Doctrine," *New York Times*, November 19, 1995, pp. A1, A13.

24. Reprinted in *Commonweal*, June 17, 1994, 4–5.

25. Congregation for the Doctrine of the Faith, "Response to a 'Dubium' on Ordaining Women to the Ministerial Priesthood," *Origins* 25, no. 24 (November 30, 1995): 401, 403.

26. Ibid., p. 401.

27. Bishop Pilla refers to another document, the pope's "Letter to Women" of June 1994, which states that women's exclusion from the priesthood "in no way detracts from the role of women . . . since all share

equally in the dignity proper to the 'common priesthood' based on baptism (No. 11)." Bishop Anthony Pilla, "Statements on Doctrinal Congregation's Action," *Origins* 25, no. 24 (November 30, 1995): 406.

28. Ibid.

29. Quoted in John B. Noss, ed., *Man's Religions*, 6th ed. (New York: Macmillan, 1980), p. 484.

30. Quoted in Peter C. Phan, "Infallibility," in Michael Glazier and Monika K. Hellwig, eds., *The Modern Catholic Encyclopedia*, p. 425 (Collegeville, Minn.: Liturgical Press, 1994).

31. Huston Smith, *The World's Religions* (San Francisco: HarperSanFrancisco, 1991), p. 349.

32. Ibid.

33. In Ann Graff and David Knight, "Infallibly Complex: Have We Heard the Final Word on Women's Ordination?" *U.S. Catholic* 61, no. 4 (April 1, 1996): 10.

34. Francis Sullivan, in Graff and Knight, "Infallibly Complex," p. 8.

35. Graff and Knight, "Infallibly Complex," p. 11.

36. Ibid., p. 13.

37. Ibid.

38. Hermann Josef Pottmeyer, "Refining the Question About Women's Ordination," *America* 175, no. 12 (1996): 16–17. Pottmeyer suggests that the proper forum for a discussion of this magnitude is a council.

39. John H. Wright, " 'That All Doubt May Be Removed,'" *America* 171, no. 3 (July 30, 1994): 18.

40. Ibid., p. 19.

41. U.S. Bishops, Statement Calling the Vatican to Collegiality, "Bishops Embrace Conference Change, More Openness," *National Catholic Reporter* 31, no. 35 (July 28, 1995): 14.

42. In Roberts, *Women Priests*, p. 57.

43. A standard definition of an apostle used in an introductory theology text is "one who is commissioned by Christ to preach the gospel or one who has witnessed the risen Christ." Alister E. McGrath, *Christian Theology: An Introduction* (Oxford: Blackwell, 1994), p. 426.

44. Elisabeth Schüssler Fiorenza, "Tablesharing and the Celebration of the Eucharist," in Mary Collins and David Power, eds., *Can We Always Celebrate the Eucharist?*, Concilium 152, pp. 7–8 (New York: Seabury, 1982).

45. This message, she admits, eventually became somewhat strangled by the tendency toward patriarchal solidification. Elisabeth Schüssler Fiorenza, "Word, Spirit, and Power: Women in Early Christian Communities," in Ruether and McLaughlin, *Women of Spirit*, p. 57.

46. Evidence for this is found in the testimony to women priests in literary and epigraphical sources. Gelasius I in 494 sent an epistle acknowledging that "women are now encouraged to officiate at the sacred altars, and to take part in all matters imputed to the offices of the male sex, to which they do not belong." An inscription from the catacomb of Tropia refers to a *presbytera*—that is, a woman who was practicing the sacerdotal ministry. Particularly significant are the writings of Bishop Atto, who in the tenth century wrote of a fourth-century canon forbidding ordination to women. Atto wrote that in the ancient Christian Church, not only men but also women were ordained and assumed the duties of preaching, directing, and teaching, the three duties defining the role of the sacrament of the priesthood. Mary Ann Rossi, "Priesthood, Precedent, and Prejudice: On Recovering the Women Priests of Early Christianity, Containing a Translation from the Italian 'Notes on the Female Priesthood in Antiquity' by Giorgio Otranto," *Journal of Feminist Studies in Religion* 7, no. 1 (Spring 1991):73–93.

47. Ruth McDonough Fitzpatrick, "WOC Delegation Visits Czechoslovakia," *New Women, New Church* 15, nos. 2–4 (March–August 1992): 1. See also Petr Fiala and Jiri Hanus, "Women's Ordination in the Czech Silent Church," *The Month* 259, no. 1567 (July 1998): 282–288.

48. See, for example, Pottmeyer, "Refining the Question," p. 18.

49. Graff and Knight, "Infallibly Complex," p. 18.

50. In Patrick McCormick, "With All Due Respect," *U.S. Catholic* 59, no. 9 (September 1994): 47.

51. Graff and Knight, "Infallibly Complex," p. 12.

52. Joan Chittester, "One, Two, Three Strikes, You're Out in the Ol' Boys' Game," *National Catholic Reporter* 30, no. 32 (June 17, 1994): 12.

53. Reprinted in Leonard Swidler and Arlene Swidler, eds., *Women Priests: A Catholic Commentary on the Vatican Declaration* (New York: Paulist Press, 1977), pp. 43–44.

54. R. A. Norris Jr., "The Ordination of Women and the 'Maleness of Christ,'" *Anglican Theological Review Supplementary Series* 6 (June 1976): 69, 76, 78.

55. John Austin Baker, "Eucharistic Presidency and Women's Ordination," *Theology* 88, no. 725 (September 1985): 352, 355.

56. Kenny, "Which Way the Pastoral?" p. 76.

57. Saint Thomas Aquinas, *Summa Theologica*, part 3, supplement, question 39, article 1. Quoted in Roberts, *Women Priests*, p. 24.

58. John Paul II, "On the Dignity and Vocation of Women," reprinted in *Origins* 18, no. 17 (October 6, 1988): 279.

59. Carl Jung, "Transformation Symbolism in the Mass," in R. F. C.

2. Gender Reversal 253

Hull, trans., *The Collected Works of C. G. Jung*, 11:201–296 (New York: Pantheon, 1958).

60. Sara Butler, "Proceedings of the Second Conference on the Ordination of Roman Catholic Women," in Maureen Dywer, ed., *New Woman, New Church, New Priestly Ministry*, p. 122 (Baltimore: Women's Ordination Conference, 1980).

61. Merlin Stone, *When God Was a Woman* (San Diego: Harcourt Brace Jovanovich, 1976).

62. John Paul II, "On the Dignity and Vocation of Women," reprinted in *Origins* 18, no. 17 (October 6, 1988): 269.

63. John Paul II, Apostolic Letter, *Mulieris Dignitatem* (1988), no. 25, cited in Roberts, *Women Priests*, p. 36.

64. Roberts, *Women Priests*, p. 37.

65. Sara Butler, "The Priest as Sacrament of Christ the Bridegroom," *Worship* 66 (November 1992): 511.

66. In Herve Legrand, "*Traditio perpetuo servata?* The Non-ordination of Women: Tradition or Simply an Historical Fact?" *Worship* 65, no. 6 (November 1991): 501.

67. Urs von Balthasar adopts the notion that only men are capable of representation from Louis Bouyer. In Legrand, "*Traditio*," p. 501.

68. Butler, "Priest as Sacrament," p. 513.

69. Ibid., p. 516.

70. See also Legrand, "*Traditio*." Legrand explains that early priests presided at the Eucharist because they presided in the church. In the Eucharist, the priest "acts in a context governed by the epiclesis which he announces in the name of the church and with the church" (p. 502). Furthermore, in his view, *all* ministers of the sacraments act *in persona Christi*: women act *in persona Christi* in the sacrament of their marriage and in the sacrament of baptism, which they have been able to administer since the eleventh century. Thus it does not make sense, according to Legrand, to argue that women cannot represent Christ in the Eucharist (p. 503).

71. David Power, "Representing Christ in Community and Sacrament," in Donald J. Goergen, ed., *Being a Priest Today*, p. 115 (Collegeville, Minn.: Liturgical Press, 1992).

72. Ibid., p. 120.

73. Kate DeSmet, "Ken, Don't Foul Up the Church Today," *The Critic* 47, no. 3 (Spring 1993): 22–23.

74. David Coffey, "Priestly Representation and Women's Ordination," in Gerald P. Gleeson, ed., *Priesthood: The Hard Questions*, p. 89 (Newtown, Australia: E. J. Dwyer, 1993).

75. This is primarily because of the influence of another theologian,

Gerald Gleeson, and his application of the notions "donative" and "receptive" to characterize masculine and feminine, respectively. Gleeson states: "What does seem to be of transcultural significance in the marriage and sexual relationship is that a man is 'donative' whereas a woman is 'receptive.' . . . In view of the structure of the sexual act, and the fact that it is the woman who 'receives' and carries the child a couple conceive, the *symbolic* description of the two spouses as donative and receptive seems undeniable." Gerald Gleeson, "The Ordination of Women and the Symbolism of Priesthood, Part One," *Astralasian Catholic Record* 67 (1990): 480. Gleeson explains that while being female is not an obstacle to exercising "donative" or leadership roles in general, a woman cannot symbolize the *specific* donative role of husband and father. Yet she *could* exercise a donative role in the community if admitted to pastoral leadership (p. 481). Gleeson concludes that it would be unreasonable to exclude women from pastoral leadership for the sole reason that they cannot symbolize "donative" in the sense of "husband."

76. Coffey, "Priestly Representation," p. 97.

77. Philip Lyndon Reynolds, "Scholastic Theology and the Case Against Women's Ordination," *Heythrop Journal* 36, no. 3 (1995): 281.

78. Ibid., p. 274.

79. John McDade, S.J., "Gender Matters: Women and Priesthood," *The Month* 255 (July 1994): 258.

80. Ibid.

81. In Richard Beauchesne, "Explorations and Responses: Scriptural/Theological Argument Against Women's Ordination (Simply Stated) and Responses," *Journal of Ecumenical Studies* 32, no. 1 (Winter 1995): 110.

82. Ibid., p. 110 n. 16.

83. Elaine Pagels, *The Gnostic Gospels* (New York: Random House, 1979), pp. 50–54.

84. Elaine Pagels, "What Became of God the Mother? Conflicting Images of God in Early Christianity," *Signs: Journal of Women in Culture and Society* 2, no. 2 (Winter 1976): 302.

85. Ritamary Bradley, "Patristic Background of the Motherhood Similitude in Julian of Norwich," *Christian Scholar's Review* 8 (1978): 104.

86. Elizabeth A. Johnson, *She Who Is: The Mystery of God in Feminist Theological Discourse* (New York: Crossroad, 1992), p. 157.

87. See, in particular, Caroline Walker Bynum, *Jesus as Mother: Studies in the Spirituality of the High Middle Ages* (Berkeley: University of California Press, 1982), and Bynum, *Fragmentation and Redemption: Essays on Gender and the Human Body in Medieval Religion* (New York:

Zone Books, 1991).
88. Bynum, *Jesus as Mother*, p. 126.
89. Ibid., p. 119.
90. Ibid., pp. 154–155.
91. Bynum, *Fragmentation and Redemption*, p. 101.
92. Ibid., p. 102.
93. Ibid., pp. 82, 117.
94. William R. Crockett, *Eucharist: Symbol of Transformation* (New York: Pueblo Publishing, 1989), p. 1.
95. Jerome Kodell, O.S.B., *The Eucharist in the New Testament* (Wilmington, Del.: Michael Glazier, 1988), p. 18.
96. Ibid., pp. 19, 56.
97. Ibid., p. 52.
98. Crockett, *Eucharist*, pp. 1–2.
99. Kodell, *The Eucharist*, p. 21.
100. Gilbert Ostdiek, "Body of Christ, Blood of Christ," in Joseph A. Komonchak, Mary Collins, and Dermot A. Lane, eds., *The New Dictionary of Theology* (Wilmington, Del.: Michael Glazier, 1988), p. 143.
101. Mitchell G. Reddish, "Body of Christ," in Watson E. Mills, ed., *Mercer Dictionary of the Bible*, p. 121 (Macon, Ga.: Mercer University Press, 1990).
102. S.K.W., "The Lord's Supper," in Paul J. Achtemeier, ed., *The HarperCollins Bible Dictionary*, p. 623 (San Francisco: HarperSanFrancisco, 1996).
103. John L. McKenzie, S.J., *Dictionary of the Bible* (Milwaukee: Bruce Publishing, 1965), p. 251.
104. Ostdiek, "Body of Christ," pp. 142–143.
105. James A. Fischer, "Body," in Carroll Stuhlmueller, ed., *The Collegeville Pastoral Dictionary*, p. 101 (Collegeville, Minn.: Liturgical Press, 1996).
106. Ostdiek, "Body of Christ," p. 143.
107. As stated by Stephen L. Harris in *Understanding the Bible*, 3d ed. (London: Mayfield, 1992), scholars believe that Ephesians was written by a later disciple who modified and updated Paul's ideas to address concerns of his own day (pp. 374–376).
108. R. Eduard Schweiser, "Body," in David Noel Friedman, ed., *The Anchor Bible Dictionary*, 1:771 (New York: Doubleday, 1992).
109. Reddish, "Body of Christ," p. 120.
110. Raymond Moloney, "Eucharist," in Komonchak, Collins, and Lane, *The New Dictionary of Theology*, p. 352.
111. Christine Gudorf, "The Power to Create: Sacraments and Men's

Need to Give Birth," *Horizons* 14, no. 2 (1987): 298.

112. Ibid., p. 299.

113. Ibid., p. 303.

114. Heather Hyuck, "To Celebrate a Whole Priesthood: The History of Women's Ordination in the Episcopal Church" (Ph.D. diss., University of Minnesota, 1981), p. 20.

115. In ibid., p. 60.

3. MATERNAL ENVY

1. Sigmund Freud, "Beyond the Pleasure Principle (1920)," in *The Pelican Freud Library*, vol. 11, *On Metapsychology: The Theory of Psychoanalysis*, ed. James Strachey, p. 288 (Harmondsworth, Middlesex, England: Penguin Books, 1984).

2. See Jeffrey Moussaieff Masson, *The Assault on Truth: Freud's Suppression of the Seduction Theory* (New York: Farrar, Strauss, and Giroux, 1984).

3. Sigmund Freud, "The Interpretation of Dreams (1900)," in *The Pelican Freud Library*, vol. 4, *The Interpretation of Dreams*, ed. James Strachey, p. 364. (Harmondsworth, Middlesex, England: Penguin Books, 1975).

4. Sigmund Freud, "The Dissolution of the Oedipus Complex (1924)," in *The Pelican Freud Library*, vol. 7, *On Sexuality*, ed. Angela Richards, p. 319 (Harmondsworth, Middlesex, England: Penguin Books, 1977).

5. Editor's Note to Sigmund Freud, "Some Psychical Consequences of the Anatomical Distinction Between the Sexes (1925)," in *The Pelican Freud Library*, vol. 7, *On Sexuality*, ed. Angela Richards, p. 326 (Harmondsworth, Middlesex, England: Penguin Books, 1977).

6. Freud, "Some Psychical Consequences," pp. 334–335.

7. Freud, "The Dissolution," p. 321; "Some Psychical Consequences," p. 340.

8. Jane Flax, "Mother-Daughter Relationships: Psychodynamics, Politics, and Philosophy," in Hester Eisenstein and Alice Jardine, eds., *The Future of Difference*, p. 22 (New Brunswick, N.J.: Rutgers University Press, 1985).

9. Diane Jonte-Pace, "Feminist Transformations in the Psychology of Religion: New Developments in Method and Theory," *Method and Theory in the Study of Religion* (in press).

10. Rosemarie Tong, *Feminist Thought: A Comprehensive Introduction* (Boulder: Westview, 1989), p. 143.

11. Simone de Beauvoir, *The Second Sex*, trans. H. M. Parshley (New York: Vintage Books, 1952), pp. 48–56.

12. Juliet Mitchell, *Psychoanalysis and Feminism* (New York: Vintage Books, 1974), p. xvi.

13. Ibid., pp. 377, 380, 402–416. See also Tong, *Feminist Thought*, pp. 168–169.

14. Jonte-Pace, "Feminist Transformations."

15. Naomi Goldenberg, "The Return of the Goddess: Psychoanalytic Reflections on the Shift From Theology to Thealogy," *Studies in Religion* 16, no. 1 (Winter 1987): 38–39.

16. Klein has been considered an object relations theorist by some for her focus on the pre-Oedipal period, but not by others because of her emphasis on instinctual drives. Like Freud, she believed feelings of love and hate were innate.

17. Janet Sayers, *Mothers of Psychoanalysis* (New York: Norton, 1991), p. 85.

18. Noreen O'Connor and Joanna Ryan, *Wild Desires and Mistaken Identities: Lesbianism and Psychoanalysis* (New York: Columbia University Press, 1993), p. 210.

19. Melanie Klein, "The Early Stages of the Oedipus Conflict," in *The Selected Melanie Klein*, ed. Juliet Mitchell, p. 74 (Harmondsworth, Middlesex, England: Penguin Books, 1986).

20. Klein's use of the spelling "phantasy" rather than "fantasy" indicates for her the unconscious nature of these desires. In Mitchell, *Psychoanalysis and Feminism*, p. 351.

21. Donald W. Winnicott, *Collected Papers: Through Paediatrics to Psycho-Analysis* (New York: Basic Books, 1958), p. 165.

22. Ibid., pp. 223–224.

23. Donald W. Winnicott, *Playing and Reality* (London and New York: Tavistock Publications, 1971), pp. 99–102.

24. Diane Jonte-Pace, "Feminism, Object Relations Theory, and Religion: The Betrayal of Mothering" (paper presented at the annual meeting of the American Academy of Religion, Atlanta, Ga., November 1986).

25. Dorothy Dinnerstein, *The Mermaid and the Minotaur: Sexual Arrangements and the Human Malaise* (New York: Harper and Row, 1976), p. 104.

26. Ibid., p. 51.

27. Ibid., pp. 163, 177.

28. Jean Bethke Elshtain, *Public Man, Private Woman: Women in Social and Political Thought* (Princeton, N.J.: Princeton University Press, 1981), p. 287.

29. Tong, *Feminist Thought*, p. 158.

30. Nancy Chodorow, *Feminism and Psychoanalytic Theory* (New Haven: Yale University Press, 1989), p. 110.

31. Ibid., p. 109.

32. Tong, *Feminist Thought*, p. 156.

33. Nancy Chodorow, *The Reproduction of Mothering: Psychoanalysis and the Sociology of Gender* (Berkeley: University of California Press, 1978), p. 218.

34. See, for example, Nancy Chodorow, *Femininities, Masculinities, Sexualities: Freud and Beyond* (Lexington: University Press of Kentucky, 1994).

35. Ellyn Kaschak, *Engendered Lives: A New Psychology of Women's Experience* (New York: Basic Books, 1992), pp. 116–118.

36. Ibid., p. 121.

37. Nancy Chodorow, "Gender as a Personal and Cultural Construction," *Signs: Journal of Women in Culture and Society* 20, no. 3 (Spring 1995): 522–523.

38. Ibid., p. 537.

39. See, for example, Paul Gray, "The Assault on Freud," *Time*, November 29, 1993, pp. 47–51; Mark Edmundson, "Save Sigmund Freud," *New York Times Magazine*, July 13, 1997, pp. 34–35.

40. Calvin S. Hall, *A Primer of Freudian Psychology* (New York: World Publishing, 1954), pp. 85–59.

41. Victor Turner, *The Forest of Symbols: Aspects of Ndembu Ritual* (Ithaca: Cornell University Press, 1967), p. 19.

42. Ronald Grimes, *Beginnings in Ritual Studies* (Washington, D.C.: University Press of America, 1982), p. 54.

43. Ibid., p. 55.

44. Ronald L. Grimes, *Ritual Criticism: Case Studies in Its Practice, Essays on Its Theory* (Columbia: University of South Carolina Press, 1990), p. 10.

45. Bruce Lincoln, *Emerging from the Chrysalis: Studies in Rituals of Women's Initiation* (Cambridge: Harvard University Press, 1981), p. 6.

46. Emile Durkheim, *The Elementary Forms of the Religious Life*, trans. Joseph Swain (Glencoe: Free Press, 1915 [1974]), pp. 37, 41. Quoted in David I. Kertzer, *Ritual, Politics, and Power* (New Haven: Yale University Press, 1988), p. 9.

47. Catherine Bell, *Ritual Theory, Ritual Practice* (New York: Oxford University Press, 1992), p. 74.

48. Ibid., p. 220.

49. Grimes, *Beginnings*, p. 35.

50. Ibid., p. 43.

51. Catherine Bell, *Ritual: Perspectives and Dimensions* (New York: Oxford University Press, 1997), p. 218.

52. Grimes, *Beginnings*, p. 62.

53. Victor Turner, *Dramas, Fields, and Metaphors: Symbolic Action in Human Society* (Ithaca: Cornell University Press, 1974), p. 274.

54. Victor Turner and Edith Turner, *Image and Pilgrimage in Christian Culture: Anthropological Perspectives* (New York: Columbia University Press, 1978), p. 21.

55. I will again use Grimes to illustrate the type of criticism that has been leveled against Turner. The term *liminoid*, for Grimes, emerged from Turner's study of ritual in ancient and preindustrial contexts. Turnerian theory, according to Grimes, requires that contemporary symbolic acts be viewed as likenesses or remnants of earlier or simpler such acts. They cannot be new creations. Grimes argues that instead of using this type of archaic template, ritual studies should begin with the relationship between performer and audience-observer. Grimes, *Beginnings*, p. 155.

56. Grimes, *Ritual Criticism*, p. 14.

57. Bell, *Ritual Theory*, pp. 92–93.

58. Grimes, *Beginnings*, p. 38.

59. Tom Driver, *The Magic of Ritual: Our Need for Liberating Rites That Transform Our Lives and Our Communities* (San Francisco: HarperSanFrancisco, 1991), p. 23.

60. Ibid., p. 26.

61. Bell, *Ritual Theory*, pp. 20–21.

62. Victor Turner, *On the Edge of the Bush: Anthropology as Experience*, ed. Edith L. B. Turner (Tucson: University of Arizona Press, 1985), p. 251.

63. Kertzer, *Ritual, Politics, and Power*, p. 12.

64. Marjorie Procter-Smith, *In Her Own Rite: Constructing Feminist Liturgical Tradition* (Nashville: Abingdon, 1990), pp. 31, 45, 59.

65. Driver, *Magic of Ritual*, p. 163.

66. Driver also explains that ritual is best understood from the perspective of a "preferential option for the poor." This phrase, which originates from Latin American liberation theology, applies to victims of political, social, and economic injustice. Driver, *Magic of Ritual*, p. 166.

67. Caroline Walker Bynum, "Women's Stories, Women's Symbols: A Critique of Victor Turner's Theory of Liminality," in Robert L. Moore and Frank E. Reynolds, eds., *Anthropology and the Study of Religion*, pp. 105–125 (Chicago: Center for the Scientific Study of Religion, 1984).

68. Lincoln, *Emerging*, pp. 97–105.

69. Lesley A. Northup, *Ritualizing Women* (Cleveland: Pilgrim Press, 1997), pp. 28–38, 45–49.

70. Ibid., p. 23.

71. Ibid., p. 93.

72. Procter-Smith, *In Her Own Rite*, p. 23.

73. David N. Power, *The Eucharistic Mystery: Revitalizing the Tradition* (New York: Crossroad, 1993). Subsequent citations to this source are indicated by parenthetical page numbers within the text.

74. Edward J. Kilmartin, "The Lima Text on Eucharist," in Michael A. Fahey, ed., *Catholic Perspectives on Baptism, Eucharist, and Ministry*, p. 135 (New York: University Press of America, 1986).

75. Johannes H. Emminghaus, *The Eucharist: Essence, Form, Celebration*, trans. Matthew J. O'Connell (Collegeville, Minn.: Liturgical Press, 1978), p. xvi.

76. Ibid., p. 23.

77. Stephen L. Harris, *Understanding the Bible*, 3d ed. (London: Mayfield, 1992), p. 324.

78. E. O. James, *Christian Myth and Ritual: An Historical Study* (Cleveland: World Publishing, 1965), pp. 124–125.

79. George Worgul, "Lima's Ecclesiology: An Inquiry," in Fahey, *Catholic Perspectives*, p. 91.

80. Emminghaus, *The Eucharist*, p. 155.

81. While virtually all Catholic theologians concur that the contemporary Eucharist is a ritual of sacrifice, theological controversy exists over whether the Eucharist originated as a sacrificial ritual. See, for example, Josef A. Jungmann, S.J., *The Early Liturgy*, trans. Francis Brunner, C.S.S.R. (Notre Dame: University of Notre Dame Press, 1959), pp. 45–46; and Gregory Dix, *The Shape of the Liturgy*, 2d ed. (London: Dacre, 1945; Adam and Charles Black, 1975), pp. 114–116.

82. David N. Power, *The Sacrifice We Offer: The Tridentine Dogma and Its Reinterpretation* (New York: Crossroad, 1987), p. 15.

83. I retain noninclusive language here both because at this juncture in history only men can serve in the function of Catholic priests and because this theology reflects the perspective of primarily male theologians.

84. Michael O'Carroll, C.S.Sp., "Priesthood," in *Corpus Christi: An Encyclopedia of the Eucharist* (Wilmington, Del.: Michael Glazier, 1988), p. 168.

85. Ibid., p. 169.

86. Power, *Sacrifice*, p. 22.

87. Edward J. Kilmartin, S.J., *Christian Liturgy: Theology and Practice*, vol. 1 (Kansas City, Mo.: Sheed and Ward, 1988), p. 318.

88. Power, *Eucharistic*, p. 262.

89. Kilmartin, "The Lima Text on Eucharist," pp. 145–146.

90. Michael O'Carroll, "Consecration," in *Corpus Christi: An Encyclopedia of the Eucharist*, p. 56.

91. This is a Catholic view of sacrament. The Protestant understanding of sacrament generally adheres to Luther's two criteria: forgiveness of sins and outward sacramental sign. See Alister E. McGrath, *Christian Theology: An Introduction* (Oxford: Blackwell, 1994), p. 431.

92. Kevin W. Irwin, "The Sacramentality of Creation and the Role of Creation in Liturgy and Sacraments," in Kevin W. Irwin and Edmund D. Pellegrino, eds., *Preserving the Creation: Environmental Theology and Ethics*, p. 71 (Washington, D.C.: Georgetown University Press, 1994).

93. Mary Ellen Ross and Cheryl Linn Ross, "Mothers, Infants, and the Psychoanalytic Study of Ritual," *Signs: Journal of Women in Culture and Society* 9 (Autumn 1983): 26–39.

94. Ibid., p. 87.

95. Turner, *Dramas, Fields, and Metaphors*, p. 274.

96. I wish to state my reasons for *not* utilizing a Jungian interpretation, for Jungian mysticism at first seems like a needed balance to Freudian rationalism. According to Carl Jung, the mass expresses powerful psychological dynamics, particularly concerning the uniting of opposites, the archetype of sacrifice, and the mass as a rite of individuation (Carl Jung, "Transformation Symbolism in the Mass," in *Psychology and Religion: West and East*, trans. R. F. C. Hull, pp. 201–296 [New York: Pantheon Books, 1958]). While Jung's theory is not antithetical to much of Catholic eucharistic theology described, I find it lacks concreteness. It is too mystical. As Naomi Goldenberg points out, almost any claims can be made about "unknown" and "unknowable" archetypes in terms of determining human thought patterns (Naomi Goldenberg, *Returning Words to Flesh: Feminism, Psychoanalysis, and the Resurrection of the Body* [Boston: Beacon, 1990], p. 88). In addition, Jung's gendered archetypes of animus and anima perpetuate sexist stereotypes about masculinity and femininity. Jung was an essentialist, claiming that masculine and feminine qualities were inherent in biology.

97. See Sigmund Freud, *Totem and Taboo (1913)*, in *The Pelican Freud Library*, vol. 13, *The Origins of Religion*, ed. Albert Dickson, pp. 53–224 (Harmondsworth, Middlesex, England: Penguin Books, 1985).

98. Eli Sagan, a more contemporary psychoanalyst, takes a route similar to Freud in proposing that as a ritual of sacrifice, the Eucharist is a

form of socialized aggression and can be traced back to primitive canni-balistic behavior. Sagan argues that three important characteristics of can-nibalistic activity are also found in the Eucharist: aggression, ambiva-lence, and a ritual rubric. Jesus is sacrificially killed yet loved, and the rit-ualized act takes on special significance. Eli Sagan, *Cannibalism: Human Aggression and Cultural Form* (New York: Psychohistory Press, 1974), p. xix.

99. Michael Balint, *The Basic Fault: Therapeutic Aspects of Regression* (New York: Brunner/Mazel, 1968).

100. Dario Zadra, "Victor Turner's Theory of Religion: Towards an Analysis of Symbolic Time," in Moore and Reynolds, *Anthropology and the Study of Religion*, p. 85.

101. Freud, "Mourning and Melancholia (1917)," in *The Pelican Freud Library*, vol. 11, ed. James Strachey, p. 252 (Harmondsworth, Middlesex, England: Penguin Books, 1984).

102. Melanie Klein, "Mourning and Manic-Depressive States," in *The Selected Melanie Klein*, p. 148.

103. Hans Loewald, *Papers on Psychoanalysis* (New Haven: Yale University Press, 1980), p. 260.

104. Ibid.

105. Rev. Cheryl Wertheimer gave me this insight.

106. Robert L. Moore, "Space and Transformation in Human Experience," in Moore and Reynolds, *Anthropology and the Study of Religion*, p. 137.

107. Hans-Gunter Heimbrock, "Ritual and Transformation: A Psychoanalytic Perspective," in Hans-Gunter Heimbrock and H. Barbara Boudewijnse, eds., *Current Studies on Rituals: Perspectives for the Psychology of Religion*, p. 40 (Amsterdam: Rodopi, 1990).

108. The term is Ralph Greenson's. Ralph R. Greenson, "Dis-identi-fying from Mother: Its Special Importance for the Boy," in Dana Breen, ed., *The Gender Conundrum: Contemporary Psychoanalytic Perspectives on Femininity and Masculinity*, p. 258 (London: Routledge, 1993).

109. Chodorow, *Feminism and Psychoanalytic Theory*, p. 109.

110. Sigmund Freud, "Analysis of a Phobia in a Five-Year-Old Boy (1909)," in *The Pelican Freud Library*, vol. 8, *Case Histories I: "Dora" and "Little Hans,"* ed. Angela Richards, pp. 246–247 (Harmondsworth, Middlesex, England: Penguin Books, 1977).

111. In Hanna Lerman, *A Mote in Freud's Eye: From Psychoanalysis to the Psychology of Women* (New York: Springer, 1986), p. 81.

112. Sigmund Freud, "Psychoanalytic Notes on an Autobiographical Account of a Case of Paranoia (Dementia Paranoides) (1911)," in *The Pelican Freud Library*, vol. 9, *Case Histories II: The "Rat Man," Schreber,*

the Wolf Man, a Case of Female Homosexuality, ed. Angela Richards, p. 165 (Harmondsworth, Middlesex, England: Penguin Books, 1979).

113. Ibid., p. 151.

114. Ibid., pp. 146–147.

115. Lerman, *A Mote in Freud's Eye*, p. 81.

116. In Karen Horney, *Feminine Psychology* (New York: Norton, 1967), p. 21.

117. Sir E. F. Im Thurn, *Among the Indians of Guiana* (London: 1883), p. 218. Cited in Bruno Bettelheim, *Symbolic Wounds: Puberty Rites and the Envious Male* (Glencoe, Ill.: Free Press, 1954), p. 209.

118. Horney, *Feminine Psychology*, p. 61. Mary O'Brien makes a similar argument to Horney's, claiming that men's focus on ideologies of productivity stems from their alienation from the reproductive process. See Mary O'Brien, *The Politics of Reproduction* (London: Routledge and Kegan Paul, 1981).

119. Greenson, "Dis-identifying from Mother," p. 259.

120. Robert J. Stoller, *Presentations of Gender* (New Haven: Yale University Press, 1985), pp. 19–21.

121. Ibid., pp. 16, 40, 182.

122. Gerald J. M. van den Aardweg, *On the Origins and Treatment of Homosexuality: A Psychoanalytic Reinterpretation* (New York: Praeger, 1986), p. 153.

123. Elizabeth Wells, "The View from Within: What It Feels Like to Be a Transsexual," in William A. W. Walters and Michael W. Ross, eds., *Transsexualism and Sex Reassignment*, p. 12 (Oxford: Oxford University Press, 1986).

124. Janice G. Raymond, *The Transsexual Empire: The Making of the She-Male* (Boston: Beacon, 1979), pp. xv–xvi.

125. Ibid., pp. vxiii, 16.

126. Michael W. Ross, "Causes of Gender Dysphoria: How Does Transsexualism Develop and Why?" in Walters and Ross, *Transsexualism and Sex Reassignment*, pp. 24–25.

127. Don Burnard and Michael W. Ross, "Psychosocial Aspects and Psychological Testing: What Can Psychological Testing Reveal?" in Walters and Ross, *Transsexualism and Sex Reassignment*, p. 56.

128. Richard C. Friedman, *Male Homosexuality: A Contemporary Psychoanalytic Perspective* (New Haven: Yale University Press, 1988), p. 74.

129. Ihsan Al-Issa, "Gender Role," in Louis Diamont, ed., *Male and Female Homosexuality: Psychological Approaches*, p. 155 (Washington: Hemisphere Publishing, 1987).

130. Kenneth Lewes, "Psychoanalysis and Male Homosexuality," in Louis Diamant and Richard D. McAnulty, eds., *The Psychology of Sexual Orientation, Behavior, and Identity: A Handbook*, p. 115 (Westport, Conn.: Greenwood, 1995).

131. Al-Issa, "Gender Role," p. 165.

132. Beverly Burch, "Gender Identities, Lesbianism, and Potential Space," in Judith M. Glassgold and Suzanne Iasenza, eds., *Lesbians and Psychoanalysis: Revolutions in Theory and Practice*, pp. 288–289 (New York: Free Press, 1995).

133. Angela Moorjani, "Fetishism, Gender Masquerade, and the Mother-Father Fantasy," in Joseph H. Smith and Afaf M. Mahfouz, eds., *Psychoanalysis, Feminism, and the Future of Gender*, p. 26 (Baltimore: Johns Hopkins University Press, 1994).

134. Ibid., p. 32.

135. Adam Limentani, "To the Limits of Male Heterosexuality: The Vagina-man," in Dana Breen, ed., *The Gender Conundrum: Contemporary Psychoanalytic Perspectives on Femininity and Masculinity*, pp. 273–285 (London: Routledge, 1993).

136. Greenson, "Dis-identifying from Mother," p. 260.

137. Melanie Klein, "A Study of Envy and Gratitude," in *The Selected Melanie Klein*, p. 213.

138. Ibid., p. 219.

139. Greenson, "Dis-identifying from Mother," p. 260.

4. SACRIFICE

1. Alasdair Heron, *Table and Tradition* (Edinburgh: Handsel, 1983), p. xii.

2. Margaret S. Mahler, Fred Pine, and Anni Bergman, *The Psychological Birth of the Human Infant: Symbiosis and Individuation* (New York: Basic Books, 1975), pp. ix–x.

3. See Margaret S. Mahler, *On Human Symbiosis and the Vicissitudes of Individuation* (New York: International Universities Press, 1968).

4. Mahler, Pine, and Bergman, *Psychological Birth*, p. 3.

5. Ibid., p. 11.

6. James W. Jones, *Contemporary Psychoanalysis and Religion: Transference and Transcendence* (New Haven: Yale University Press, 1991), pp. 91–92.

7. Robert D. Nye, *Three Psychologies: Perspectives from Freud, Skinner, and Rogers*, 4th ed. (Pacific Grove, Calif.: Brooks/Cole Publishing, 1992), p. 36.

8. Jones, *Contemporary Psychoanalysis*, pp. 62–67.

9. Nancy Chodorow, "Reflections on the Authority of the Past in Psychoanalytic Thinking," *Psychoanalytic Quarterly* 65, no. 1 (1996): 41.

10. Ibid., pp. 35–37.

11. Jones, *Contemporary Psychoanalysis*, pp. 65–66.

12. Ibid., p. 65.

13. W. W. Meissner, *Psychoanalysis and Religious Experience* (New Haven: Yale University Press, 1984), p. 18.

14. Roy Schafer, *Aspects of Internalization* (Madison, Conn.: International Universities Press, 1968), p. 9.

15. Mary Daly, *Beyond God the Father: Toward a Philosophy of Women's Liberation* (Boston: Beacon, 1973), p. 77.

16. Ibid., pp. 75–77.

17. Joanne Carlson Brown and Rebecca Parker, "For God So Loved the World?" in Joanne Carlson Brown and Carole R. Bohn, eds., *Christianity, Patriarchy, and Abuse: A Feminist Critique*, pp. 3, 23 (New York: Pilgrim, 1989).

18. Ibid., p. 23.

19. Henri Hubert and Marcel Mauss, *Sacrifice: Its Nature and Function*, trans. W. D. Halls (Chicago: University of Chicago Press, 1898), p. 35.

20. Ibid., p. 97.

21. Ivan Strenski, "Reading Between the Lines of Sacrifice" (paper presented at the annual meeting of the American Academy of Religion, Chicago, November 1994).

22. In Burton Mack, "Introduction: Religion and Ritual," in Walter Burkert, René Girard, and Jonathan Z. Smith, *Violent Origins: Ritual Killing and Cultural Formation*, pp. 6–9 (Stanford: Stanford University Press, 1987).

23. Mary Daly makes a similar argument with regard to Jesus as sacrificial victim in *Beyond God the Father*, p. 76.

24. From a womanist perspective, Delores Williams explains that a major theological problem in any theology significantly informed by the experience of African American women with surrogacy is the place of the cross. Both coerced surrogacy—in the areas of nurturance, field labor, and sexuality in the pre–Civil War period—and voluntary surrogacy, particularly in the role of the "mammy" during the postbellum period, are part of the history of African American women. Williams asserts that theologians in mainline Christian churches teach that Jesus, in taking human sin upon himself, represents the ultimate surrogate figure. Surrogacy thus takes on the aura of the sacred. Williams argues that "the womanist theologian must show that redemption of humans can have

nothing to do with any kind of surrogate or substitute role Jesus was reputed to have played in a bloody act that supposedly gained victory over sin and/or evil." Delores S. Williams, *Sisters in the Wilderness: The Challenge of Womanist God-Talk* (Maryknoll, N.Y.: Orbis, 1993), p. 165. For Williams, to glorify the cross is to glorify sin. See also Williams, "Black Women's Surrogacy Experience and the Christian Notion of Redemption," in Paula M. Cooey, William R. Eakin, and Jay B. McDaniel, eds., *After Patriarchy: Feminist Transformations of the World Religions*, pp. 1–14 (Maryknoll, N.Y.: Orbis, 1991). My theory of sacrifice does not include surrogacy.

25. Susan Nowak points out that Girard does have a notion of "positive mimesis," which is nonacquisitive and nonconflictual. She argues that his concept of difference conceives of differentiation not in terms of dichotomous oppositionality but in terms of separation and identity, or distinctiveness and similarity. In her reading of Girard, differentiation can take place without violence, for it is the collapse of difference that leads to victimage. Susan Nowak, "The Girardian Theory and Feminism: Critique and Appropriation," *Contagion: Journal of Violence, Mimesis, and Culture* 1 (1994): 27. While Nowak's theory is intriguing, in my view Girard's lack of gender analysis obfuscates the usefulness of positive mimesis to explore women as other than scapegoats for male violence. Future feminist scholarship may obviate this problem.

26. The earlier work is William Robertson Smith's *Lectures on the Religion of the Semite* (London, 1894). Sigmund Freud, *Totem and Taboo (1913)*, in *The Pelican Freud Library*, vol. 13, *The Origins of Religion*, ed. Albert Dickson (Harmondsworth, Middlesex, England: Penguin, 1985), pp. 193–217.

27. A more recent effort by Martin Bergmann integrates Oedipal theory with scapegoat psychology to posit that Christ is the universal scapegoat and that Christianity "reintroduced the celebratory killing and eating of the god." Martin Bergmann, *In the Shadow of Moloch: The Sacrifice of Children and Its Impact on Western Religions* (New York: Columbia University Press, 1992), p. 5. Here, sacrifice is based on the primary process idea that ritualistic destruction is pleasing to the deity and that one life can be purchased by the taking of another (p. 47)—in other words, that aggression and displacement are inherent in both gods and human beings.

28. René Girard, *Violence and the Sacred*, trans. Patrick Gregory (Baltimore: Johns Hopkins University Press, 1977), pp. 169–170.

29. Ibid., pp. 173, 201.

30. Bergmann suggests that we cannot completely accept the idea that Abraham sacrificed Isaac or that God sacrificed Jesus without feelings of

hostility. Bergmann, *In the Shadow*, p. 7.

31. While much has been written concerning Freud's treatment of women, his relationship with his mother, and blatant misogyny in his theories, the impact of the Oedipal slant of his thought on his theories about culture has been less fully investigated. Eli Sagan suggests that while inadequacies in Freudian theory arise from repression of the pre-Oedipal mother, it would be a mistake to look for their source in some lack in Freud's psyche or character, for the same pre-Oedipal ambivalence runs through all of Western culture. Eli Sagan, *Freud, Women, and Morality: The Psychology of Good and Evil* (New York: Basic Books, 1988), p. 9. Sagan attempts to demonstrate that Freud's anxiety about women produced not only antifeminist theory on matters directly concerning women but also rendered crucially important theoretical distortions in areas that, on the surface, do not bear directly on the question of male-female equality. He proposes that no adequate theory of morality, civilization, science, and reason can be constructed as long as it is erected upon a primarily Oedipal foundation (pp. 62–64).

32. Nancy Jay, *Throughout Your Generations Forever: Sacrifice, Religion, and Paternity* (Chicago: University of Chicago Press, 1992), p. 32. Subsequent citations to this source are indicated by parenthetical page numbers within the text.

33. Nancy Jay, "Throughout Your Generations Forever: A Sociology of Blood Sacrifice" (Ph.D. diss., Brandeis University, 1982), pp. 4, 276.

34. Jay, *Throughout*, p. 133.

35. William Beers, *Women and Sacrifice: Male Narcissism and the Psychology of Religion* (Detroit: Wayne State University Press, 1992), p. 140.

36. Ibid., 140–141.

37. William Beers, "Real Food for Real People: A Sociocultural and Psychological Perspective on Sacrifice" (paper presented at the annual meeting of the American Academy of Religion, Chicago, November 1994).

38. Diane Jonte-Pace, "New Directions in the Feminist Psychology of Religion: An Introduction," *Journal of Feminist Studies in Religion* 13, no. 1 (Spring 1997): 68.

39. Jay, *Throughout*, p. 112.

40. Jay, "Throughout," pp. 288, 290.

41. Jay, *Throughout*, pp. 126–127.

42. Beers, *Women and Sacrifice*, p. 167.

43. Jay, *Throughout*, p. 62.

44. Jon D. Levenson, *The Death and Resurrection of the Beloved Son: The Transformation of Sacrifice in Judaism and Christianity* (New Haven:

Yale University Press, 1993), p. 138. Subsequent citations to this source are indicated by parenthetical page numbers within the text.

46. Alister E. McGrath, *Christian Theology: An Introduction* (Oxford: Blackwell, 1994), pp. 351–352.

47. Michael Balint is one exception. See Michael Balint, *The Basic Fault: Therapeutic Aspects of Regression* (New York: Brunner/Mazel, 1968).

48. Margaret S. Mahler, "On the First Three Subphases of the Separation-Individuation Process," in Peter Buckley, ed., *Essential Papers on Object Relations*, p. 223 (New York and London: New York University Press, 1986).

49. In Mahler, Pine, and Bergman, *Psychological Birth*, p. 10.

50. Marija Gimbutas, *The Civilization of the Goddess* (San Francisco: HarperSanFrancisco, 1991), pp. 244, 294, 344.

51. Balint, *The Basic Fault*, p. 66.

52. Ibid., p. 65.

53. D. W. Winnicott, *Collected Papers: Through Paediatrics to Psycho-Analysis* (New York: Brunner/Mazel, 1958), pp. 219–242.

54. Mahler, Pine, and Bergman, *Psychological Birth*, pp. 39–40.

55. Mary Grey uses "right relation" as a model for atonement. Mary Grey, *Feminism, Redemption, and the Christian Tradition* (Mystic, Conn.: Twenty-third Publications, 1990), pp. 160, 165, 170, 186.

56. Mary Ellen Ross and Cheryl Linn Ross, "Mothers, Infants, and the Psychoanalytic Study of Ritual," *Signs: Journal of Women in Culture and Society* 9 (Autumn 1983), p. 34.

57. Eva P. Lester, "Gender and Identity Issues in the Analytic Process," *International Journal of Psycho-Analysis* 71 (1990): 438. While research on this topic is not conclusive, even Freud suggested that female analysts may be better able to perceive concerns involved in the first attachment to the mother than male analysts. See Freud, "Female Sexuality (1931)," in *The Pelican Freud Library*, vol. 7, *On Sexuality*, ed. Angela Richards, p. 373 (Harmondsworth, Middlesex, England: Penguin Books, 1977).

58. Nancy Chodorow, "Gender, Relation, and Difference in Psychoanalytic Perspective," in Hester Eisenstein and Alice Jardine, eds., *The Future of Difference*, pp. 10–11 (New Brunswick, N.J.: Rutgers University Press, 1987).

59. Ibid., p. 10.

60. Edwina Hunter, "Reflections on the Christa from a Christian Theologian," *Journal of Women Religion* 4, no. 2 (Winter 1985): 30.

61. Johannes H. Emminghaus, *The Eucharist: Essence, Form, Celebration*, trans. Matthew J. O'Connell (Collegeville, Minn.: Liturgical

Press, 1978), p. xxi. In turn, Kilmartin states that sacrifice revolves around the self-offering of God, Christ, and Christians, visibly exemplified in the eucharistic meal. Edward J. Kilmartin, S.J., *Church, Eucharist, and Priesthood* (New York: Paulist Press, 1981), pp. 9–11.

62. Lucien Deiss, *It's the Lord's Supper: The Eucharist of Christians*, trans. Edmond Bonin (New York: Paulist Press, 1976), pp. 71–76.

63. David N. Power, *The Eucharistic Mystery: Revitalizing the Tradition* (New York: Crossroad, 1993), p. 56. Subsequent citations to this source are indicated by parenthetical page numbers within the text.

64. Vatican Council (Second: 1962–1965), *The Documents of Vatican II* (Grand Rapids, Mich.: Eerdmans, 1975), p. 20.

65. Karl Rahner, *The Church and the Sacraments*, trans. W. J. O'Hara (New York: Herder and Herder, 1963), p. 83.

66. Grey, *Feminism*, p. 160. Grey observes that at-one-ment based on the theme of the will to communion, or the dynamic of mutuality, has many similarities to a psychotherapeutic approach. The essence of the therapeutic relationship is the cure and change (salvation/redemption) of brokenness in human relationship, and restoration of mutuality (p. 165).

67. Ibid., p. 170.

68. Ibid., p. 186.

69. Elizabeth Johnson, "Redeeming the Name of Christ," in Catherine Mowry LaCugna, ed., *Freeing Theology: The Essentials of Theology in Feminist Perspective*, p. 125 (San Francisco: HarperSanFrancisco, 1993).

70. Isabel Carter Heyward, *The Redemption of God: A Theology of Mutual Relation* (Lanham, Md.: University Press of America, 1982), p. 6.

71. Brown and Parker, "For God So Loved the World?" p. 26.

72. Sally B. Purvis, *The Power of the Cross: Foundations for a Christian Feminist Ethic of Community* (Nashville: Abingdon, 1993), p. 88.

73. Ibid., p. 97.

74. Marjorie Procter-Smith, *In Her Own Rite: Constructing Feminist Liturgical Tradition* (Nashville: Abingdon, 1990), p. 143.

75. Marjorie Procter-Smith, *Praying with Our Eyes Open: Engendering Feminist Liturgical Prayer* (Nashville: Abingdon, 1995), pp. 101–102.

76. Elisabeth Schüssler Fiorenza, "Tablesharing and the Celebration of the Eucharist," in Mary Collins and David Power, eds., *Can We Always Celebrate the Eucharist?*, Concilium 152, p. 4 (New York: Seabury, 1982). Cited in Procter-Smith, *In Her Own Rite*, p. 150.

77. This phrase was first used by Catherine Keller in *From a Broken Web: Separation, Sexism, and Self* (Boston: Beacon, 1986).

78. Kelly Oliver, *Reading Kristeva: Unraveling the Double-Bind* (Bloomington: Indiana University Press, 1993), p. 64.

5. CHRIST AS A WOMAN

1. Sheila Greeve Davaney, "Continuing the Story, but Departing the Text: A Historicist Interpretation of Feminist Norms in Theology," in Rebecca S. Chopp and Sheila Greeve Davaney, eds., *Horizons in Feminist Theology: Identity, Tradition, and Norms*, p. 207 (Minneapolis: Fortress, 1997).

2. Anne E. Carr, *Transforming Grace: Christian Tradition and Women's Experience* (San Francisco: Harper and Row, 1988), pp. 124–126.

3. Hester Eisenstein, introduction to Hester Eisenstein and Alice Jardine, eds., *The Future of Difference* (New Brunswick, N.J.: Rutgers University Press, 1985), p. xvi.

4. Shulamith Firestone, *The Dialectic of Sex: The Case for Feminist Revolution* (New York: Bantam, 1970).

5. Adrienne Rich, *Of Woman Born: Motherhood as Experience and Institution* (New York: Norton, 1976).

6. Eisenstein, "Introduction," p. xviii.

7. Virginia Sapiro, *Women in American Society: An Introduction to Women's Studies*, 3d ed. (Mountain View, Calif.: Mayfield Publishing, 1994), pp. 89–117.

8. Martha Long Ice, *Clergy Women and Their Worldviews: Calling for a New Age* (New York: Praeger, 1987), p. 4.

9. Carol Gilligan and Grant Wiggins, "The Origins of Morality in Early Childhood," in Carol Gilligan, Janie Victoria Ward, Jill McLean Taylor, with Betty Bardige, eds., *Mapping the Moral Domain: A Contribution of Women's Thinking to Psychological Theory and Education*, pp. 111-117 (Cambridge: Harvard University Press, 1988).

10. Lesley Stevens, "Different Voice/Different Voices: Anglican Women in Ministry," *Review of Religious Research* 30, no. 3 (March 1989): 262.

11. Ibid., p. 262. See Carol Gilligan, *In a Different Voice: Psychological Theory and Women's Development* (Cambridge: Harvard University Press, 1982).

12. For elaboration of these critiques and Gilligan's response, see Linda K. Kerber et al., "On *In a Different Voice*: An Interdisciplinary Forum," *Signs: Journal of Women in Culture and Society* 11, no. 2 (Winter 1986): 305–333.

13. Rosemarie Tong, *Feminine and Feminist Ethics* (Belmont, Calif.: Wadsworth, 1993), pp. 5–6. Tong finds problems with each of these schools of thought.

14. See ibid., p. 56.

15. For example, Mary Daly, *Gyn/ecology: The Metaethics of Radical Feminism* (Boston: Beacon, 1978), and Daly, *Pure Lust* (Boston: Beacon, 1984).

16. Sheila Greeve Davaney, "The Limits of the Appeal to Women's Experience," in Clarissa W. Atkinson, Constance H. Buchanan, and Margaret R. Miles, eds., *Shaping New Vision: Gender and Values in American Culture*, p. 41 (Ann Arbor: UMI Research Press, 1987).

17. In contrast, Daly, states Davaney, "grounds her claims of epistemological privilege primarily in the assumption that women possess a distinctive nature, with innate female faculties that are capable of non-distorted, adequate, and true knowledge of Being." Ibid., p. 42.

18. Carol Christ, *Diving Deep and Surfacing: Women Writers on Spiritual Quest* (Boston: Beacon, 1980).

19. Mary Daly, *Beyond God the Father: Toward a Philosophy of Women's Liberation* (Boston: Beacon, 1973); Daly, *Gyn/ecology*.

20. Naomi R. Goldenberg, *Changing of the Gods: Feminism and the End of Traditional Religion* (Boston: Beacon, 1979).

21. Judith Plaskow, *Sex, Sin, and Grace: Women's Experience and the Theologies of Reinhold Niebuhr and Paul Tillich* (Washington, D.C.: University Press of America, 1980).

22. Rosemary Radford Ruether, *New Woman/New Earth: Sexist Ideologies and Human Liberation* (New York: Seabury, 1975).

23. See, for example, Carol P. Christ and Judith Plaskow, eds., *Womanspirit Rising: A Feminist Reader in Religion* (San Francisco: Harper and Row, 1979).

24. Davaney, "Continuing the Story," p. 199.

25. Serene Jones, "Women's Experience Between a Rock and a Hard Place: Feminist, Womanist, and *Mujerista* Theologies in North America," in Chopp and Devaney, *Horizons in Feminist Theology*, pp. 33–53.

26. Jones examines three types of approaches used by women scholars that she claims essentialize experience: phenomenological, process/psychoanalytic, and literary/textual. She also analyzes two frameworks that consciously use experience as historically localized and culturally specific: cultural anthropology and poststructuralism. I will give some attention to her analysis of the process/psychoanalytic and poststructuralist approaches.

Jones explains that the methodology associated with the process/psychoanalytic approach emphasizes universalizing structures that organize a "relational self"—in other words, relationality becomes the locus of a new "essence" or structural coherence of the subject. Using as representative texts Rita Nakashima Brock's *Journeys by Heart: A Christology of Erotic Power* (New York: Crossroad, 1988) and Catherine Keller's *From a Broken Web: Separation, Sexism, and Self* (Boston: Beacon, 1986), Jones critiques their uncritical deployment of such categories as feeling, memory, and creativity without reference to the constructed character of such terminology (p. 40). She also faults both texts for "systematizing experience." In addition, she argues that there is a tendency within psychoanalysis to posit the triadic family, with its distributed social roles, as a universal given.

Concerning poststructuralist accounts of women's experience, Jones observes that their methodology relies upon conceptual tools rather than an analytic scheme. This approach, illustrated in Rebecca Chopp's *The Power to Speak: Feminism, Language, God* (New York: Crossroad, 1989) attempts to honor unique discursive practices of historically marginalized voices by celebrating differences while simultaneously discerning unifying themes (p. 51). Jones asks: "Is a rhetoric which celebrates the fragmentation of the subject strategically well suited for persons who are struggling to claim a sense of wholeness and stability, having been oppressively fractured by their time on the margin?" (p. 52). I share Jones's criticisms of a poststructuralist approach, yet I find this methodology useful in deconstructing androcentric Catholic dogma. Sometimes, fragmentation of the subject is actually advantageous to women's status (see chapter 6).

27. Davaney, "Continuing the Story," pp. 209, 212, 214.

28. Nancy Chodorow, "Gender as a Personal and Cultural Construction," *Signs: Journal of Women in Culture and Society* 20, no. 3 (1995): 518, 522.

29. See Sapiro, *Women in American Society*, pp. 358–393.

30. Mircea Eliade, *Myths, Rites, Symbols: A Mircea Eliade Reader*, vol. 1, ed. Wendell Beane and William G. Doty (New York: Harper and Row, 1975), p. 88.

31. Paul Tillich, "Symbols of Faith," in Ronald E. Santoni, ed., *Religious Language and the Problem of Religious Knowledge*, pp. 136–137 (Bloomington: Indiana University Press, 1968).

32. Clifford Geertz, *The Interpretation of Cultures* (New York: Basic Books, 1973), p. 90.

33. Ibid., p. 91.

34. Ibid., p. 93.

35. Carol P. Christ, "Why Women Need the Goddess: Phenomenological, Psychological, and Political Reflections," in Charlene Spretnak, ed., *The Politics of Women's Spirituality*, p. 73 (Garden City, N.Y.: Anchor Books, 1982).

36. Daly, *Beyond God the Father*, p. 19.

37. Ross Shepard Kraemer, *Her Share of the Blessings: Women's Religions Among Pagans, Jews, and Christians in the Greco-Roman World* (New York: Oxford University Press, 1992), pp. 14, 16, 201. Kraemer utilizes a classification strategy proposed by anthropologist Mary Douglas. "Grid" also measures the degree to which people hold common beliefs about the way things are. Where grid is strong, people utilize language and symbols to communicate those beliefs in condensed forms (p. 14).

38. David Kinsley, *The Goddesses' Mirror: Visions of the Divine from East and West* (Albany: State University of New York Press, 1989), p. 215.

39. W. W. Meissner, *Psychoanalysis and Religious Experience* (New Haven: Yale University Press, 1984), p. 171.

40. W, W. Meissner, "The Role of Transitional Conceptualization in Religious Thought," in Joseph H. Smith, ed., *Psychoanalysis and Religion*, p. 105 (Baltimore: Johns Hopkins University Press, 1990).

41. Ernest Wallwork, "Sigmund Freud: The Psychoanalytic Diagnosis—Infantile Illusion," in Roger A. Johnson et al., eds., *Critical Issues in Modern Religion*, 2d ed., p. 132 (Englewood Cliffs, N.J.: Prentice Hall, 1990).

42. Sigmund Freud, *Totem and Taboo (1913)*, in *The Pelican Freud Library*, vol. 13, *The Origins of Religion*, ed. Albert Dickson, pp. 211, 215 (Harmondsworth, Middlesex, England: Penguin Books, 1985).

43. Meissner, "Role of Transitional Conceptualization," p. 105.

44. Ana-Maria Rizzuto, *The Birth of the Living God: A Psychoanalytic Study* (Chicago: University of Chicago Press, 1979), pp. 185–186.

45. In James Jones, *Contemporary Psychoanalysis and Religion: Transference and Transcendence* (New Haven: Yale University Press, 1991), pp. 42–43.

46. Rizzuto, *Birth of the Living God*, pp. 48, 179.

47. Meissner, "Role of Transitional Conceptualization," pp. 109–112.

48. Gerald F. O'Hanlon, S.J., *The Immutability of God in the Theology of Hans Urs von Balthasar* (Cambridge: Cambridge University Press, 1990), pp. 9–10.

49. Alister E. McGrath, *Christian Theology: An Introduction* (Oxford: Blackwell, 1994), pp. 137–139.

50. Marcus J. Borg, *Meeting Jesus Again for the First Time: The Historical Jesus and the Heart of Contemporary Faith* (San Francisco: Harper, 1994), pp. 109–111.

51. Rosemary Radford Ruether, "Can Christology Be Liberated from Patriarchy?" in Maryanne Stevens, ed., *Reconstructing the Christ Symbol: Essays in Feminist Christology*, p. 12 (New York: Paulist Press, 1993).

52. Ibid., pp. 23–24.

53. Mary Hembrow Snyder, *The Christology of Rosemary Radford Ruether: A Critical Introduction* (Mystic, Conn.: Twenty-third Publications, 1988), p. 68.

54. Ibid., p. 69.

55. Hwain Chang Lee, *Confucius, Christ, and Co-Partnership: Competing Liturgies for the Soul of Korean American Women* (Lanham, Md.: University Press of America, 1994), p. 80.

56. Chung Hyun Kyung, *Struggle to Be the Sun Again: Introducing Asian Women's Theology* (Maryknoll, N.Y.: Orbis, 1990), p. 64.

57. Ibid., pp. 65–66.

58. Ibid., p. 66. Asian American ethicist Young Mi Angela Pak informed me that this is not the typical view of Korean Christians.

59. Elizabeth A. Johnson, "Wisdom Was Made Flesh and Pitched Her Tent Among Us," in Maryanne Stevens, *Reconstructing the Christ Symbol*, p. 103.

60. Elizabeth A. Johnson, *She Who Is: The Mystery of God in Feminist Theological Discourse* (New York: Crossroad, 1992), pp. 90–91.

61. Ibid., p. 95.

62. Ibid., p. 99.

63. Elisabeth Schüssler Fiorenza, *Jesus: Miriam's Child, Sophia's Prophet* (New York: Continuum, 1994), pp. 148, 152, 157.

64. Borg, *Meeting Jesus*, p. 102.

65. Ibid., p. 108.

66. Ibid., p. 111.

67. Jacqueline Grant, "Womanist Theology: Black Women's Experience as a Source for Doing Theology, with Special Reference to Christology," *Journal of the Interdenominational Theological Center* 13, no. 2 (Spring 1986), p. 210. Cited in Kelly Brown Douglas, *The Black Christ* (Maryknoll, N.Y.: Orbis, 1994), p. 109.

68. Kelly Delaine Brown, "God Is as Christ Does: Toward a Womanist Theology," *Journal of Religious Thought* 46, no. 1 (Summer–Fall 1989): 16.

69. Douglas, *The Black Christ*, p. 108.

70. From Maria Pilar Aquino, *Our Cry for Life: Feminist Theology from Latin America*, trans. Dinah Livingstone (Maryknoll, N.Y.: Orbis, 1993), p. 145.

71. Ibid., p. 149.

72. Quoted in Ada María Isasi-Díaz, *Mujerista Theology: A Theology for the Twenty-first Century* (Maryknoll, N.Y.: Orbis, 1996), p. 183.

73. Ibid., p. 198.

74. Ibid., p. 189.

75. Johnson, *She Who Is*, pp. 70, 73.

76. Goldenberg, *Changing of the Gods*, p. 9.

77. Susan Cady, Marian Ronan, and Hall Taussig, *Sophia: The Future of Feminist Spirituality* (San Francisco: Harper and Row, 1986), p. 83.

78. Mary Douglas, *Cultural Bias* (occasional paper no. 35 of the Royal Anthropological Institute of Great Britain and Ireland, London, 1978). Cited in Kraemer, *Her Share of the Blessings*, p. 20.

79. Christ, "Why Women Need the Goddess," pp. 74–84.

80. Nelle Morton, *The Journey Is Home* (Boston: Beacon, 1985), p. 143.

81. Jann Aldredge Clanton, *In Whose Image? God and Gender* (New York: Crossroad, 1991), p. 68.

82. Ibid., pp. 72, 76.

83. Ibid., p. 96.

84. James Fowler, *Stages of Faith: The Psychology of Human Development and the Quest for Meaning* (San Francisco: Harper and Row, 1981), pp. 128–129. Subsequent citations to this source are indicated by parenthetical page numbers within the text.

85. Robert Coles, *The Spiritual Life of Children* (Boston: Houghton Mifflin, 1990), pp. 57–59.

86. Julia Wally Rath, "Faith, Hope, and Education: African-American Parents of Children in Catholic Schools and their Social and Religious Accommodation to Catholicism" (Ph.D. diss., University of Chicago, 1995), p. 244.

87. Ibid., pp. 244–245.

88. Robert D. Nye, *Three Psychologies: Perspectives from Freud, Skinner, and Rogers*, 4th ed. (Pacific Grove, Calif.: Brooks/Cole, 1992), p. 20.

89. I. Hendrick, "Early Development of the Ego: Identification in Infancy," in George H. Pollock, ed., *Pivotal Papers on Identification*, p. 127 (Madison, Conn.: International Universities Press, 1993), p. 127.

90. R. Schafer, "Identification: A Comprehensive and Flexible Definition," in Pollock, *Pivotal Papers*, pp. 307, 325.

91. Ibid., p. 307.

92. Kelley Ann Raab, "Christology Crossing Boundaries: The Threat of Imaging Christ as Other Than a White Male," *Pastoral Psychology* 45, no. 5 (1997): 389–399.

93. Nancy Chodorow, *The Reproduction of Mothering: Psychoanalysis and the Sociology of Gender* (Berkeley: University of California Press, 1978), pp. 205–209.

94. Nancy Chodorow, *Feminism and Psychoanalytic Theory* (New Haven: Yale University Press, 1989), p. 111.

95. Ibid., p. 111.

96. Kenneth B. Clark and Mamie K. Clark, "The Development of Consciousness of Self and the Emergence of Racial Identification in Negro Preschool Children," *Journal of Psychology, SPSSI Bulletin* 10 (1939): 591–599.

97. Ibid., p. 594.

98. Sharon-Ann Gopaul-McNicol, "Racial Identification and Racial Preference of Black Preschool Children in New York and Trinidad," in A. Kathleen Hoard Burlew, W. Curtis Banks, Harriette Pipe McAdoo, and Daudi Ajani ya Azibo, eds., *African American Psychology: Theory, Research, and Practice*, pp. 190–193 (Newbury Park, Calif.: Sage, 1992).

99. Among the places *Christa* opened were Stanford University and the Bade Museum. Mary Cross, "Introduction from the Publisher," *Journal of Women and Religion* 4, no. 2 (Winter 1985): 3–4.

100. Eleanor McLaughlin, "Feminist Christologies: Re-Dressing the Tradition," in Maryanne Stevens, *Reconstructing the Christ Symbol*, p. 127.

101. Edwina Hunter, "Reflections on the Christa from a Christian Theologian," *Journal of Women and Religion*, 4, no. 2 (Winter 1985): 26.

102. Cross, "Introduction," pp. 3–4.

103. Hunter, "Reflections," pp. 25–26.

104. In ibid., p. 26.

105. In Sandra Winter Park, "Reflections on the Christa from a Theological Educator," *Journal of Women and Religion* 4, no. 2 (Winter 1985): 49.

106. Rev. Dr. Gloria Smallwood, "Reflections on the Christa from a Pastor," *Journal of Women and Religion* 4, no. 2 (Winter 1985): 41–42.

107. McLaughlin, "Feminist Christologies," p. 127.

6. GENDER, SEX, AND GOD

1. Ellie Ragland-Sullivan, *Jacques Lacan and the Philosophy of Psychoanalysis* (Urbana: University of Illinois Press, 1986), pp. 284, 287.

2. Kelly Oliver, *Reading Kristeva: Unraveling the Double-Bind* (Bloomington: Indiana University Press, 1993), p. 179.

3. Kelly Oliver, "Julia Kristeva's Feminist Revolutions," *Hypatia* 8, no. 3 (Summer 1993): 96.

4. Julia Kristeva, *New Maladies of the Soul*, trans. Ross Guberman (New York: Columbia University Press, 1995), pp. 103–104.

5. Kristeva's semiotic is also equivalent to Freud's primary process and is similar to Lacan's concept of the imaginary. See Anika Lemaire, *Jacques Lacan*, trans. David Macey (London: Routledge and Kegan Paul, 1977), pp. 60–61.

6. Chris Weedon, *Feminist Practice and Poststructuralist Theory* (Oxford: Blackwell, 1987), p. 161.

7. Toril Moi, *Sexual/Textual Politics: Feminist Literary Theory* (London: Methuen, 1985), p. 166.

8. Moi, *Sexual/Textual*, p. 165; Weedon, *Feminist Practice*, p. 69.

9. Diane Jonte-Pace, "Feminist Transformations in the Psychology of Religion: New Developments in Method and Theory," *Method and Theory in the Study of Religion*, in press.

10. Jane Flax, *Thinking Fragments: Psychoanalysis, Feminism, and Postmodernism in the Contemporary West* (Berkeley: University of California Press, 1990), p. 178.

11. Luce Irigaray, *This Sex Which Is Not One*, trans. Catherine Porter (Ithaca: Cornell University Press, 1985), pp. 23–33.

12. Rosemarie Tong, *Feminist Thought: A Comprehensive Introduction* (Boulder: Westview, 1989), p. 232.

13. Kristeva, *New Maladies*, pp. 118–119.

14. Luce Irigaray, "Equal to Whom?" *Differences* 1, no. 2 (1989): 70.

15. Ibid., p. 72.

16. Morny Joy, "Equality or Divinity: A False Dichotomy?" *Journal of Feminist Studies in Religion* 6 (Spring 1990): 9–24.

17. Cleo McNelly Kearns, "Kristeva and Feminist Theology," in C. W. Maggie Kim, Susan M. St. Ville, and Susan M. Simonaitis, eds., *Transfigurations: Theology and the French Feminists*, pp. 66, 75 (Minneapolis: Fortress, 1993).

18. Julia Kristeva, *Powers of Horror: An Essay on Abjection*, trans. Leon S. Roudiez (New York: Columbia University Press, 1982), pp. 119, 188.

19. According to Kristeva, the Eucharist represents the individual as divided and lapsing, a split subject with regard to Christ the ideal. Christ alone, a heterogeneous body, is without sin, and temporarily gives back childhood innocence by means of communion. Ibid., pp. 118–120.

20. Kristeva, *New Maladies*, pp. 173–174.

21. Ibid., p. 178.

22. Luce Irigaray, "The Bodily Encounter with the Mother," in Margaret Whitford, ed., *The Irigaray Reader*, pp. 45–46 (Oxford: Blackwell, 1991).

23. Luce Irigaray, *Sexes and Genealogies*, trans. Gillian C. Gill (New York: Columbia University Press, 1993), p. 26 n. 3.

24. Kristeva, *Powers*, pp. 77, 96.

25. Martha Reineke, "The Mother in Mimesis: Kristeva and Girard on Violence and the Sacred," in David R. Crownfield, ed., *Body/Text in Julia Kristeva: Religion, Women, and Psychoanalysis*, p. 75 (Albany: State University of New York Press, 1992).

26. Ibid., p. 81.

27. David Crownfield, "Inter-Text 4," in ibid., p. 88.

28. Irigaray uses the example of the murder of Clytemnestra by her son Orestes in the *Oresteia*. See Irigaray, "Bodily Encounter," p. 37.

29. Diane Jonte-Pace, "Julia Kristeva and the Psychoanalytic Study of Religion: Rethinking Freud's Cultural Texts," in Janet Liebman Jacobs and Donald Capps, eds., *Religion, Society, and Psychoanalysis: Readings in Contemporary Theory*, p. 253 (Boulder: Westview, 1997).

30. Julia Kristeva, *Black Sun: Depression and Melancholia*, trans. Leon S. Roudiez (New York: Columbia University Press, 1989), pp. 27–28.

31. Martha J. Reineke, *Sacrificed Lives: Kristeva on Women and Violence* (Bloomington: Indiana University Press, 1997), p. 30.

32. Ibid., p. 37.

33. Ibid., p. 69.

34. Luce Irigaray, "Women, the Sacred, and Money," *Paragraph* 8 (1986): 10–11.

35. Reineke, "The Mother in Mimesis," pp. 67–68.

36. Irigaray, "Bodily Encounter," p. 46.

37. *Fertility* in this context does not refer to ritual prostitution.

38. Luce Irigaray, "Women-Amongst-Themselves: Creating a Woman-to-Woman Sociality," in Whitford, *The Irigaray Reader*, p. 193.

39. Margaret Whitford, *Luce Irigaray: Philosophy in the Feminine* (London: Routledge, 1991), p. 146.

40. Elizabeth Gross, "The Body of Signification," in John Fletcher and Andrew Benjamin, eds., *Abjection, Melancholia, and Love: The Work of Julia Kristeva*, p. 92 (London: Routledge, 1990).

41. Ibid., p. 87.

42. Julia Kristeva, *Desire in Language: A Semiotic Approach to Literature and Art*, ed. Leon S. Roudiez, trans. Thomas Gora, Alice Jardine, and Leon S. Roudiez (New York: Columbia University Press, 1980), p. 286.

43. Gross, "The Body of Signification," p. 95.

44. Kristeva, *New Maladies*, p. 219.

45. Gross, "The Body of Signification," p. 96.

46. David Fisher, "Kristeva's *Chora* and the Subject of Postmodern Ethics," in Crownfield, *Body/Text in Julia Kristeva*, p. 98.

47. Julia Kristeva, *Tales of Love*, trans. Leon S. Roudiez (New York: Columbia University Press, 1987), p. 254.

48. David Crownfield, "Inter-Text 5," in Crownfield, *Body/Text in Julia Kristeva*, p. 108.

49. Ewa Ziarek, "At the Limits of Discourse: Heterogeneity, Alterity, and the Maternal Body in Kristeva's Thought," *Hypatia* 7, no. 2 (Spring 1992): 92.

50. Janet Martin Soskice, "Blood and Defilement: Feminism and the Atonement" (lecture given at Harvard Divinity School, Cambridge, November 1994).

51. David Crownfield states that through the mediation of the death of Christ, the "unbearable ambiguity of the flesh has been transfigured into a signifier of the stainless body . . . thus re-marking the life of the communicant as bearable, as . . . one with the symbolic, with God." David Crownfield, "The Seminal Trace: Presence, Difference, and Transsubstantiation," *Journal of the American Academy of Religion* 59, no. 2 (Summer 1991): 370.

52. Denise G. Haines, "Women's Ordination: What Difference Has It Made?" *Christian Century* 103, no. 30 (October 15, 1986), p. 888.

53. In affirming that Christ is both truly human and truly divine, the doctrine of hypostatic union attempted to quell heresies that Christ only appeared to take on fleshly form and therefore did not suffer and die or that Christ was not really God. See Alister McGrath, *Christian Theology: An Introduction* (Oxford: Blackwell, 1994), pp. 291, 295.

54. Delores Williams, *Sisters in the Wilderness: The Challenge of Womanist God-Talk* (Maryknoll, N.Y.: Orbis, 1993), p. 203.

55. Elizabeth Schüssler Fioreza, *Jesus: Miriam's Child, Sophia's Prophet* (New York: Continuum, 1994), p. 22.

56. Karl Rahner, *A Rahner Reader*, ed. Gerald A. McCool (New York: Seabury, 1975), p. 170.

57. Eleanor McLaughlin, "Feminist Christologies: Re-Dressing the Tradition," in Maryanne Stevens, ed., *Reconstructing the Christ Symbol: Essays in Feminist Christology*, p. 131 (New York: Paulist Press, 1993).

58. Oliver, "Julia Kristeva's Feminist Revolutions," p. 99.

59. Ibid., p. 100.

60. In contrast, she sees the pre-Oedipal mother as a figure encompassing both masculinity and femininity.

61. In John Morgan, *Women Priests* (Bristol, Ind.: Wyndam Hall, 1985), p. 155.

62. Alexina Murphy, "Self-Awareness in the Image of God," in Alyson Peberdy, ed., *Women Priests?*, p. 75 (Basingstoke, Hants, U.K.:

Marshall Pickering, 1988).

63. Kristeva notes that for Renaissance painters, Jesus had a sexuality, but she does not pursue the topic further. *New Maladies*, p. 157.

64. Whitford, *Luce Irigaray*, p. 93.

65. Maria-Teresa Porcile-Santiso, "Roman Catholic Teachings on Female Sexuality," in Jeanne Becher, ed., *Women, Religion, and Sexuality: Studies on the Impact of Religious Teachings on Women*, p. 198 (Philadelphia: Trinity Press International, 1991).

66. Ibid., p. 198.

67. Quoted in ibid., p. 204.

68. Ibid.

69. Rosemary Radford Ruether, "Catholicism, Women, Body and Sexuality: A Response," in Becher, *Women, Religion, and Sexuality*, p. 231.

70. Ibid., p. 230.

71. Ibid., p. 223.

72. Rita Nakashima Brock, *Journeys by Heart: A Christology of Erotic Power* (New York: Crossroad, 1988), p. 25.

73. Carol Christ, "In Praise of Aphrodite: Sexuality as Sacred," in Elizabeth Dodson Gray, ed., *Sacred Dimensions of Women's Experience*, p. 226 (Wellesley: Roundtable Press, 1988).

74. Carter Heyward, *Speaking of Christ: A Lesbian Feminist Voice*, ed. Ellen C. Davis (New York: Pilgrim Press, 1989), p. 22. See also Carter Heyward, *Touching Our Strength: The Erotic as Power and the Love of God* (San Francisco: Harper and Row, 1989). "Christa" for Heyward refers to a female symbol of Christ, of which the sculpture *Christa* is one example.

75. Kathleen M. Sands, "Uses of the Thea(o)logian: Sex and Theodicy in Religious Feminism," *Journal of Feminist Studies in Religion* 8, no. 1 (Spring 1992): 7–33.

76. Ibid., p. 8.

77. Alla Bozarth-Campbell, *Womanpriest: A Personal Odyssey* (New York: Paulist Press, 1978), p. 171.

78. Pamela W. Darling, *New Wine: The Story of Women Transforming Leadership and Power in the Episcopal Church* (Cambridge: Cowley Publications, 1994), pp. 201–202.

79. Ed Stannard, "Sexuality Statement Made More Conservative," *Episcopal Life*, September 1998, p. 4; Ed Stannard, "Lambeth Showcases Conservative Anglican World," *Episcopal Life*, September 1998, p. 1.

80. Irigaray, "Equal to Whom?" p. 68.

81. Ibid.

82. Robert Goss, *Jesus Acted Up: A Gay and Lesbian Manifesto* (New York: HarperCollins, 1993), pp. 64, 69.

83. Irigaray, "Equal to Whom?" p. 65.

84. Ibid., p. 62.

85. Ibid., p. 64.

86. Elizabeth Grosz, "Irigaray and the Divine," in Kim, St. Ville, and Simonaitis, *Transfigurations*, p. 204.

87. Luce Irigaray, *An Ethics of Sexual Difference*, trans. Carolyn Burke and Gillian C. Gill (Ithaca: Cornell University Press, 1993), p. 10.

88. Ibid., pp. 101–102.

89. Luce Irigaray, "The Limits of the Transference," in Whitford, *The Irigaray Reader*, p. 105.

90. Irigaray, "Bodily Encounter," p. 43.

91. Whitford, *Luce Irigaray*, p. 43.

92. Irigaray, *Sexes and Genealogies*, p. 195.

93. Ibid., p. 196.

94. Whitford, *Luce Irigaray*, pp. 76–77.

95. Irigaray, *Sexual Difference*, p. 10.

96. Luce Irigaray, *I Love to You: Sketch for a Felicity Within History*, trans. Alison Martin (New York: Routledge, 1995), p. 46.

97. Luce Irigaray, *Je, Tu, Nous: Toward a Culture of Sexual Difference*, trans. Alison Martin (New York: Routledge, 1993), pp. 46–47.

98. Irigaray, "Bodily Encounter," p. 44.

99. Irigaray, *This Sex Which Is Not One*, p. 28.

100. Irigaray, "Women-Amongst-Themselves," p. 190.

101. Its capacity for destructiveness is well known. See, for example, Sands, "Uses of the Thea(o)logian," and Brock, *Journeys by Heart*.

102. Goss, *Jesus Acted Up*, p. 84. The "queer Christ," for Goss, attempts to construct a Christological discourse that interprets Jesus' embodied practices in a positive, queer-affirming theology. See also Goss's discussion of Jesus as gay on pp. 77–85.

103. Marcus J. Borg, *Meeting Jesus Again for the First Time: The Historical Jesus and the Heart of Contemporary Faith* (San Francisco: Harper, 1994), pp. 31–36.

104. Edward Schillebeeckx, O.P., *Christ the Sacrament* (London: Sheed and Ward, 1963), p. 15.

105. Schüssler Fiorenza, *Jesus*, pp. 50–57.

106. Whitford, *Luce Irigaray*, p. 144.

107. Grosz, "Irigaray and the Divine," p. 207.

108. Irigaray, *Sexual Difference*, p. 148.

109. Ibid., p. 112.

110. Grosz, "Irigaray and the Divine," p. 207.

111. Irigaray, *I Love to You*, p. 104.

112. Irigaray, *Je, Tu, Nous*, p. 111.

113. Whitford, *Luce Irigaray*, p. 89.

114. Grosz, "Irigaray and the Divine," p. 212.

115. Whitford, *Luce Irigaray*, p. 142.

116. The sensible transcendental indicates the aim of this redistribution. Whitford, *Luce Irigaray*, p. 93.

117. Ibid., p. 47; Irigaray, *I Love to You*, p. 27.

118. Irigaray, *Sexes and Genealogies*, p. 112.

119. Irigaray, *Sexual Difference*, p. 82.

120. Grosz, "Irigaray and the Divine," p. 204.

121. Irigaray, *I Love to You*, pp. 31, 104.

122. Mary Daly, *Beyond God the Father: Toward a Philosophy of Women's Liberation* (Boston: Beacon, 1973), pp. 33–34.

123. John B. Cobb Jr. and David Ray Griffin, *Process Theology: An Introductory Exposition* (Philadelphia: Westminster, 1976), p. 47.

124. McGrath, *Christian Theology*, p. 239.

125. Sally McFague, *The Body of God: An Ecological Theology* (Minneapolis: Fortress, 1993), pp. 182–183.

126. Paula M. Cooey, "The Redemption of the Body: Post-Patriarchal Reconstruction of Inherited Christian Doctrine," in Paula M. Cooey, William R. Eakin, and Jay B. McDaniel, eds., *After Patriarchy: Feminist Transformations of the World Religions*, p. 121 (Maryknoll, N.Y.: Orbis, 1991).

7. WHEN WOMEN BECOME PRIESTS

1. Ruth A. Wallace, *They Call Her Pastor: A New Role for Catholic Women* (Albany: State University of New York Press, 1992), p. 9. Wallace obtained her information from Richard A. Schoenherr and Lawrence A. Young, *The Catholic Priest in the United States: Demographic Investigations* (Madison: University of Wisconsin–Madison Comparative Religious Organization Studies Publications, 1990).

2. Daniel J. Wakin, "Vatican Closes Theological Dissent Loophole," *Lincoln Journal Star*, July 4, 1998, p. 3C.

3. The Vatican ordained some married Episcopal priests who converted to Catholicism in the 1980s and perhaps continues to do so. For one account, see Mary Vincent Dally, *Married to a Catholic Priest* (Chicago: Loyola University Press, 1988).

4. In John Morgan, *Women Priests* (Bristol, Ind.: Wyndam Hall, 1985), p. 162.

5. Mary Sudman Donovan, "Beyond the Parallel Church: Strategies of Separatism and Integration in the Governing Councils of the Episcopal Church," in Catherine M. Prelinger, ed., *Episcopal Women: Gender, Spirituality, and Commitment in an American Mainline Denomination*, p. 133 (New York: Oxford University Press, 1992).

6. Pamela W. Darling, *New Wine: The Story of Women Transforming Leadership and Power in the Episcopal Church* (Cambridge: Cowley Publications, 1994), p. 104.

7. Heather Hyuck, "To Celebrate a Whole Priesthood: The History of Women's Ordination in the Episcopal Church" (Ph.D. diss., University of Minnesota, 1981), pp. 16–17; Darling, *New Wine*, p. 110.

8. Darling, *New Wine*, pp. 111–112.

9. Suzanne R. Hiatt, "How We Brought the Good News from Graymoor to Minneapolis: An Episcopal Paradigm," *Journal of Ecumenical Studies* 20, no. 4 (Fall 1983): 578.

10. Hyuck, "To Celebrate a Whole Priesthood," p. 98.

11. Darling, *New Wine*, pp. 113, 115.

12. Hiatt, "How We Brought," p. 581.

13. Darling, *New Wine*, p. 129.

14. Hiatt, "How We Brought," p. 582.

15. Darling, *New Wine*, pp. 133, 135, 147; Hiatt, "How We Brought," p. 582.

16. Hiatt, "How We Brought," pp. 576–577.

17. Ibid., p. 582.

18. Norene Carter, "The Episcopalian Story," in Rosemary Radford Ruether and Eleanor McLaughlin, eds., *Women of Spirit: Female Leadership in the Jewish and Christian Traditions*, p. 364 (New York: Simon and Schuster, 1979).

19. Michael Hirsley, "A Bishop-elect Stirs Religious Rift," *Chicago Tribune*, October 7, 1988, sec. 2, p. 8. See also Richard N. Ostling, "The Bishop Is a Lady," *Time*, December 26, 1988, p. 81.

20. Darling, *New Wine*, p. 164.

21. Suzanne R. Hiatt, "Women's Ordination in the Anglican Communion: Can This Church Be Saved?" in Catherine Wessinger, ed., *Religious Institutions and Women's Leadership: New Roles Inside the Mainstream*, pp. 213–214 (Columbia: University of South Carolina Press, 1996).

22. Ibid., p. 218.

23. In Carter I. Heyward, Alla Bozarth-Campbell, Nancy Hatch Wittig, and Merrill Bittner, "The Witness: Women of the Episcopal Church Ten Years After Philadelphia," *Journal of Women and Religion* 4, no. 1 (Winter 1984): 24.

24. Ibid.

25. According to Stevens's 1989 study of 108 Anglican clergy-women, discussed in chapter 1, 39 percent of the women earned a salary of less than $10,000 a year (only 10 percent of the male clergy were in that category). In addition, of those women working in parish ministry, fewer than one-half (47 percent) were in charge, as sole or senior minister—compared with 88 percent of clergymen. Lesley Stevens, "Different Voice/Different Voices: Anglican Women in Ministry," *Review of Religious Research* 30, no. 3 (March 1989): 264–265. John Morgan also observes that women priests are sorely underpaid on the whole, indicating that many earn below the poverty level. According to his study of 350 women priests—selected randomly across the United States—the average income was only $13,500. Morgan did not disclose what the average income was for male Episcopal priests. Morgan, *Women Priests*, p. 48.

26. Barbara Brown Zikmund, Adair T. Lummis, and Patricia Mei Yin Chang, *Clergy Women: An Uphill Calling* (Louisville: Westminster John Knox, 1998), appendix 4.2, p. 156.

27. Louie Crew, "Female Priests in the Episcopal Church," http://newark.rutgers.edu/~7Elcrew/womenpr.html, January 6, 1999.

28. Paula D. Nesbitt, "Dual Ordination Tracks: Differential Benefits and Costs for Men and Women Clergy," in William H. Swatos, Jr., ed., *Gender and Religion*, pp. 29, 33, 35, 42 (New Brunswick: Transaction Publishers, 1994).

29. Constance Buchanan, "The Anthropology of Vitality and Decline: The Episcopal Church in a Changing Society," in Prelinger, *Episcopal Women*, pp. 312–313.

30. E. T. Malone Jr. and Katie Sherrod, "Traditionalists Get Boost from Action on Women," *Episcopal Life*, September 1998, p. 7.

31. Quoted in ibid.

32. Philip Lyndon Reynolds, "Scholastic Theology and the Case Against Women's Ordination," *Heythrop Journal* 36, no. 3 (1995): 251.

33. John McDade, S.J., "Gender Matters: Women and Priesthood," *The Month* 255 (July 1994): 254–259.

34. Wallace, *They Call Her Pastor*, p. 6. Subsequent citations to this source are indicated by parenthetical page numbers within the text.

35. Lavinia Byrne, *Woman at the Altar: The Ordination of Women in the Roman Catholic Church* (New York: Continuum, 1998), pp. 3, 96.

36. See, for example, Susan K. Wood, "Priestly Identity: Sacrament of the Ecclesial Community," *Worship* 69 (March 1995): 122.

37. Susan McNamara, "Corpus Christi: A Church in Transition," *Rochester Democrat and Chronicle*, August 23, 1998, p. A1.

38. Jeff Blackwell and Doug Mandelaro, "Corpus Christi Pastor Is 'Fired,'" *Rochester Democrat and Chronicle*, August 16, 1998, p. A1. Subsequent citations to this source are indicated by parenthetical page numbers within the text.

39. Doug Mandelaro, "A Question of Faith," *Rochester Democrat and Chronicle*, September 17, 1998, p. C6; Doug Mandelaro, "Church Stands Firm," *Rochester Democrat and Chronicle*, October 16, 1998, pp. A1, A8; Doug Mandelaro, "Woman and Priest Again Lead Mass," *Rochester Democrat and Chronicle*, December 3, 1998, pp. B1, B2; Nadya Labi, "Not Doing as the Romans Do," *Time*, November 30, 1998, p. 8.

40. Doug Mandelaro, "Bishop Suspends Callan Indefinitely," *Rochester Democrat and Chronicle*, December 8, 1998, p. A1.

41. Sheila Durkins Dierks, *WomenEucharist* (Boulder, Col.: WovenWord Press, 1997), p. 15.

42. Bishop John S. Cummins, "Bishop Addresses Misuse of Eucharist," *Catholic Voice*, 36, no. 5 (March 9, 1998): 1.

43. Dierks, *WomenEucharist*, p. 156.

44. Victoria Rue, Kaye Ashe, Monica Kaufer, Mary Fran Michaels, Kate O'Day, Nora Schaffer, and Karen Schwarz, "A Critical Mass: Women Celebrating Eucharist, a Theology Position Paper" (Critical Mass press packet, July 1998).

45. Jane Redmont, "Women Stake Claim to Rites," *National Catholic Reporter* 33, no. 44 (October 17, 1977): 4–5.

46. Dierks, *WomenEucharist*, p. 62.

47. James W. Jones, *Religion and Psychology in Transition: Psychoanalysis, Feminism, and Theology* (New Haven: Yale University Press, 1996), p. 126.

48. James W. Fowler, *Stages of Faith: The Psychology of Human Development and the Quest for Meaning* (San Francisco: Harper and Row, 1981).

49. Mary Daly, *Gyn/ecology: The Metaethics of Radical Feminism* (Boston: Beacon, 1978), p. 46.

50. Naomi R. Goldenberg, "A Feminist, Psychoanalytic Reflection on 'The Cat in the Hat Comes Back': Exploring the Male Claim to the Ownership of Sacred Texts" (lecture given at Nebraska Wesleyan University, Lincoln, October 1997).

51. Naomi R. Goldenberg, *Changing of the Gods: Feminism and the End of Traditional Religions* (Boston: Beacon, 1979).

52. Pamela Schaeffer, "Woman Cuts Into Liturgy, Asks to Be Priest," *National Catholic Reporter*, February 6, 1998, p. 5.

BIBLIOGRAPHY

Achtemeier, Paul J., ed. *The HarperCollins Bible Dictionary*. San Francisco: HarperSanFrancisco, 1996.

Al-Issa, Ihsan. "Gender Role." In Louis Diamont, ed., *Male and Female Homosexuality: Psychological Approaches*, pp. 155–167. Washington: Hemisphere, 1987.

Aquino, Maria Pilar. *Our Cry for Life: Feminist Theology from Latin America*. Trans. Dinah Livingstone. Maryknoll, N.Y.: Orbis, 1993.

Baker, John Austin. "Eucharistic Presidency and Women's Ordination." *Theology* 88, no. 725 (September 1985): 350–357.

Balint, Michael. *The Basic Fault: Therapeutic Aspects of Regression*. New York: Brunner/Mazel, 1968.

Beauchesne, Richard. "Explorations and Responses: Scriptural/Theological Argument Against Women's Ordination (Simply Stated) and Responses." *Journal of Ecumenical Studies* 32, no. 1 (Winter 1995): 107–113.

Beers, William. *Women and Sacrifice: Male Narcissism and the Psychology of Religion*. Detroit: Wayne State University Press, 1992.

———. "Real Food for Real People: A Sociocultural and Psychological Perspective on Sacrifice." Paper presented at the annual meeting of the American Academy of Religion, Chicago, November 1994.

Bell, Catherine. *Ritual Theory, Ritual Practice*. New York: Oxford University Press, 1992.

———. *Ritual: Perspectives and Dimensions*. New York: Oxford University Press, 1997.

Bergmann, Martin. *In the Shadow of Moloch: The Sacrifice of Children and Its Impact on Western Religions*. New York: Columbia University Press, 1992.

Bettelheim, Bruno. *Symbolic Wounds: Puberty Rites and the Envious Male*. Glencoe, Ill.: Free Press, 1954.

Blackwell, Jeff, and Doug Mandelaro. "Corpus Christi Pastor Is 'Fired.'" *Rochester Democrat and Chronicle*, August 16, 1998, pp. A1, A14.

Borg, Marcus J. *Meeting Jesus Again for the First Time: The Historical*

Jesus and the Heart of Contemporary Faith. San Francisco: Harper, 1994.

Bozarth-Campbell, Alla. *Womanpriest: A Personal Odyssey.* New York: Paulist Press, 1978.

Bradley, Ritamary. "Patristic Background of the Motherhood Similitude in Julian of Norwich." *Christian Scholar's Review* 8 (1978): 101–113.

Breen, Dana, ed. *The Gender Conundrum: Contemporary Psychoanalytic Perspectives on Femininity and Masculinity.* London: Routledge, 1993.

Brock, Rita Nakashima. *Journeys by Heart: A Christology of Erotic Power.* New York: Crossroad, 1988.

Brown, Joanne Carlson, and Rebecca Parker. "For God So Loved the World?" In Joanne Carlson Brown and Carole R. Bohn, eds., *Christianity, Patriarchy, and Abuse: A Feminist Critique,* pp. 1–30. New York: Pilgrim, 1989.

Brown, Kelly Delaine. "God Is as Christ Does: Toward a Womanist Theology." *Journal of Religious Thought* 46, no. 1 (Summer–Fall 1989): 7–16.

Buckley, Peter, ed. *Essential Papers on Object Relations.* New York: New York University Press, 1986.

Burch, Beverly. "Gender Identities, Lesbianism, and Potential Space." In Judith M. Glassgold and Suzanne Iasenza, eds., *Lesbians and Psychoanalysis: Revolutions in Theory and Practice,* pp. 287–307. New York: Free Press, 1995.

Burkert, Walter, René Girard, and Jonathan Z. Smith. *Violent Origins: Ritual Killing and Cultural Formation.* Stanford: Stanford University Press, 1987.

Butler, Sara. "The Priest as Sacrament of Christ the Bridegroom." *Worship* 66 (November 1992): 498–517.

Bynum, Caroline Walker. *Jesus as Mother: Studies in the Spirituality of the High Middle Ages.* Berkeley: University of California Press, 1982.

———. "Women's Stories, Women's Symbols: A Critique of Victor Turner's Theory of Liminality." In Robert L. Moore and Frank E. Reynolds, eds., *Anthropology and the Study of Religion,* pp. 105–125. Chicago: Center for the Scientific Study of Religion, 1984.

———. *Fragmentation and Redemption: Essays on Gender and the Human Body in Medieval Religion.* New York: Zone Books, 1991.

Byrne, Lavinia. *Woman at the Altar: The Ordination of Women in the Roman Catholic Church.* New York: Continuum, 1998.

Cady, Susan, Marian Ronan, and Hall Taussig. *Sophia: The Future of Feminist Spirituality.* San Francisco: Harper and Row, 1986.

Carmody, Denise. *Women and World Religions.* 2d ed. Englewood Cliffs, N.J.: Prentice-Hall, 1989.

Carr, Anne E. *Transforming Grace: Christian Tradition and Women's Experience.* San Francisco: Harper and Row, 1988.

Chittester, Joan. "One, Two, Three Strikes, You're Out in the Ol' Boys' Game." *National Catholic Reporter* 30, no. 32 (June 17, 1994): 12.

Chodorow, Nancy. *The Reproduction of Mothering: Psychoanalysis and the Sociology of Gender.* Berkeley: University of California Press, 1978.

——. "Gender, Relation, and Difference in Psychoanalytic Perspective." In Hester Eisenstein and Alice Jardine, eds., *The Future of Difference,* pp. 3–19. New Brunswick, N.J.: Rutgers University Press, 1987.

——. *Feminism and Psychoanalytic Theory.* New Haven: Yale University Press, 1989.

——. *Femininities, Masculinities, Sexualities: Freud and Beyond.* Lexington: University Press of Kentucky, 1994.

——. "Gender as a Personal and Cultural Construction." *Signs: Journal of Women in Culture and Society* 20, no. 3 (Spring 1995): 516–544.

——. "Reflections on the Authority of the Past in Psychoanalytic Thinking." *Psychoanalytic Quarterly* 65, no. 1 (1996): 32–51.

Chopp, Rebecca S. *The Power to Speak: Feminism, Language, God.* New York: Crossroad, 1989.

Chopp, Rebecca S., and Sheila Greeve Davaney, eds. *Horizons in Feminist Theology: Identity, Tradition, and Norms.* Minneapolis: Fortress, 1997.

Christ, Carol. *Diving Deep and Surfacing: Women Writers on Spiritual Quest.* Boston: Beacon, 1980.

——. "Why Women Need the Goddess: Phenomenological, Psychological, and Political Reflections." In Charlene Spretnak, ed., *The Politics of Women's Spirituality,* pp. 71–86. Garden City, N.Y.: Anchor, 1982.

——. "In Praise of Aphrodite: Sexuality as Sacred." In Elizabeth Dodson Gray, ed., *Sacred Dimensions of Women's Experience,* pp. 220–227. Wellesley: Roundtable, 1988.

Christ, Carol P., and Judith Plaskow, eds. *Womanspirit Rising: A Feminist Reader in Religion.* San Francisco: Harper and Row, 1979.

Chung, Hyun Kyung. *Struggle to Be the Sun Again: Introducing Asian Women's Theology.* Maryknoll, N.Y.: Orbis, 1990.

Clanton, Jann Aldredge. *In Whose Image? God and Gender.* New York: Crossroad, 1991.

Clark, Kenneth B., and Mamie K. Clark. "The Development of

Consciousness of Self and the Emergence of Racial Identification in Negro Preschool Children." *Journal of Psychology, SPSSI Bulletin* 10 (1939): 591–599.

Cobb, John B., Jr., and David Ray Griffin. *Process Theology: An Introductory Exposition*. Philadelphia: Westminster, 1976.

Coffey, David. "Priestly Representation and Women's Ordination." In Gerald P. Gleeson, ed., *Priesthood: The Hard Questions*, pp. 79–99. Newtown, Australia: Dwyer, 1993.

Coles, Robert. *The Spiritual Life of Children*. Boston: Houghton Mifflin, 1990.

Congregation for the Doctrine of the Faith. "The Vatican Declaration: Women in the Ministerial Priesthood." *Origins* 6 (February 3, 1977): 517–524.

——. "Response to a 'Dubium' on Ordaining Women to the Ministerial Priesthood." *Origins* 25, no. 24 (November 30, 1995): 401, 403.

Connell, R. W. *Gender and Power: Society, the Person, and Sexual Politics*. Stanford: Stanford University Press, 1987.

Cooey, Paula M. "The Redemption of the Body: Post-Patriarchal Reconstruction of Inherited Christian Doctrine." In Paula M. Cooey, William R. Eakin, and Jay B. McDaniel, eds., *After Patriarchy: Feminist Transformations of the World Religions*, pp. 106–130. Maryknoll, N.Y.: Orbis, 1991.

Cowell, Alan. "Pope Rules Out Debate on Making Women Priests." *New York Times*, May 31, 1994, p. A8.

Crew, Louie. "Female Priests in the Episcopal Church." http://newark.rutgers.edu/~7Elcrew/womenpr.html, January 6, 1999.

Crockett, William R. *Eucharist: Symbol of Transformation*. New York: Pueblo, 1989.

Cross, Mary. "Introduction from the Publisher." *Journal of Women and Religion* 4, no. 2 (Winter 1985): 3–4.

Crownfield, David. "The Seminal Trace: Presence, Difference, and Transubstantiation." *Journal of the American Academy of Religion* 59, no. 2 (Summer 1991): 361–371.

—, ed. *Body/Text in Julia Kristeva: Religion, Women, and Psychoanalysis*. Albany: State University of New York Press, 1992.

Cummins, Bishop John S. "Bishop Addresses Misuse of Eucharist." *Catholic Voice* 36, no. 5 (March 9, 1998): 1.

Dally, Mary Vincent. *Married to a Catholic Priest*. Chicago: Loyola University Press, 1988.

Daly, Mary. *Beyond God the Father: Toward a Philosophy of Women's Liberation.* Boston: Beacon, 1973.
——. *Gyn/ecology: The Metaethics of Radical Feminism.* Boston: Beacon, 1978.
——. *Pure Lust.* Boston: Beacon, 1984.
Darling, Pamela W. *New Wine: The Story of Women Transforming Leadership and Power in the Episcopal Church.* Cambridge: Cowley, 1994.
Davaney, Sheila Greeve. "The Limits of the Appeal to Women's Experience." In Clarissa W. Atkinson, Constance H. Buchanan, and Margaret R. Miles, eds., *Shaping New Vision: Gender and Values in American Culture*, pp. 31–49. Ann Arbor: UMI Research Press, 1987.
——. "Continuing the Story, but Departing the Text: A Historicist Interpretation of Feminist Norms in Theology." In Rebecca S. Chopp and Sheila Greeve Davaney, eds., *Horizons in Feminist Theology: Identity, Tradition, and Norms*, pp. 198–214. Minneapolis: Fortress, 1997.
de Beauvoir, Simone. *The Second Sex.* Trans. H. M. Parshley. New York: Vintage Books, 1952.
Deiss, Lucien. *It's the Lord's Supper: The Eucharist of Christians.* Trans. Edmond Bonin. New York: Paulist Press, 1976.
DeSmet, Kate. "Ken, Don't Foul Up the Church Today." *The Critic* 47, no. 3 (Spring 1993): 14–29.
Dierks, Sheila Durkins. *WomenEucharist.* Boulder, Col.: WovenWord, 1997.
Dinnerstein, Dorothy. *The Mermaid and the Minotaur: Sexual Arrangements and the Human Malaise.* New York: Harper and Row, 1976.
Dix, Gregory. *The Shape of the Liturgy.* 2d ed. London: Dacre, 1945; Adam and Charles Black, 1975.
Donovan, Mary D. *Women Priests in the Episcopal Church: The Experience of the First Decade.* Cincinnati: Forward Movement Publications, 1988.
Douglas, Kelly Brown. *The Black Christ.* Maryknoll, N.Y.: Orbis, 1994.
Driver, Tom. *The Magic of Ritual: Our Need for Liberating Rites That Transform Our Lives and Our Communities.* San Francisco: HarperSanFrancisco, 1991.
Dywer, Maureen, ed. *New Woman, New Church, New Priestly Ministry.* Baltimore: Women's Ordination Conference, 1980.
Edmundson, Mark. "Save Sigmund Freud." *New York Times Magazine*, July 13, 1997, pp. 34–35.

Eisenstein, Hester. Introduction to Hester Eisenstein and Alice Jardine, eds., *The Future of Difference*, pp. xv–xxiv. New Brunswick, N.J.: Rutgers University Press, 1985.

Eisler, Riane. *The Chalice and the Blade: Our History, Our Future*. San Francisco: Harper and Row, 1987.

Eliade, Mircea. *Myths, Rites, Symbols: A Mircea Eliade Reader*, vol. 1. Ed. Wendell Beane and William G. Doty. New York: Harper and Row, 1975.

Elshtain, Jean Bethke. *Public Man, Private Woman: Women in Social and Political Thought*. Princeton, N.J.: Princeton University Press, 1981.

Emminghaus, Johannes H. *The Eucharist: Essence, Form, Celebration*. Trans. Matthew J. O'Connell. Collegeville, Minn.: Liturgical Press, 1978.

Fahey, Michael A., ed. *Catholic Perspectives on Baptism, Eucharist, and Ministry*. New York: University Press of America, 1986.

Faludi, Susan. *Backlash: The Undeclared War Against American Women*. New York: Anchor, 1992.

Fiala, Petr, and Jiri Hanus. "Women's Ordination in the Czech Silent Church." *The Month* 259, no. 1567 (July 1998): 282–288.

Firestone, Shulamith. *The Dialectic of Sex: The Case for Feminist Revolution*. New York: Bantam, 1970.

Fischer, James A. "Body." In Carroll Stuhlmueller, ed., *The Collegeville Pastoral Dictionary*, pp. 100–102. Collegeville, Minn.: Liturgical Press, 1996.

Fitzpatrick, Ruth McDonough. "WOC Delegation Visits Czechoslovakia." *New Women, New Church* 15, nos. 2–4 (March–August 1992): 1, 7, 8, 10.

Flax, Jane. "Mother-Daughter Relationships: Psychodynamics, Politics, and Philosophy." In Hester Eisenstein and Alice Jardine, eds., *The Future of Difference*, pp. 20–40. New Brunswick, N.J.: Rutgers University Press, 1985.

——. *Thinking Fragments: Psychoanalysis, Feminism, and Postmodernism in the Contemporary West*. Berkeley: University of California Press, 1990.

Fletcher, John, and Andrew Benjamin, eds. *Abjection, Melancholia, and Love: The Work of Julia Kristeva*. London: Routledge, 1990.

Fowler, James W. *Stages of Faith: The Psychology of Human Development and the Quest for Meaning*. San Francisco: Harper and Row, 1981.

Freud, Sigmund. "The Interpretation of Dreams (1900)." In *The Pelican Freud Library*, vol. 4, *The Interpretation of Dreams*, ed. James Strachey, pp. 57–783. Harmondsworth, Middlesex, England: Penguin, 1975.

———. "Analysis of a Phobia in a Five-Year-Old Boy (1909)." In *The Pelican Freud Library*, vol. 8, *Case Histories I: "Dora" and "Little Hans,"* ed. Angela Richards, pp. 169–305. Harmondsworth, Middlesex, England: Penguin, 1977.

———. "Psychoanalytic Notes on an Autobiographical Account of a Case of Paranoia (Dementia Paranoides) (1911)." In *The Pelican Freud Library*, vol. 9, *Case Histories II: The "Rat Man," Schreber, the Wolf Man, a Case of Female Homosexuality*, ed. Angela Richards, pp. 138–223. Harmondsworth, Middlesex, England: Penguin, 1979.

———. *Totem and Taboo* (1913). In *The Pelican Freud Library*, vol. 13, *The Origins of Religion*, ed. Albert Dickson, pp. 53–224. Harmondsworth, Middlesex, England: Penguin, 1985.

———. "Mourning and Melancholia (1917)." In *The Pelican Freud Library*, vol. 11, *On Metapsychology: The Theory of Psychoanalysis*, ed. James Strachey, pp. 251–268. Harmondsworth, Middlesex, England: Penguin, 1984.

———. "Beyond the Pleasure Principle (1920)." In *The Pelican Freud Library*, vol. 11, *On Metapsychology: The Theory of Psychoanalysis*, ed. James Strachey, pp. 275–338. Harmondsworth, Middlesex, England: Penguin, 1984.

———. "The Dissolution of the Oedipus Complex (1924)." In *The Pelican Freud Library*, vol. 7, *On Sexuality*, ed. Angela Richards, pp. 315–322. Harmondsworth, Middlesex, England: Penguin, 1977.

———. "Some Psychical Consequences of the Anatomical Distinction Between the Sexes (1925)." In *The Pelican Freud Library*, vol. 7, *On Sexuality*, ed. Angela Richards, pp. 325–343. Harmondsworth, Middlesex, England: Penguin, 1977.

———. "Female Sexuality (1931)." In *The Pelican Freud Library*, vol. 7, *On Sexuality*, ed. Angela Richards, pp. 371–392. Harmondsworth, Middlesex, England: Penguin, 1977.

Friedman, Richard C. *Male Homosexuality: A Contemporary Psychoanalytic Perspective*. New Haven: Yale University Press, 1988.

Geertz, Clifford. *The Interpretation of Cultures*. New York: Basic Books, 1973.

Gilligan, Carol. *In a Different Voice: Psychological Theory and Women's Development*. Cambridge: Harvard University Press, 1982.

Gilligan, Carol, and Grant Wiggins. "The Origins of Morality in Early Childhood." In Carol Gilligan, Janie Victoria Ward, Jill McLean Taylor, with Betty Bardige, eds., *Mapping the Moral Domain: A Contribution of Women's Thinking to Psychological Theory and Education*, pp. 111–138. Cambridge: Harvard University Press, 1988.

Gimbutas, Marija. *The Civilization of the Goddess*. San Francisco: Harper, 1991.

Girard, René. *Violence and the Sacred*. Trans. Patrick Gregory. Baltimore and London: Johns Hopkins University Press, 1977.

Gleeson, Gerald. "The Ordination of Women and the Symbolism of Priesthood, Part One." *The Astralasian Catholic Record* 67 (1990): 472–481.

Goldenberg, Naomi R. *Changing of the Gods: Feminism and the End of Traditional Religion*. Boston: Beacon, 1979.

——. "The Return of the Goddess: Psychoanalytic Reflections on the Shift from Theology to Thealogy." *Studies in Religion* 16, no. 1 (Winter 1987): 37–52.

——. *Returning Words to Flesh: Feminism, Psychoanalysis, and the Resurrection of the Body*. Boston: Beacon, 1990.

——. "A Feminist, Psychoanalytic Reflection on 'The Cat in the Hat Comes Back': Exploring the Male Claim to the Ownership of Sacred Texts." Lecture given at Nebraska Wesleyan University, Lincoln, October 1997.

Gopaul-McNicol, Sharon-Ann. "Racial Identification and Racial Preference of Black Preschool Children in New York and Trinidad." In A. Kathleen Hoard Burlew, W. Curtis Banks, Harriette Pipe McAdoo, and Daudi Ajani ya Azibo, eds., *African American Psychology: Theory, Research, and Practice*, pp. 190–193. Newbury Park, Calif.: Sage, 1992.

Goss, Robert. *Jesus Acted Up: A Gay and Lesbian Manifesto*. New York: HarperCollins, 1993.

Graff, Ann, and David Knight. "Infallibly Complex: Have We Heard the Final Word on Women's Ordination?" *U.S. Catholic* 61, no. 4 (April 1, 1996): 6–13.

Gray, Paul. "The Assault on Freud." *Time*, November 29, 1993, pp. 47–51.

Grey, Mary. *Feminism, Redemption, and the Christian Tradition*. Mystic, Conn.: Twenty-third Publications, 1990.

Greider, Kathleen J. "The Authority of Our Ambivalence: Women and Priestly Ministry." *Quarterly Review* 10, no. 4 (Winter 1990): 22–39.

Grimes, Ronald. *Beginnings in Ritual Studies*. Washington, D.C.: University Press of America, 1982.

——. *Ritual Criticism: Case Studies in Its Practice, Essays on Its Theory*. Columbia: University of South Carolina Press, 1990.

Gudorf, Christine. "The Power to Create: Sacraments and Men's Need to Give Birth." *Horizons* 14, no. 2 (1987): 296–309.

Haines, Denise G. "Women's Ordination: What Difference Has It Made?" *Christian Century* 103, no. 30 (October 15, 1986): 888–889.

Hall, Calvin S. *A Primer of Freudian Psychology.* New York: World Publishing, 1954.

Harris, Stephen L. *Understanding the Bible.* 3d ed. London: Mayfield, 1992.

Heimbrock, Hans-Gunter. "Ritual and Transformation: A Psychoanalytic Perspective." In Hans-Gunter Heimbrock and H. Barbara Boudewijnse, eds., *Current Studies on Rituals: Perspectives for the Psychology of Religion*, pp. 33–42. Amsterdam: Rodopi, 1990.

Herdt, Gilbert. *Guardians of the Flutes: Idioms of Masculinity.* New York: McGraw-Hill, 1981.

——. *The Sambia: Ritual and Gender in New Guinea.* New York: Holt, Rinehart, and Winston, 1987.

Heron, Alasdair. *Table and Tradition.* Edinburgh: Handsel, 1983.

Heyward, Carter I., Alla Bozarth-Campbell, Nancy Hatch Wittig, and Merrill Bittner. "The Witness: Women of the Episcopal Church Ten Years After Philadelphia." *Journal of Women and Religion* 4, no. 1 (Winter 1984): 22–25.

Heyward, Isabel Carter. *The Redemption of God: A Theology of Mutual Relation.* Lanham, Md.: University Press of America, 1982.

——. *Speaking of Christ: A Lesbian Feminist Voice.* Ed. Ellen C. Davis. New York: Pilgrim Press, 1989.

——. *Touching Our Strength: The Erotic as Power and the Love of God.* San Francisco: Harper and Row, 1989.

Hiatt, Suzanne R. "How We Brought the Good News from Graymoor to Minneapolis: An Episcopal Paradigm." *Journal of Ecumenical Studies* 20, no. 4 (Fall 1983): 576–584.

——. "Women's Ordination in the Anglican Communion: Can This Church Be Saved?" In Catherine Wessinger, ed., *Religious Institutions and Women's Leadership: New Roles Inside the Mainstream*, pp. 211–227. Columbia: University of South Carolina Press, 1996.

Hirsley, Michael. "A Bishop-elect Stirs Religious Rift." *Chicago Tribune,* October 7, 1988, sec. 2, p. 8.

Horney, Karen. *Feminine Psychology.* New York: Norton, 1967.

Hubert, Henri, and Marcel Mauss. *Sacrifice: Its Nature and Function.* Trans. W. D. Halls. Chicago: University of Chicago Press, 1898.

Hunt, Mary. "Thinking Anew About Ordination." *New Women, New Church* 14, nos. 4–6; 15, no. 1 (July 1991–February 1992): 3–5.

Hunter, Edwina. "Reflections on the Christa from a Christian Theologian." *Journal of Women and Religion* 4, no. 2 (Winter 1985): 22–32.

Hwain, Chang Lee. *Confucius, Christ, and Co-Partnership: Competing Liturgies for the Soul of Korean American Women.* Lanham, Md.: University Press of America, 1994.

Hyuck, Heather. "To Celebrate a Whole Priesthood: The History of Women's Ordination in the Episcopal Church." Ph.D. diss., University of Minnesota, 1981.

Iadorola, Antoinette. "The American Catholic Bishops and Woman: From the Nineteenth Amendment to ERA." In Yvonne Yazbeck Haddad and Ellison Banks Findly, eds., *Women, Religion and Social Change,* pp. 457–476. Albany: State University of New York Press, 1985.

Ice, Martha Long. *Clergy Women and Their Worldviews: Calling for a New Age.* New York: Praeger, 1987.

Irigaray, Luce. *This Sex Which Is Not One.* Trans. Catherine Porter. Ithaca: Cornell University Press, 1985.

——. "Women, the Sacred, and Money." *Paragraph* 8 (1986): 6–18.

——. "Equal to Whom?" *Differences* 1, no. 2 (1989): 59–76.

——. *An Ethics of Sexual Difference.* Trans. Carolyn Burke and Gillian C. Gill. Ithaca: Cornell University Press, 1993.

——. *Je, Tu, Nous: Toward a Culture of Sexual Difference.* Trans. Alison Martin. New York: Routledge, 1993.

——. *Sexes and Genealogies.* Trans. Gillian C. Gill. New York: Columbia University Press, 1993.

——. *I Love to You: Sketch for a Felicity Within History.* Trans. Alison Martin. New York: Routledge, 1995.

Irwin, Kevin W. "The Sacramentality of Creation and the Role of Creation in Liturgy and Sacraments." In Kevin W. Irwin and Edmund D. Pellegrino, eds., *Preserving the Creation: Environmental Theology and Ethics,* pp. 67–111. Washington, D.C.: Georgetown University Press, 1994.

Isasi-Díaz, Ada María. *Mujerista Theology: A Theology for the Twenty-first Century.* Maryknoll, N.Y.: Orbis, 1996.

James, E. O., *Christian Myth and Ritual: An Historical Study.* Cleveland: World Publishing, 1965.

Jay, Nancy. "Throughout Your Generations Forever: A Sociology of Blood Sacrifice." Ph.D. diss., Brandeis University, 1982.

——. *Throughout Your Generations Forever: Sacrifice, Religion, and Paternity.* Chicago: University of Chicago Press, 1992.

John Paul II. "On the Dignity and Vocation of Women." Reprinted in *Origins* 18, no. 17 (October 6, 1988): 262–283.

——. *Ordinatio Sacerdotalis*. Reprinted in *Commonweal*, June 17, 1994, pp. 4–5.

Johnson, Elizabeth A. *She Who Is: The Mystery of God in Feminist Theological Discourse*. New York: Crossroad, 1992.

——. "Redeeming the Name of Christ." In Catherine Mowry LaCugna, ed., *Freeing Theology: The Essentials of Theology in Feminist Perspective*, pp. 115–137. San Francisco: HarperSanFrancisco, 1993.

——. "Wisdom Was Made Flesh and Pitched Her Tent Among Us." In Maryanne Stevens, ed., *Reconstructing the Christ Symbol: Essays in Feminist Christology*, pp. 95–117. New York: Paulist Press, 1993.

Jones, James. *Contemporary Psychoanalysis and Religion: Transference and Transcendence*. New Haven: Yale University Press, 1991.

——. *Religion and Psychology in Transition: Psychoanalysis, Feminism, and Theology*. New Haven: Yale University Press, 1996.

Jones, Serene. "Women's Experience Between a Rock and a Hard Place: Feminist, Womanist, and *Mujerista* Theologies in North America." In Rebecca S. Chopp and Sheila Greeve Davaney, eds., *Horizons in Feminist Theology: Identity, Tradition, and Norms*, pp. 35–53. Minneapolis: Fortress, 1997.

Jonte-Pace, Diane. "Feminism, Object Relations Theory and Religion: The Betrayal of Mothering." Paper presented at the annual meeting of the American Academy of Religion. Atlanta, November 1986.

——. "Julia Kristeva and the Psychoanalytic Study of Religion: Rethinking Freud's Cultural Texts." In Janet Liebman Jacobs and Donald Capps, eds., *Religion, Society, and Psychoanalysis: Readings in Contemporary Theory*, pp. 240–268. Boulder: Westview, 1997.

——. "New Directions in the Feminist Psychology of Religion: An Introduction." *Journal of Feminist Studies in Religion* 13, no. 1 (Spring 1997): 63–74.

——. "Feminist Transformations in the Psychology of Religion: New Developments in Method and Theory." *Method and Theory in the Study of Religion*. In press.

Joy, Morny. "Equality or Divinity: A False Dichotomy?" *Journal of Feminist Studies in Religion* 6 (Spring 1990): 9–24.

Jung, Carl. "Transformation Symbolism in the Mass." In *Psychology and Religion: West and East*, vol. 11 of *The Collected Works of C. G. Jung*. Trans. R. F. C. Hull, pp. 201–296. New York: Pantheon, 1958.

Jungmann, Josef A., S.J. *The Early Liturgy*. Trans. Francis Brunner, C.S.S.R. Notre Dame: University of Notre Dame Press, 1959.

Kaschak, Ellyn. *Engendered Lives: A New Psychology of Women's Experience*. New York: Basic Books, 1992.

Keller, Catherine. *From a Broken Web: Separation, Sexism, and Self.* Boston: Beacon, 1986.

Kenny, Michael H. "Which Way the Pastoral?" *America* 167, no. 4 (August 22, 1992): 76–77.

Kerber, Linda K., et al. "On *In a Different Voice*: An Interdisciplinary Forum." *Signs: Journal of Women in Culture and Society* 11, no. 2 (Winter 1986): 305–333.

Kertzer, David I. *Ritual, Politics, and Power*. New Haven: Yale University Press, 1988.

Kilmartin, Edward J., S.J. *Church, Eucharist, and Priesthood*. New York: Paulist Press, 1981.

——. *Christian Liturgy: Theology and Practice*. Vol. 1. Kansas City, Mo.: Sheed and Ward, 1988.

Kim, C. W. Maggie, Susan M. St. Ville, and Susan M. Simonaitis, eds. *Transfigurations: Theology and the French Feminists*. Minneapolis: Fortress, 1993.

Kinsley, David. *The Goddesses' Mirror: Visions of the Divine from East and West*. Albany: State University of New York Press, 1989.

Kodell, Jerome, O.S.B. *The Eucharist in the New Testament*. Wilmington, Del.: Michael Glazier, 1988.

Kraemer, Ross Shepard. *Her Share of the Blessings: Women's Religions Among Pagans, Jews, and Christians in the Greco-Roman World*. New York: Oxford University Press, 1992.

Kristeva, Julia. *Desire in Language: A Semiotic Approach to Literature and Art*. Ed. Leon S. Roudiez. Trans. Thomas Gora, Alice Jardine, and Leon S. Roudiez. New York: Columbia University Press, 1980.

——. *Powers of Horror: An Essay on Abjection*. Trans. Leon S. Roudiez. New York: Columbia University Press, 1982.

——. *Tales of Love*. Trans. Leon S. Roudiez. New York: Columbia University Press, 1987.

——. *Black Sun: Depression and Melancholia*. Trans. Leon S. Roudiez. New York: Columbia University Press, 1989.

——. *New Maladies of the Soul*. Trans. Ross Guberman. New York: Columbia University Press, 1995.

Labi, Nadya. "Not Doing as the Romans Do." *Time*, November 30, 1998, p. 8.

Legrand, Herve. "*Traditio perpetuo servata?* The Non-ordination of Women: Tradition or Simply an Historical Fact?" *Worship* 65, no. 6 (November 1991): 482–508.

Lemaire, Anika. *Jacques Lacan.* Trans. David Macey. London: Routledge and Kegan Paul, 1977.

Lerman, Hanna. *A Mote in Freud's Eye: From Psychoanalysis to the Psychology of Women.* New York: Springer, 1986.

Lester, Eva P. "Gender and Identity Issues in the Analytic Process." *International Journal of Psycho-Analysis* 71 (1990): 435–444.

Levenson, Jon D. *The Death and Resurrection of the Beloved Son: The Transformation of Sacrifice in Judaism and Christianity.* New Haven: Yale University Press, 1993.

Lewes, Kenneth. "Psychoanalysis and Male Homosexuality." In Louis Diamant and Richard D. McAnulty, eds., *The Psychology of Sexual Orientation, Behavior, and Identity: A Handbook,* pp. 105–120. Westport, Conn.: Greenwood, 1995.

Lincoln, Bruce. *Emerging from the Chrysalis: Studies in Rituals of Women's Initiation.* Cambridge: Harvard University Press, 1981.

Loewald, Hans. *Papers on Psychoanalysis.* New Haven: Yale University Press, 1980.

"The Lord's Supper." In Paul J. Achtemeier, ed., *The Harper Collins Bible Dictionary,* pp. 622–624. San Francisco: Harper, 1996.

Luckett, Rosemary. "Women Make Eucharist Too." *New Women, New Church* 15, nos. 2–4 (March–August 1992): 18.

Mahler, Margaret S. *On Human Symbiosis and the Vicissitudes of Individuation.* New York: International Universities Press, 1968.

Mahler, Margaret S., Fred Pine, and Anni Bergman. *The Psychological Birth of the Human Infant: Symbiosis and Individuation.* New York: Basic Books, 1975.

Malone, E. T., Jr., and Katie Sherrod. "Traditionalists Get Boost from Action on Women." *Episcopal Life,* September 1998, p. 7.

Mandelaro, Doug. "A Question of Faith." *Rochester Democrat and Chronicle,* September 17, 1998, pp. C1, C6.

——. "Church Stands Firm." *Rochester Democrat and Chronicle,* October 16, 1998, pp. A1, A8.

——. "Woman and Priest Again Lead Mass." *Rochester Democrat and Chronicle,* December 3, 1998, pp. B1, B2.

——. "Bishop Suspends Callan Indefinitely." *Rochester Democrat and Chronicle,* December 8, 1998, pp. A1, A10.

Masson, Jeffrey Moussaieff. *The Assault on Truth: Freud's Suppression of the Seduction Theory.* New York: Farrar, Strauss, and Giroux, 1984.

McCormick, Patrick. "With All Due Respect." *U.S. Catholic* 59, no. 9 (September 1994): 46–49.

McDade, John, S.J. "Gender Matters: Women and Priesthood." *The Month* 255 (July 1994): 254–259.

McFague, Sally. *The Body of God: An Ecological Theology*. Minneapolis: Fortress, 1993.

McGrath, Alister E. *Christian Theology: An Introduction*. Oxford: Blackwell, 1994.

McGuire, Daniel. "The Exclusion of Women From Orders: A Moral Evaluation." Cross Currents: 1984. Reprinted by Priests for Equality and the Women's Ordination Conference.

McKenzie, John L., S.J. *Dictionary of the Bible*. Milwaukee: Bruce Publishing, 1965.

McNamara, Susan. "Corpus Christi: A Church in Transition." *Rochester Democrat and Chronicle*, August 23, 1998, pp. A1, A8.

Meissner, W. W. *Psychoanalysis and Religious Experience*. New Haven: Yale University Press, 1984.

———. "The Role of Transitional Conceptualization in Religious Thought." In Joseph H. Smith, ed., *Psychoanalysis and Religion*, pp. 95–116. Baltimore: Johns Hopkins University Press, 1990.

Mitchell, Juliet. *Psychoanalysis and Feminism*. New York: Vintage, 1974.

———, ed. *The Selected Melanie Klein*. Harmondsworth, Middlesex, England: Penguin, 1986.

Moi, Toril. *Sexual/Textual Politics: Feminist Literary Theory*. London: Methuen, 1985.

Moloney, Raymond. "Eucharist." In Joseph A. Komonchak, Mary Collins, and Dermot A. Lane, eds., *The New Dictionary of Theology*, pp. 342–355. Wilmington, Del.: Michael Glazier, 1988.

Moore, Robert L., and Frank E. Reynolds, eds. *Anthropology and the Study of Religion*. Chicago: Center for the Scientific Study of Religion, 1984.

Moorjani, Angela. "Fetishism, Gender Masquerade, and the Mother-Father Fantasy." In Joseph H. Smith and Afaf M. Mahfouz, eds., *Psychoanalysis, Feminism, and the Future of Gender*, pp. 22–41. Baltimore: Johns Hopkins University Press, 1994.

Morgan, John. *Women Priests*. Bristol, Ind.: Wyndam Hall, 1985.

Morton, Nelle. *The Journey Is Home*. Boston: Beacon, 1985.

Murphy, P. Francis. "Let's Start Over: A Bishop Appraises the Pastoral on Women." *Commonweal*, September 15, 1992, pp. 11–15.

Nesbitt, Paula D. "Dual Ordination Tracks: Differential Benefits and Costs for Men and Women Clergy." In William H. Swatos Jr., ed., *Gender and Religion*, pp. 27–44. New Brunswick, N.J.: Transaction Publishers, 1994.

Norris, R. A., Jr. "The Ordination of Women and the 'Maleness of Christ.'" *Anglican Theological Review Supplementary Series* 6 (June 1976): 69–80.

Northup, Lesley A. *Ritualizing Women*. Cleveland: Pilgrim Press, 1997.

Noss, John B., ed. *Man's Religions*. 6th ed. New York: Macmillan, 1980.

Nowak, Susan. "The Girardian Theory and Feminism: Critique and Appropriation." *Contagion: Journal of Violence, Mimesis, and Culture* 1 (1994): 19–30.

Nye, Robert D. *Three Psychologies: Perspectives from Freud, Skinner, and Rogers*. 4th ed. Pacific Grove, Calif.: Brooks/Cole Publishing, 1992.

O'Brien, Mary. *The Politics of Reproduction*. London: Routledge and Kegan Paul, 1981.

O'Carroll, Michael. *Corpus Christi: An Encyclopedia of the Eucharist*. Wilmington, Del.: Michael Glazier, 1988.

O'Connor, Noreen, and Joanna Ryan. *Wild Desires and Mistaken Identities: Lesbianism and Psychoanalysis*. New York: Columbia University Press, 1993.

O'Hanlon, Gerald F., S.J. *The Immutability of God in the Theology of Hans Urs von Balthasar*. Cambridge: Cambridge University Press, 1990.

Oliver, Kelly. "Julia Kristeva's Feminist Revolutions." *Hypatia* 8, no. 3 (Summer 1993): 94–114.

———. *Reading Kristeva: Unraveling the Double-Bind*. Bloomington: Indiana University Press. 1993.

Ostdiek, Gilbert. "Body of Christ, Blood of Christ." In Joseph A. Komonchak, Mary Collins, and Dermot A. Lane, eds., *The New Dictionary of Theology*, pp. 141–144. Wilmington, Del.: Michael Glazier, 1988.

Ostling, Richard N. "The Bishop Is a Lady." *Time*, December 26, 1988, p. 81.

Pagels, Elaine. "What Became of God the Mother? Conflicting Images of God in Early Christianity." *Signs: Journal of Women in Culture and Society* 2, no. 2 (Winter 1976): 293–303.

———. *The Gnostic Gospels*. New York: Random House, 1979.

Park, Sandra Winter. "Reflections on the Christa from a Theological Educator." *Journal of Women and Religion* 4, no. 2 (Winter 1985): 47–62.

Peberdy, Alyson, ed. *Women Priests?* Basingstoke, Hants, U.K.: Marshall Pickering, 1988.

Phan, Peter C. "Infallibility." In Michael Glazier and Monika K. Hellwig, eds., *The Modern Catholic Encyclopedia*, pp. 425–426. Collegeville, Minn.: Liturgical Press, 1994.

Pilla, Bishop Anthony. "Statements on Doctrinal Congregation's Action." *Origins* 25, no. 24 (November 30, 1995): 406.

Plaskow, Judith. *Sex, Sin, and Grace: Women's Experience and the Theologies of Reinhold Niebuhr and Paul Tillich.* Washington, D.C.: University Press of America, 1980.

Pollock, George H., ed. *Pivotal Papers on Identification.* Madison, Conn.: International Universities Press, 1993.

Porcile-Santiso, Maria-Teresa. "Roman Catholic Teachings on Female Sexuality." In Jeanne Becher, ed., *Women, Religion, and Sexuality: Studies on the Impact of Religious Teachings on Women,* pp. 192–220. Philadelphia: Trinity Press International, 1991.

Pottmeyer, Hermann Josef. "Refining the Question About Women's Ordination." *America* 175, no. 12 (1996): 16–18.

Power, David N. *The Sacrifice We Offer: The Tridentine Dogma and Its Reinterpretation.* New York: Crossroad, 1987.

———. "Representing Christ in Community and Sacrament." In Donald J. Goergen, ed., *Being a Priest Today,* pp. 97–123. Collegeville, Minn.: Liturgical Press, 1992.

———. *The Eucharistic Mystery: Revitalizing the Tradition.* New York: Crossroad, 1993.

Prelinger, Catherine M., ed. *Episcopal Women: Gender, Spirituality, and Commitment in an American Mainline Denomination.* New York: Oxford University Press, 1992.

Procter-Smith, Marjorie. *In Her Own Rite: Constructing Feminist Liturgical Tradition.* Nashville: Abingdon, 1990.

———. *Praying with Our Eyes Open: Engendering Feminist Liturgical Prayer.* Nashville: Abingdon, 1995.

Purvis, Sally B. *The Power of the Cross: Foundations for a Christian Feminist Ethic of Community.* Nashville: Abingdon, 1993.

Raab, Kelley Ann. "Christology Crossing Boundaries: The Threat of Imaging Christ as Other Than a White Male." *Pastoral Psychology* 45, no. 5 (1997): 389–399.

Ragland-Sullivan, Ellie. *Jacques Lacan and the Philosophy of Psychoanalysis.* Urbana: University of Illinois Press, 1986.

Rahner, Karl. *The Church and the Sacraments.* Trans. W. J. O'Hara. New York: Herder and Herder, 1963.

———. *A Rahner Reader.* Ed. Gerald A. McCool. New York: Seabury, 1975.

Rath, Julia Wally. "Faith, Hope, and Education: African-American Parents of Children in Catholic Schools and Their Social and Religious Accommodation to Catholicism." Ph.D. diss., University of Chicago, 1995.

Raymond, Janice G. *The Transsexual Empire: The Making of the She-Male.* Boston: Beacon, 1979.

Reddish, Mitchell G. "Body of Christ." In Watson E. Mills, ed., *Mercer Dictionary of the Bible*, pp. 120–121. Macon, Ga.: Mercer University Press, 1990.

Redmont, Jane. "Women Stake Claim to Rites." *National Catholic Reporter* 33, no. 44 (October 17, 1977): 4–5.

Reineke, Martha J. *Sacrificed Lives: Kristeva on Women and Violence.* Bloomington: Indiana University Press, 1997.

Reynolds, Philip Lyndon. "Scholastic Theology and the Case Against Women's Ordination." *Heythrop Journal* 36, no. 3 (1995): 249–285.

Rich, Adrienne. *Of Woman Born: Motherhood as Experience and Institution.* New York: Norton, 1976.

Rizzuto, Ana-Maria. *The Birth of the Living God: A Psychoanalytic Study.* Chicago: University of Chicago Press, 1979.

Roberts, James R. *Women Priests: Reflections on Papal Teaching.* Vancouver: Langara College, 1994.

Ross, Mary Ellen, and Cheryl Linn Ross. "Mothers, Infants, and the Psychoanalytic Study of Ritual." *Signs: Journal of Women in Culture and Society* 9 (Autumn 1983): 26–39

Rossi, Mary Ann. "Priesthood, Precedent, and Prejudice: On Recovering the Women Priests of Early Christianity, Containing a Translation from the Italian 'Notes on the Female Priesthood in Antiquity' by Giorgio Otranto." *Journal of Feminist Studies in Religion* 7, no. 1 (Spring 1991): 73–93.

Rue, Victoria, Kaye Ashe, Monica Kaufer, Mary Fran Michaels, Kate O'Day, Nora Schaffer, and Karen Schwarz. "A Critical Mass: Women Celebrating Eucharist. A Theology Position Paper." Critical Mass press packet, July 1998.

Ruether, Rosemary Radford. *New Woman/New Earth: Sexist Ideologies and Human Liberation.* New York: Seabury, 1975.

———. "Catholicism, Women, Body and Sexuality: A Response." In Jeanne Becher, ed., *Women, Religion, and Sexuality: Studies on the Impact of Religious Teachings on Women*, pp. 221–232. Philadelphia: Trinity Press International, 1991.

———. "Can Christology Be Liberated from Patriarchy?" In Maryanne Stevens, ed., *Reconstructing the Christ Symbol: Essays in Feminist Christology*, pp. 7–29. New York: Paulist Press, 1993.

Ruether, Rosemary Radford, and Eleanor McLaughlin, eds. *Women of Spirit: Female Leadership in the Jewish and Christian Traditions.* New York: Simon and Schuster, 1979.

Sagan, Eli. *Cannibalism: Human Aggression and Cultural Form.* New York: Psychohistory Press, 1974.

————. Freud, Women, and Morality: The Psychology of Good and Evil. New York: Basic Books, 1988.

Sands, Kathleen M. "Uses of the Thea(o)logian: Sex and Theodicy in Religious Feminism." Journal of Feminist Studies in Religion 8, no. 1 (Spring 1992): 7–33.

Sapiro, Virginia. Women in American Society: An Introduction to Women's Studies. 3d ed. Mountain View, Calif.: Mayfield Publishing, 1994.

Sayers, Janet. Mothers of Psychoanalysis. New York: Norton, 1991.

Schaeffer, Pamela. "Woman Cuts Into Liturgy, Asks to Be Priest." National Catholic Reporter 34 (February 6, 1998): 5.

Schafer, Roy. Aspects of Internalization. Madison, Conn.: International Universities Press, 1968.

Schillebeeckx, E., O.P. Christ the Sacrament. London: Sheed and Ward, 1963.

Schüssler Fiorenza, Elisabeth. "Tablesharing and the Celebration of the Eucharist." In Mary Collins and David Power, eds., Can We Always Celebrate the Eucharist?, Concilium 152, pp. 3–12. New York: Seabury, 1982.

————. Jesus: Miriam's Child, Sophia's Prophet. New York: Continuum, 1994.

Schweiser, R. Eduard. "Body." In David Noel Friedman, ed., The Anchor Bible Dictionary, 1:767–772. New York: Doubleday, 1992.

Smallwood, Rev. Dr. Gloria. "Reflections on the Christa from a Pastor." Journal of Women and Religion 4, no. 2 (Winter 1985): 41–43.

Smith, Huston. The World's Religions. San Francisco: HarperSanFrancisco, 1991.

Snyder, Mary Hembrow. The Christology of Rosemary Radford Ruether: A Critical Introduction. Mystic, Conn.: Twenty-third Publications, 1988.

Soskice, Janet Martin. "Blood and Defilement: Feminism and the Atonement." Lecture given at Harvard Divinity School, Cambridge, November 1994.

Stannard, Ed. "Lambeth Showcases Conservative Anglican World." Episcopal Life, September 1998, pp. 1, 3, 4.

————. "Sexuality Statement Made More Conservative." Episcopal Life, September 1998, pp. 4, 8.

Steinfels, Peter. "Vatican Says the Ban on Women as Priests Is 'Infallible' Doctrine." New York Times, November 19, 1995, pp. A1, A13.

Stevens, Lesley. "Different Voice/Different Voices: Anglican Women in Ministry." Review of Religious Research 30, no. 3 (March 1989): 262–275.

Stevens, Maryanne, ed. *Reconstructing the Christ Symbol: Essays in Feminist Christology*. New York: Paulist Press, 1993.

Stoller, Robert J. *Presentations of Gender*. New Haven: Yale University Press, 1985.

Stone, Merlin. *When God Was a Woman*. San Diego: Harcourt Brace Jovanovich, 1976.

Strenski, Ivan. "Reading Between the Lines of Sacrifice." Paper presented at the annual meeting of the American Academy of Religion, Chicago, November 1994.

Suhor, Mary Lou, ed. "Women Clergy Double Over Five Years." *Witness* 70, no. 10 (October 1987): 13.

Swidler, Leonard, and Arlene Swidler, eds. *Women Priests: A Catholic Commentary on the Vatican Declaration*. New York: Paulist Press, 1977.

Tillich, Paul. "Symbols of Faith." In Ronald E. Santoni, ed., *Religious Language and the Problem of Religious Knowledge*, pp. 136–145. Bloomington: Indiana University Press, 1968.

Tong, Rosemarie. *Feminist Thought: A Comprehensive Introduction*. Boulder: Westview, 1989.

——. *Feminine and Feminist Ethics*. Belmont, Calif.: Wadsworth, 1993.

Turner, Victor. *The Forest of Symbols: Aspects of Ndembu Ritual*. Ithaca: Cornell University Press, 1967.

——. *Dramas, Fields, and Metaphors: Symbolic Action in Human Society*. Ithaca: Cornell University Press, 1974.

——. *On the Edge of the Bush: Anthropology as Experience*. Ed. Edith L. B. Turner. Tucson: University of Arizona Press, 1985.

Turner, Victor, and Edith Turner. *Image and Pilgrimage in Christian Culture: Anthropological Perspectives*. New York: Columbia University Press, 1978.

Untener, Kenneth. "Forum: The Ordination of Women: Can the Horizons Widen?" *Worship* 65 (January 1991): 50–59.

U.S. Bishops. "Partners in the Mystery of Redemption: A Pastoral Response to Women's Concerns for Church and Society." *Origins* 17, no. 45 (April 21, 1988): 757–788.

——. Second Draft of Pastoral on Women ("One in Christ Jesus: A Pastoral Response to the Concerns of Women for Church and Society"). *Origins* 19, no. 44 (April 5, 1990): 717–740.

——. Third Draft of Proposed Pastoral Response to the Concerns of Women for Church and Society ("Called to Be One in Christ Jesus"). *Origins* 21, no. 46 (April 23, 1992): 761–776.

——. Fourth Draft of Response to the Concerns of Women for Church and Society ("One in Christ Jesus"). *Origins* 22, no. 13 (September

10, 1992): 221–240.

——. Statement Calling the Vatican to Collegiality ("Bishops Embrace Conference Change, More Openness"). *National Catholic Reporter* 31, no. 35 (July 28, 1995): 12–14.

van den Aardweg, Gerald J. M. *On the Origins and Treatment of Homosexuality: A Psychoanalytic Reinterpretation.* New York: Praeger, 1986.

Vatican Council (Second: 1962–1965). *The Documents of Vatican II.* Grand Rapids, Mich.: Eerdmans, 1975.

Wakeman, Hilary, ed. *Women Priests: The First Years.* London: Darton, Longman, and Todd, 1996.

Wakin, Daniel J. "Vatican Closes Theological Dissent Loophole." *Lincoln Journal Star,* July 4, 1998, p. 3C.

Wallace, Ruth A. *They Call Her Pastor: A New Role for Catholic Women.* Albany: State University of New York Press, 1992.

Wallwork, Ernest. "Sigmund Freud: The Psychoanalytic Diagnosis—Infantile Illusion." In Roger A. Johnson et al., eds., *Critical Issues in Modern Religion,* pp. 118–145. 2d ed. Englewood Cliffs, N.J.: Prentice Hall, 1990.

Walrond-Skinner, Sue, ed. *Crossing the Boundary: What Will Women Priests Mean?* London: Mowbray, 1994.

Walters, William A. W., and Michael W. Ross, eds. *Transsexualism and Sex Reassignment.* Oxford: Oxford University Press, 1986.

Weaver, Mary Jo. *New Catholic Women: A Contemporary Challenge to Traditional Religious Authority.* San Francisco: Harper and Row, 1986.

Weedon, Chris. *Feminist Practice and Poststructuralist Theory.* Oxford: Basil Blackwell, 1987.

Whitford, Margaret. *Luce Irigaray: Philosophy in the Feminine.* London: Routledge, 1991.

——, ed. *The Irigaray Reader.* Oxford: Basil Blackwell, 1991.

Williams, Delores, "Black Women's Surrogacy Experience and the Christian Notion of Redemption." In Paula M. Cooey, William R. Eakin, and Jay B. McDaniel, eds., *After Patriarchy: Feminist Transformations of the World Religions,* pp. 1–14. Maryknoll, N.Y.: Orbis, 1991.

——. *Sisters in the Wilderness: The Challenge of Womanist God-Talk.* Maryknoll, N.Y.: Orbis, 1993.

Winnicott, Donald W. *Collected Papers: Through Paediatrics to Psycho-Analysis.* New York: Basic Books, 1958.

——. *Collected Papers: Through Paediatrics to Psycho-Analysis.* New York: Brunner/Mazel, 1958.

———. *Playing and Reality.* London: Tavistock Publications, 1971.
Women's Ordination Conference. *Women and Priesthood: A Bibliography,* Parts I and II. Fairfax, Va.: Women's Ordination Conference, 1995.
Wood, Susan K. "Priestly Identity: Sacrament of the Ecclesial Community." *Worship* 69 (March 1995): 109–127.
Wright, John H. " 'That All Doubt May be Removed.'" *America* 171, no. 3 (July 30, 1994): 16–19.
Ziarek, Ewa. "At the Limits of Discourse: Heterogeneity, Alterity, and the Maternal Body in Kristeva's Thought." *Hypatia* 7, no. 2 (Spring 1992): 91–108.
Zikmund, Barbara Brown, Adair T. Lummis, and Patricia Mei Yin Chang. *Clergy Women: An Uphill Calling.* Louisville: Westminster John Knox Press, 1998.

INDEX